500

quilt blocks

500

quilt blocks

the only compendium of quilt blocks you'll ever need

Lynne Goldsworthy & Kerry Green

Search Press

A Quintet Book

First published in the UK in 2013 by
Search Press Ltd
Wellwood
North Farm Road
Tunbridge Wells
Kent TN2 3DR
United Kingdom

www.searchpress.com

ISBN: 978-1-84448-967-1
QTT.QUIL

This book was conceived, designed, and produced by
Quintet Publishing Limited
6 Blundell Street
London N7 9BH
United Kingdom

Photographer: Sussie Bell
Flat Photography: Freshpak Photo
Designer: Tania Field
Art Director: Michael Charles
Editor: Margaret Swinson
Publisher: Mark Searle

10 9 8 7 6 5 4 3 2 1

Printed in China by 1010 Printing International Ltd.

contents

introduction

This book is the ultimate source of inspiration for quilters, whether they enjoy modern or traditional designs. There are instructions for 500 different quilt blocks suitable for the complete beginner through to the advanced quilter. We have included traditional blocks, variations on traditional blocks, new, original, and modern blocks. We have used a wide selection of fabrics and a huge variety of colour and pattern combinations in the hope that you will be as inspired by the fabric choices as you are by the finished blocks themselves. Whether you are starting a new project from scratch, joining a quilting group, thinking of designing a quilt of your own, or interested in trying new ideas, we hope you will find plenty of inspiration in these pages.

The art of piecing and quilting goes back centuries and it has seen a revival in recent years with the increased popularity of homemade over store-bought items. The internet has also breathed new life into the quilting community, with quilters able to share ideas and inspiration around the globe through blogs, social media, and photo-sharing websites. In past times, local quilters would get together in a quilting bee to make a joint quilt; quilters now join worldwide groups online to sew blocks for each other and make quilts from the blocks they have received.

This revival has coincided with a whole new generation of quilting fabric designers. New fabric lines are shown twice a year at places like Quilt Market and at festivals, and quilters worldwide clamour to get their hands on the exciting new designs. In *500 Quilt Blocks* we have mixed new, old, vintage and modern fabrics to inspire you to try unexpected combinations of your own.

Alongside the 500 blocks in this book are 20 projects, each one made from a block featured in the book. We aim to give you examples of how you might use these blocks to create something for your home or as a gift. From small projects like decorated dish towels or pincushions right through to bed-size quilts, there is a project for everyone at all skill levels. We hope you enjoy this book as much as we enjoyed putting it together.

Lynne Goldsworthy and *Kerry Green*

tools and equipment

The following equipment is essential for quilters of all levels:

- rotary cutter: sold in metric sizes, with 45mm as the standard size but 28mm will give additional control on smaller shapes.

- quilting ruler (inches or cm): a good starting size is 6in x 12in (15cm x 30cm) but you can always add to your collection. There are many specialty rulers to help with making Dresden plates, kaleidoscope blocks, hexagons, equilateral triangles etc.

- cutting mat: this provides a self-healing surface for a rotary cutter. Buy the largest size you can.

- scissors: a pair for fabric, a pair for paper, and a small pair for snipping thread.

- patchwork pins: strong, thin, and have extra-fine points. Glass-ended pins are helpful as they will not melt if caught by an iron.

- needles: for sewing machines and hand sewing.

- thread: 50wt 100% cotton thread will cover all piecing needs. A selection of light and dark neutrals blend with most fabrics. Heavier weights such as 40wt and 28wt can also be used for quilting.

- marking tools: we use mechanical pencils or Frixion pens for marking the wrong side of fabrics and a Hera marking tool for marking straight quilting lines. If you use pens or pencils on the right side of your fabric, make sure you test a sample first to ensure that the marks will vanish completely when washed.

- seam ripper: a good quality one is a worthwhile investment. Everyone makes mistakes!

- quilting safety pins for basting: these have a bend in them to pin through multiple layers of fabric.

- sewing machine: while you can piece by hand, a sewing machine will speed things up a great deal. Quilting and piecing can be sewn with a straight stitch as long as you can alter the length of your stitch on your machine. Use a short length for foundation paper piecing (1.5), longer for piecing (2.0 or so), and longer for quilting (3–5). There are machines for quilters with extra stitches built in, improved feed to handle multiple layers, built-in walking foot, and additional space in the throat of the machine to accommodate larger quilts.

- quarter-inch foot: this saves a lot of time worrying about the accuracy of your 1/4in (6mm) seam.

- free-motion or darning foot: allows you to be more creative in your quilting.

- walking foot: keeps the fabric feed steady when machine quilting, so that layers do not shift (and therefore reducing wrinkles and puckers). This feature is built into some machines, but if not, a specialty foot will need to be purchased.

- iron and ironing board: for smaller piecing you can use a travel iron. A portable ironing board is useful in a small working space.

templates

Templates need to be copied by either tracing, scanning, or photocopying. Some templates need enlarging; check instructions. A range of paper can be used. If using standard printer paper, the templates can be cut out and then stuck onto card stock to make a template that can be drawn around with a sharp pencil. Freezer paper can be used to trace the templates and can then be ironed to the fabric and cut around using a quilt ruler and rotary cutter or scissors. If tracing, look out for grainline arrows or other marks that will need to be transferred as you trace.

Alternatively, use template plastic, which can be drawn on and is semi-transparent, to make your own templates and produce sturdy, reusable shapes to draw around. Instructions should indicate if the templates include seam allowances or if these need to be added, except in the case of EPP and appliqué templates, which do not usually have seam allowances added. Templates are generally used on the wrong side of fabrics.

buying fabric

When you first take up quilting, the array of fabric choices, lines, and cuts can seem bewildering. We recommend visiting one or two quilting shops and spending time browsing the aisles and chatting to the staff. Online fabric stores are also a great place to find a wide range of prints, and it is always worth contacting the owner via email for advice on putting together colours and prints.

Small cuts like fat quarters are aimed at quilters so you can buy a selection of fabric and start to build your stash. Pre-cut fabric packs such as layer cakes, jelly rolls, and charm packs are great for buying a lot of different prints without spending a fortune. Stick to cotton when you start out and broaden your selection of fabrics and prints as your skills improve and your taste develops. Quilting cotton is a little heavier than standard dressmaking cotton such as poplin, and has strength and durability.

Purchase some all-over patterns like florals or spots and mix these with solid colours or shot cottons when making your first blocks. These colours and prints are easier to place in a block as an all-over print can't be upside down. Directional prints like stripes and pictorial prints can be used once you are familiar with basic block construction. As your confidence and skills increase, you can start adding fussy cut pieces for interest and focus. Vintage fabrics can mix with modern prints, but prewash and test for strength first. Combining similar fabric weights together will make for a flatter, more even result.

abbreviations

The instructions in this book have been written using some abbreviations, all of which can be found in the table below.

Abbreviation	Full term
BKG	background
CF	centre front
col	colour
CST	corner-square triangle
Diag	diagonal
EPP	English paper piecing
FMQ	free-motion quilting
HST	half-square triangle
LOF	length of fabric
Lrg	large
Med	medium
QST	quarter-square triangle
Rects	rectangles
RS	right side
SA	seam allowance
Sml	small
Sqs	squares
Tog	together
WOF	width of fabric
WS	wrong side
Yd	yard

block sizes

Throughout the book, block sizes refer to the size of the quilt block once pieced into the quilt. For example, where a block is stated to be 12in (30.5cm), you will be instructed to make a block that measures 12 1/2in (31.7cm) before it is pieced into a quilt. All blocks and projects are made with 1/4in (6mm) seams unless stated otherwise.

projects

All main block patterns within the book have variations. 20 blocks have full projects such as quilts, pillows, doorstops and potholders.

cutting

rotary cutting

A rotary cutter is incredibly useful and produces quick and accurate results when cutting fabric. It is, however, a sharp and dangerous blade and needs to be handled with great care. Always retract the blade even when you are in between cuts. The blade will dull over time so replace it regularly.

Always cut away from the body, on a self-healing cutting mat and with a quilt ruler. It is a good idea to practise using a rotary cutter with some spare fabric. Ensure your fabric is ironed and without wrinkles. Fabric can be folded or stacked since a rotary cutter can cut through more than one layer. The ruler is placed onto the fabric covering the area to be cut; the cutting line is aligned with the edge of the fabric. Check your ruler before cutting — measure twice, cut once! One hand rests firmly on the quilt ruler, fingers well away from the edge; the other hand pushes the rotary cutter away from the body so the blade runs along the edge of the quilt ruler. Once you have made your cut, retract the blade and put the piece cut to one side before preparing to make your next cut.

Always position yourself so it is comfortable to cut, never cut at an awkward angle, instead move the fabric to the right position or turn your mat, reposition your ruler and then make your cut. For cuts longer than your ruler or mat, move your ruler and your fabric, if needed, to continue the cut. Small pieces of fine sandpaper can be stuck under your quilt ruler to stop it from sliding, and plastic gripper dots can be bought for the same purpose. There are also gripper/suction devices for holding the ruler in place while keeping your fingers further away from the rotary blade. It helps to try a variety of rotary cutters and quilt rulers to see what you like best. The majority of blocks in this book have been designed with straightforward measurements especially for rotary cutting.

fussy cutting

There are a few techniques that can be used to isolate shapes, motifs, and patterns for fussy cutting. Remember to include seam allowance.

For simple regular shapes like squares, use a quilt ruler. The markings on a ruler can help you visualise squares of different sizes, and place your fussy cut accordingly. You can use masking tape to make the square the finished size. Remember to remove the tape afterwards.

For irregular shapes, use template plastic so you see the fabric beneath the shape. Draw around the template and cut out.

Freezer paper can be used instead of template plastic. It is harder to see through but it is effective for high contrast or light colours.

die cutting

Over the past couple of years, die cutting machines have been made for quilters which take a lot of the hard work out of cutting by enabling you to cut accurately and quickly by placing fabric on the die mat and rolling it through the cutter.

We have used die cutters to speed up the construction of many of the blocks in this book. Dies that we both use on a regular basis include half-square triangles, quarter-square triangles, tumblers, drunkards path, Dresden, apple core, squares and rectangles of various sizes and strips.

For anyone with wrist, hand, or arm issues or who wants to be able to cut a lot of shapes quickly and easily, these die cutters are a great investment and can really speed up the process of making many designs of blocks and quilt tops.

cutting isosceles triangles

Many quilt block designs call for the use of isosceles triangles (see diagram below). These are triangles with two sides of equal length — a bit like an ice cream cone. It is a useful skill to understand how to cut these on the cutting mat using the rotary cutter rather than always needing to use rulers or templates.

For a cut (not finished) isosceles triangle 5in (12.7cm) wide and 6in (15.2cm) tall, cut a strip of fabric 6in (15.2cm) wide. Since the triangles are symmetrical, the first angled line starts at the bottom left corner of the triangle and is angled across to the top middle of the

triangle, 2 1/2in (6.3cm) along from the corner. Cut the fabric. The second cut will go from top middle to bottom right and so will be angled from the top middle to a point 2 1/2in (6.3cm) further along, or 5in (12.7cm) away from the bottom left corner.

The next triangle can be cut in the same way but by using the line you have just cut as the first cut of the next triangle. Continue in this way until you have cut all the triangles you need from your strip of fabric.

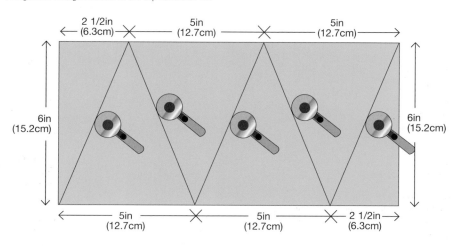

hand stitches

The direction in which you sew is likely to follow from whether you are right- or left-handed. Right-handed — sew right to left; left-handed — sew left to right.

slip stitch

A hand stitch used in many of the projects to close openings and secure bindings.

1 Press the seam on the edges that will be closed.

The crease acts as a guideline for where the stitches will be sewn. Choose a thread that will blend into the fabrics. Thread the needle and come up through the fold of the seam to place the knot on the WS of fabric and the needle and thread on the RS.

2 Push the needle into the fold on the opposite side of the seam, let it slide under the crease and come up approx 1/4in (6mm) along that side.

3 Now insert needle directly opposite, and repeat so the needle again slips into the opposite crease and travels 1/4in (6mm). Continue until opening is sewn. Secure at the end. Also used for hand appliqué - the needle travels under the basic fabric, comes up and just catches the edge of the shape before going down again.

whip stitch

This stitch joins pieces of fabric together and is essential for EPP. It is not invisible but if done carefully, small whip stitches will lie flat to join fabric for EPP. For EPP, hold the two pieces to be joined, e.g., hexagons, RS together so they lie against each other and the fabric edges folded over the paper templates are at the top.

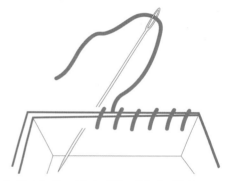

1 Choose a thread that will blend into the fabrics. Thread the needle and come up through a corner fold so the knot is hidden. Insert your needle straight through, catching just the very top threads at the folds of both fabrics and, being careful not to catch the paper template, push the needle through.

2 Loop the thread over the top; take the needle to the same side you started from but slightly further along and repeat, pushing the needle through as before. In EPP, aim for 12-15 stitches per inch sewn. Secure each completed edge with a knot just in case any should become loose.

quarter-inch seams

While much of the world uses the metric system, most quilt designs and patterns are written and made using inches. Mastering the quarter-inch seam will make your patchwork seams align well, and without puckers and stretches. A quarter-inch foot is helpful though not essential.

Step 1. If you have a quarter-inch foot, use it as your guide, aligning the seam edges along the 1/4in (6mm) line or guide.

Step 2. If you don't have a 1/4in (6mm) foot, you can mark a guideline on your machine using strips of masking or painter's tape placed 1/4in (6mm) to the right of the place where the needle drops. Several strips, one on top of another, will provide you with a physical as well as visual guide for the edge of your fabric. A stack of Post-it note strips also work for this.

Step 3. Whether using a quarter-inch foot or masking tape, test the accuracy of your 1/4in (6mm) seam by sewing together two 4 1/2in (11.4cm) squares and measuring the finished piece to make sure it measures exactly 8 1/2in (21.6cm).

Step 4. If longer or shorter than exactly 8 1/2in (21.6cm), the accuracy of your piecing will be compromised. Play around with the position of the needle, the masking tape, or the position of the fabric in relation to the quarter-inch foot until you know you have the perfect 1/4in (6mm) seam.

All blocks and projects in this book are made using 1/4in (6 mm) seams unless stated otherwise.

chain piecing

When you are making quilt blocks and have pre-cut fabrics for a number of blocks, the quickest way to piece the fabrics together is to chain piece them. To chain piece, prepare a pile of pairs to be pieced together. Sew the first pair together, sewing a few stitches beyond the end of the fabric and then insert the next pair without cutting the thread or lifting the presser foot. Continue with the whole pile of pairs until you have one long string of pairs of fabric pieces sewn together. Remove from the machine and snip the threads in between each section.

needle sizes

It is important to choose the correct needle size to match your fabric type and weight. In both sizing systems, the higher the number, the thicker the needle.

European size (mm)	American size	fabric weight
60	8	silks
70/75	10/11	lightweight, cotton, lawn, voile
80	12	medium weight, quilting cotton
90	14	medium to heavyweight, standard quilting layers
100	16	heavyweight, denim, thick quilting layers

measurement conversion

These conversion charts include a margin of error or rounding in each case and are included to give an idea of the sizes of finished blocks and the amount of fabric needed. They should not be used to convert measurements in the patterns. The blocks and projects have been designed and written in imperial measurements and will not piece together accurately if converted into approximately similar metric measurements.

quick conversion reference

Note that metric measurements have been rounded up/down to 1 decimal place maximum.

imperial	metric·
1/8in	3mm
1/4in	6mm
3/8in	9mm
1/2in	1.3cm
5/8in	1.6cm
3/4in	1.9cm
7/8in	2.2cm
1in	2.5cm
6in	15.2cm
12in	30.5cm

pressing

Quilters do not iron, they press. Pressing is an up and down motion rather than the sliding motion that you would use to remove wrinkles when ironing clothes. Use a hot iron and gentle pressure to flatten your seams or create deliberate creases and folds, such as on binding. Some quilters use steam but be careful as it can distort shapes.

Seams can be pressed open or to one side (see Block Construction: 4-patch) and different quilters have different preferences. It is good to bear in mind the bulk that can be created with different seams (half-square triangles for example) and the opacity of some fabrics so that seams can show through, and adapt pressing accordingly. For items that are going to be quilted, it is good to press the seams to the direction that reduces bulk. Pressing seams open can leave seams more vulnerable to being torn open so consider the purpose of the item you are making and whether strength and durability are a factor.

Starch can be used when pressing to control lightweight fabrics such as lawns or shot cottons, difficult fabrics like voile, linen, and silk, or bias-cut pieces.

making the blocks

block construction

These construction methods below are common to many different types of blocks:

1 **Rows:** Where pieces are joined horizontally. The 4-patch (see below) is the simplest example.

2 **Columns:** Where pieces are joined vertically. The numbers blocks use columns in their construction.

3 **Diagonal construction:** Similar to rows but running diagonally corner to corner rather than horizontally. See the granny square block.

The **4-patch** block (below) is constructed horizontally and is the basis for many quilt blocks. At its simplest, 4 squares are joined together in pairs to make two rows (1) and the seams are pressed to opposite sides (2). The rows are then joined together; this seam can be pressed open or to one side and the opposing seams nest together to make an accurate centre point where they meet (3).

Seams can also be pressed open throughout although more pinning will be required to ensure seams meet accurately. The seams on the right side should meet neatly (4).

The **9-patch** is similar to the 4-patch but uses multiples of 3 rather than 4. At its most basic it is 9 squares joined together. Like the 4-patch the squares are joined first in rows, 3 rows of 3. The rows are then joined matching the seam points. The same seam-pressing technique can be used to help alignment as the rows are stitched together.

For blocks where many points meet in the centre, try this trick: Take a pin and slide it through the point on one of the halves of the block from wrong side to right, and then on the other half of the block from right side to wrong so that the pin goes through both centre points and the 2 pieces of the block are held right sides together with the pin perpendicular to the fabric. Take the two halves of the block with the pin still inserted and slide under the sewing machine needle. Slide the pin out of the centre point and drop the sewing machine needle into the centre point. Sew one half of the seam from the centre point to the edge of the fabric, flip, and sew the second half of the seam, again starting at the centre point.

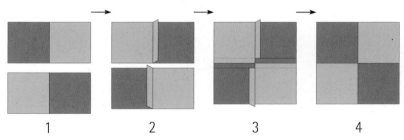

1　　　　　2　　　　　3　　　　　4

half-square triangles

There are various ways to make half-square triangle units — a square made of two half square triangles. A die cutter is a quick way to cut a lot of triangles which are ready to sew into pairs to make HST units (and have their corners already trimmed). If you do not have one or need to make HST units to a different size than the die, do this:

1 Cut two squares 1in (2.5cm) bigger than the finished HST unit. For example, for a finished HST unit of 2in (5.1cm), cut two 3in (7.6cm) squares. This will yield two HST units.

2 Draw a line along the diagonal on the wrong side of one of the triangles as a guide. The intended seam lines are also shown here.

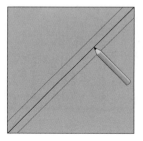

3 Place the two squares right sides together and sew two seams, 1/4in (6mm) either side of the drawn diagonal line.

4 Cut the unit in half along the drawn diagonal line.

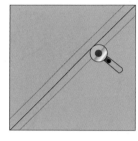

5 Press seams open or towards the darker fabric if you prefer.

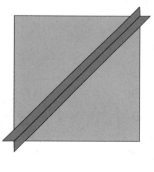

6 Trim to 2 1/2in (6.3cm) square (or 1/2in (1.3cm) bigger than whatever your finished square will be) taking care to align the diagonals of the square on the ruler with the diagonals of the seams on the HST unit when trimming. This stage also removes dog ears created when you sew with triangles.

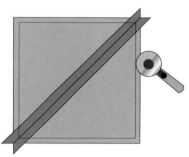

quarter-square triangles

Quarter-square triangle units are usually made in pairs, like half-square triangle units.

1 Take two squares of fabric 1 1/2in (3.8cm) bigger than the finished QST unit will be. This will make two QST units.

2 Sew these into two HST units following steps 2 to 5 in the HST instructions.

3 Press the seams to the darker side. There is no need to trim the units at this stage although you may wish to. If so, trim them to 1in larger than the finished QST unit size.

4 Draw a diagonal line on the wrong side of one of the HST units running perpendicular to the diagonal seam.

6 Sew two seams, 1/4in (6mm) away from the diag line on each side.

8 Press seams open or to one side.

5 Put the two squares right sides together, making sure that the seams nest together so that the right side of the darker fabric is next to the right side of the lighter fabric on each side of the nested seams.

7 Cut the unit in half along the drawn diagonal line.

9 Trim to 1/2in (1.3cm) bigger than the finished QST unit size. As with the HST units, take care to align the diagonals of the square on the ruler with the diagonals of the seams on the QST unit when trimming.

corner-square triangles

Adding HST triangles to the corners of squares either within a block or at the block corners themselves can be done quickly and accurately using the corner-square triangles technique. This method is similar to flying geese (see next page).

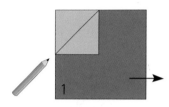 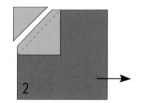 

1 Mark diagonal lines on the WS of the smaller square in pencil or by lightly pressing a crease with an iron.

2 Place the smaller square right sides together with the larger square over the corner where the triangle will be created and sew along the marked diag line. Trim both fabrics 1/4in (6mm) beyond the line.

3 Open out the fabric to reveal the triangle at the corner. Press.

4 The same technique can be used with a rectangle replacing either or both of the squares. The process is similar but the rectangle is placed perpendicular to the corner where the triangle is to be created. See right.

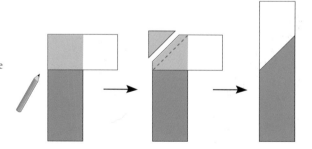

flying geese

Flying geese are made by taking one rectangle made up of two squares and adding HSTs to the corners. For a finished flying geese unit 2in x 4in (5.1cm x 10.2cm), you will need a rectangle 2 1/2in x 4 1/2in (6.3cm x 11.4cm) and two 2 1/2in (6.3cm) squares. For a 3in x 6in (7.6cm x 15.2cm) unit, you will need a rectangle 3 1/2in x 6 1/2in (8.9cm x 16.5cm) and two 3 1/2in (8.9cm) squares, etc.

1 Mark diagonal lines on the wrong side of each square.

2 Place one square right sides together with one half of the rectangle. Sew along the marked diag line.

3 Trim both fabrics 1/4in (6mm) beyond the line.

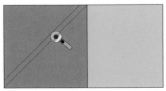

4 Press seam open (or towards the darker fabric, if you prefer) and trim off corners.

5 Repeat step 2, sewing the second square to the other half of the rectangle.

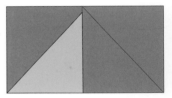

6 Again, trim seam allowance, press open, and trim corners to make the finished flying geese unit.

foundation paper piecing

Foundation paper piecing is a form of piecing which gives very accurate results. Blocks or part blocks are pieced using a printed block template as a guide for the seam lines. The paper is torn away once the block is made. It can feel like a counterintuitive process at first as you are working from the back, and in mirror image!

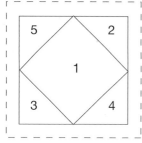

1 Print out the paper template(s).

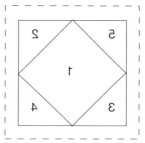

2 Shorten the stitch length to 1.5. This will make the paper easier to tear away at the end.

3 Each segment within the template will be numbered. The first piece of fabric goes on segment 1, the second on segment 2, etc.

4 Although you sew on the right side of the paper, the block is pieced on the wrong side of the paper – this means that the image produced will be the reverse of the image printed on the paper – important to remember if you are foundation-piecing nonsymmetrical images such as letters of the alphabet.

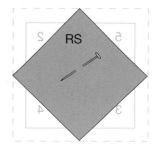

5 Take a piece of fabric which is big enough to cover segment 1 including a 1/4in (6mm) seam all around. Pin it to the back of the template, holding the paper template up to the light, if needed, to ensure that the fabric covers the whole of segment 1 plus seam allowance. The wrong side will be facing the back of the template and the right side facing you.

6 Pin a second piece of fabric with the wrong side facing you so it will be right sides together with the first piece of fabric. Place the pin along the seam line so that you can be sure that, when the seam is sewn and the fabric is flipped

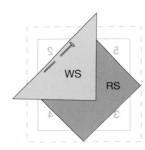

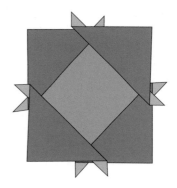

over, it will completely cover segment 2 plus seam allowance.

8 Repeat the process with all the remaining segments on the template.

9 Flip the template over and trim away excess fabric and paper, cutting along the seam allowance lines.

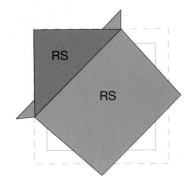

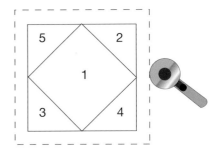

7 Sew the seam, which means sewing along the line between segments 1 and 2 (and extend the seam 1/4in (6mm) beyond each end of the line), flip, and press the fabric. Trim seam allowance on segments 1 and 2 to 1/4in (6mm), taking care not to cut the paper or the fabric other than seam allowance.

10 Finally remove the paper from the back of the block.

English paper piecing (EPP)

English paper piecing is a traditional hand-piecing method using paper templates. Paper templates can be bought online or can be homemade by printing shapes onto printer paper and cutting them out. No seam allowance is included on the templates as the seam allowance is wrapped around the template edges. This method is most commonly used for hexagons but can also be used for any tessellating shapes.

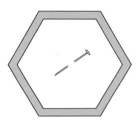

1 Pin or glue (using a fabric glue stick) the template to the wrong side of a piece of fabric. Cut around the template leaving a seam allowance of at least 1/4in (6mm).

2 Fold the seam allowance to the back of the template and baste in place either using a long basting stitch or again using a glue stick. Fold and baste first one side, then fold neatly under at the corner before folding and basting the next side, and continue until the whole shape is basted in place.

3 Take two basted shapes and hold them right sides together with the two sides to be sewn together aligned.

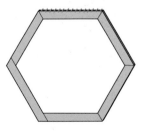

4 Sew them together along one edge using whip stitch.

5 Once any shapes are completely surrounded on all sides, you can remove basting stitches and the template paper.

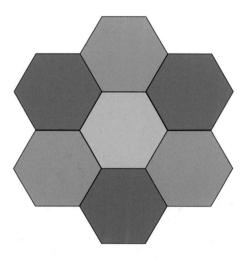

6 When appliquéing EPP to a background, appliqué the finished piece to the background with the papers still in place, cut away the background fabric up to 1/4in (6mm) away from the appliqué stitches, and remove the paper from the back.

hand appliqué

Using slip stitch and turning the fabric edge in using an iron or the point of a needle, hand appliqué is a simple way to add small fabric shapes to quilts.

1 Trace the required shape onto card stock or freezer paper. Cut out and either draw around the card stock template with a pencil onto the WS of the fabric, or iron freezer paper shape to fabric WS (nonsymmetrical designs will need to be reversed).

2 Cut out shape adding a scant 1/4in (6mm) seam allowance.

3 The raw fabric edges need to be turned inwards. Either use your finger or an iron to press the edges in around the template outline edge or freezer paper (a spray of starch helps to control and smooth curved edges), then pin and sew the turned edge shape to the background, or you can pin your shape to the fabric background and use the point of the needle to turn and fold the raw edges in as the shape is sewn down. Appliqué pins are extra small and hold tricky shapes neatly and accurately but you can also use standard pins or appliqué glue. If using freezer paper, remember to remove the freezer paper when sewing is almost complete.

4 Use slip stitch and a fine thread to hand sew the shape to the background. There are specific appliqué needles that are finer and more flexible than a standard needle to aid the needle turn process.

Alternatively, the raw edge appliqué fusible web technique can be used to apply the shape, and a decorative edge hand stitch can be used such as blanket stitch to finish the edges.

machine appliqué

There are various types of fusible web for raw edge appliqué including Bondaweb, Steam-a-Seam and Wonder-Under. They all work in fundamentally the same way but you will need to follow the manufacturer's instructions which vary from brand to brand.

1 Trace or draw your design onto the fusible web backing paper. Remember to draw your image in reverse. Cut out the shape roughly, i.e., leaving 1/2in to 1in (1.3cm to 2.5cm) excess around the edge of the shape.

2 Fuse the fusible web to the WS of the fabric. This is usually done using a hot iron.

3 Cut out the design and peel away the backing paper.

4 Position the web-backed fabric onto the BKG fabric.

5 Following manufacturer's instructions, fuse in place again, usually using a hot iron.

6 Machine sew along or close to the edge of the fused fabric to finish and hold in place. You might use a straight, blanket, or zigzag stitch.

sashing

Many quilts and even quilt blocks are made up of a basic block sashed together with other blocks that may be the same or may all be different, as in a sampler. Sashing strips are the strips of fabric that attach the blocks together.

1 To sash two blocks together, take a strip of fabric 1/2in (1.3cm) wider than the finished sashing, so a 2in (5.1cm) wide finished sashing requires strips 2 1/2in (6.3cm) wide.

2 The strip needs to be the same length as the unfinished block being sashed; so for a 6in (15.2cm) finished block, the block to be sashed will be 6 1/2in (16.5cm) square so a 2 1/2in x 6 1/2in (6.3cm x 16.5cm) strip will be needed.

3 Sew the strip to the side of one block and then to the side of the other.

4 Sashing strips can then be used to sash two halves of a block, or several strips of a quilt, together and final sashing strips can be used to add a border to the whole of the quilt top by adding strips first to the sides and then to the top and bottom.

finishing the quilt

making a quilt sandwich

After the quilt top has been sewn you will need to
make a quilt sandwich with batting and backing fabric,
and join the layers together in preparation for quilting.
This is often referred to as basting a quilt. It can
include basting/tacking stitches or the use of safety
pins and temporary spray fabric adhesive. There are a
variety of basting methods and it is important to
consider the size of the project as well as personal
preference. Good preparation is key. Iron the backing
and the quilt top so that all wrinkles are removed and
seams are flat. You will need a clean surface big
enough to spread out your quilt back flat. This can be
a table or a hard floor. If necessary, a carpeted floor
can be used, too! If using basting spray, make sure you
are in a well-ventilated area.

1   Cut the batting and the quilt backing so that they
    are 4in (10.2cm) larger all around than the quilt
    top. This allows for some shrinkage as the batting
    gets pulled in slightly during the quilting process.

2   Lay the quilt back on the floor, RS downwards.
    Working from the centre out, smooth wrinkles
    outwards and tape the edges but not the corners
    to the floor/table. The aim is for flat, even fabric.
    If the fabric is stretched too tightly it will distort.

3   Place the batting/wadding layer over the backing.
    For a large quilt, fold the batting, start in the
    centre, and fold out. Smooth out the layer as
    before. For spray basting, work on one half of the
    batting at a time, spray evenly on the side that
    will lie against the quilt back, and then repeat on
    the other side.

4   The quilt top is placed on top of the batting RS
    upwards. Smooth out any wrinkles. If you are
    spray basting, repeat as for step 3, spraying the
    batting and this time laying the quilt top over
    it, working in two halves. For large quilts, it is
    often easier to work with pins rather than spray.
    Starting from the centre, place safety pins about
    6–8in (15–20cm) apart, work outwards and push
    the pins through all 3 layers. Curved safety pins
    are easiest to work with. These are removed during
    the quilting process. There is a tool especially
    designed to help clip the safety pins together and
    save your fingers! As an alternative, you can use
    long hand-basting/tacking stitches to hold the
    layers together. Sew in a grid, from the centre
    outwards. Basting stitches will be removed by
    hand at a later stage when you quilt by hand or
    machine. This is a good method for hand quilting
    where safety pins could get in the way of a
    hoop frame.

5   Once basted, the quilt can be rolled and stored
    until ready to quilt. For small projects, even up
    to baby quilt size, spray basting is quick and
    efficient. Larger projects are harder to spray and are
    best pinned.

hand quilting

Any hand stitch that holds the layers of your quilt sandwich together is a form of hand quilting. Small projects can be quilted by basting the layers, either with basting spray or basting stitches, and then held in your hands for hand quilting. Larger projects will be easier to quilt using a quilt hoop specifically for hand quilting. The thickness of thread depends upon the effect you want to create, from finer 40wt thread through to perle cotton. For fine thread, small "between" needles are many quilters' preference. Chenille needles work well on thicker embroidery style threads. The stitching is a variation on a simple running stitch but with a rocking action from the dominant hand. The needle is pushed down through the layers by the dominant hand and the other hand helps to push it back up creating a hump and using a thimble to feel for the point of the needle from the WS. Single or multiple stitches can be taken at a time. The aim is to keep the stitches even on each side. Once the quilting is complete, trim the edges allowing 1/4in (6mm) seam allowance ready for binding. The padded tablet case project is hand quilted and a small project like this is a good way to practise hand quilting.

straight-line quilting

Many quilters take their quilts to long arm quilters or have their own long arm quilting machines. We both quilt on domestic machines which have a larger throat space to handle larger quilts. But small and medium quilts can still be quilted on almost all domestic sewing machines. For straight-line quilting, you will need a walking foot. This ensures that all three layers to be

quilted are pulled through the machine at the same rate to avoid slippage and puckering. If you do not have a walking foot, you should be able to buy one that fits your machine.

1 Although it is tempting to straight-line quilt following the lines in the patchwork, you will not end up with very straight lines. We prefer to mark the lines as a guide.

2 One of the best ways of doing this is with a Hera marker. This is a plastic tool, similar to a butter knife, which leaves a visible crease line on the quilt top. The line disappears once the quilt is washed and ironed.

3 Mark a grid or a series of lines to be quilted – for example start by marking lines 5in (12.7cm) apart and later mark and sew the lines between these guide lines.

4 If you are quilting some lines closer together, e.g. 1/2in to 1in (1.3cm to 2.5cm) apart, you can use a quilting guide which may come with your walking foot or sewing machine and enables you to quilt using previously quilted lines as a guide.

Once the quilting is complete, trim the edges allowing 1/4in (6mm) seam allowance ready for binding.

free-motion quilting

You will need a darning or free-motion quilting foot for your machine. It's best to lower your feed dogs, although you can still free-motion quilt if the feed dogs cannot be lowered. If you have not free-motion quilted before, try it on a quilting sandwich used just for "playing".

1 Attach the free-motion quilting foot and lower your feed dogs.

2 Start quilting in the centre and work your way outward.

3 Turn the needle manually through one rotation; bring the lower thread up through the sandwich. Pull both threads away from the area to be quilted.

4 Free-motion quilting takes practise. It helps to imagine the needle as a pencil and the stitches as doodles. Practise drawing your quilting patterns on paper before trying them on your quilt. Soon you will be able to sew wavy lines, flowers, hearts and other patterns.

5 Keep on quilting until you have finished the design, or that part of the design, or your thread runs out.

6 Bury the thread ends in the quilt sandwich using a hand needle.

binding

Binding can be used to finish the edges of a quilt. It frames the design and adds durability. It can be double or single folded, and straight or bias cut. Double-fold binding is used on quilts that will get heavy use. Single-fold binding is a neat finish with less bulk and is good for smaller items like coasters and potholders. Bias binding is durable and can also be used for design purposes — vertical stripes become diagonal — as well as for items with rounded corners, avoiding the need to miter corners (see potholder for a project with bias binding).

double-fold binding with mitered corners

1 Measure the perimeter of the quilt; add 20in (51cm) to allow for turning corners and joining ends.

2 Cut 2 1/2in (6.3cm) or 2 1/4in (5.7cm) strips across WOF. Wider strips make a wide binding (easier for beginners); narrower strips make a tighter binding. For bias binding, cut

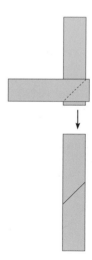

2 1/2in (6.3cm) strips for double-fold.

3   Join strips to make a continuous strip. You can use standard 1/4in (6mm) straight seams or join diagonally by placing the strips RS together and at right angles. Use your quilt ruler and pencil to mark a 45-degree line and sew a diagonal seam, trimming away the excess. *See diagram left.* Press seam open. Fold the strip in half lengthwise, WS together and press along the length of the strip. Roll up the binding until ready to use.

4   Prepare the quilt edges so they are trimmed and square, remembering to allow for 1/4in (6mm) SA around the edge. Trim the beginning of the binding to a straight edge and turn and press 1/4in (6mm) inwards to neaten the start of the binding. This will provide a pocket for the end of the binding.

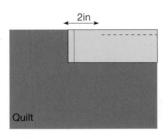

5   Start the binding part way down one side of the quilt, at least 4in (10.2cm) from a corner, place the binding RS against quilt top and align raw edges of quilt and binding. Start sewing 2in (5.1cm) in from the start of the binding and using 1/4in (6mm) seam. *See below.*

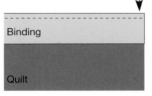

6   As you approach a corner, stop sewing the binding when you are exactly 1/4in (6mm) from the end of the fabric edge and secure with a few backstitches. Some machines have marks on the footplate to help with this.

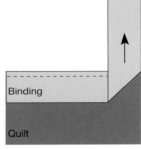

7   Fold binding away from quilt (see arrow) at an angle of 45 degrees. Press the diag crease.

8   Keeping diag crease in place, fold the binding strip down and onto the next edge to be bound. Press and, if necessary, pin to keep everything in place. Sew along this edge starting at the very top of the corner, using 1/4in (6mm) seam allowance as before. Keep sewing until you reach the next corner; repeat steps 1–4 for all the corners.

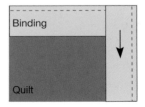

9 When you come to within 2in (5.1cm) of where the binding started, stop and secure your seam. The end of the binding will be slipping into the pocket created at the start so check the length, allowing room to tuck the end inside and trim the binding end. Tuck the binding inside and continue from where the seam stopped and sew to where the binding started. The binding should be continuously attached all around the quilt edge. The join can be closed with slip stitch.

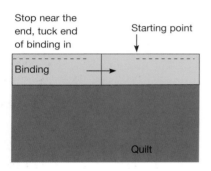

Stop near the end, tuck end of binding in

Starting point

Binding

Quilt

10 Press the binding away from the seam line. Turn the folded edge of the binding to the WS of the quilt. The binding can be sewn down by slip stitch or by machine. If machining, pin the folded edge so it just covers the binding seam line. Turn over and stitch from the RS using a thread colour that blends on both sides, and sewing in the ditch of the seam, slipping out the pins just before you reach them. This machine method takes some practise!

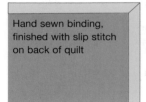

Hand sewn binding, finished with slip stitch on back of quilt

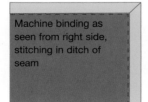

Machine binding as seen from right side, stitching in ditch of seam

Machine binding as seen from wrong side. The stitching just catches the folded edge of the binding

Note: The same method with variations can be used with other types of binding. Single-fold binding uses 1 1/4in (3.2cm) WOF strips but is otherwise sewn the same way and is best finished with handsewn slip stitch. Bias-cut single-fold binding uses 1 1/2in (3.8cm) strips to allow stretching when going around rounded corners.

hints and tips

- Press fabrics before cutting to ensure accuracy.

- Read through the block instructions before starting to check that you have what you need and understand the construction methods involved.

- Take time to play with your fabrics and check for contrast and harmony before you cut into them. Some block designs will disappear if the fabrics used don't have sufficient contrast.

- Use small stitches (under 1/8in (3mm)) so you won't have to worry about securing the beginning and end of seams.

- Invest in a 1/4in (6mm) foot for your machine, it will be worth every penny and your accurate seam allowance will make block construction so much easier!

- Match needle size to fabric weight — 80/12 for quilting weight, 70/10 for lawn and voile, 90/14 and above for canvas, heavier fabrics, and quilting.

- Replace machine sewing needles regularly and if you do a lot of quilting, consider using titanium needles. They are more expensive but they last longer.

- Keep separate machine needles for foundation paper piecing as the paper blunts the needles. The same rule applies for scissors and rotary cutters. Mark your tools for different usage so no one can ruin your best sewing scissors.

- Think safety with all your equipment. Keep sharp tools, especially rotary cutters, safely away from small children and pets, and consider yourself and your feet as you are bound to drop equipment! Pick up dropped scissors, seam rippers, pins and needles right away.

- However tempting it is, don't hold pins in your mouth — an intake of breath at the wrong time could have serious consequences.

- Use a good-quality cotton thread in your machine. A 50/2 thread will double up for piecing, machine quilting, and even hand piecing and appliqué. Good-quality thread costs more but runs through your machine more smoothly, depositing less lint and fibres, and your machine will thank you, especially when it comes to be serviced!

- Leave at least 1/4in (6mm) when snipping threads, to stop seams unravelling.

- Prewash dark colours, e.g. red, with a colour catcher. Some quilters prewash all fabrics to avoid colour bleed and shrinkage. Linens and flannel have a tendency to shrink and should be prewashed.

- Practise more challenging blocks or new construction techniques on scraps first, or cut up old clothes.

- Keep your cutting, sewing and pressing areas close together. You do not need to use a large ironing board; portable foldaway boards work well and small irons, even travel irons, can be helpful for getting the iron into those small seams.

blocks for everyone

In this chapter you will find quilt blocks ideal for beginners, but quilters of all abilities can have fun making quilts with these. Some of the most famous traditional blocks are among the simplest, including broken dishes, courthouse steps, economy square, log cabin, nine-patch, pinwheel and shoofly. You will be using some of the basic block making techniques including half square triangles and corner square triangles and cutting out a range of commonly used shapes. The colourful dish towel combines brightly coloured cotton scraps with linen for a practical and pretty starter project.

basket weave

see other variations page 62

main block [BWE1 — 6in (15.2cm) block]

1 Take 1 light and 2 dark strips, arrange dark, light, dark. Join along 7in (17.8cm) edges. Cut into 2 x 3 1/2in (8.9cm) sqs. Repeat with 2 light and 1 dark strips.
2 Using photograph for reference, arrange sqs to make 4-patch. Sew to make 2 rows, join rows.

Note: Block pictured left at top.

materials
■ **light:**
  3 x 1 1/2in x 7in (3.8cm x 17.8cm) strips
■ **dark:**
  3 x 1 1/2in x 7in (3.8cm x 17.8cm) strips

variation 1 [BWE2 — 6in (15cm) block]

1 Arrange strips light, med, dark. Join along 15in (38.1cm) edges. Cut into 4 x 3 1/2in (8.9cm) sqs, discard remainder.

2 Arrange sqs as in photograph, and join as for BWE1.

materials
■ **light:** 1 1/2in x 15in (3.8cm x 38.1cm) strip
■ **med:** 1 1/2in x 15in (3.8cm x 38.1cm) strip
■ **dark:** 1 1/2in x 15in (3.8cm x 38.1cm) strip

bento

see other variations page 63

main block [BE1 — 12in (30.5cm) block]

1   Make as CST4 using materials A. Repeat with materials B.

2   Cut each block into half lengthwise and half again widthwise to make 4 equal sqs.

3   From each block swap top right and bottom left sqs. Sew one block as 4-patch. Use remaining 4 sqs for BE2.

materials

block A
- **centre sq dark:** 5in (12.7cm) sq
- **inner border light:** 2 x 2 1/2in x 5in (6.3cm x 12.7cm), 2 x 2 1/2in x 9in (6.3cm x 22.9cm)
- **outer border dark:** 2 x 2 1/2in x 9in (6.3cm x 22.7cm), 2 x 2 1/2in x 13in (6.3cm x 33cm)

block B
- as A but inner border dark/ outer border light

note: this makes 2 blocks, BE1/BE2

variation 1 [BE2 — 12in (30.5cm) block]

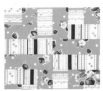

1   Arrange sqs as block photograph so the outer edges are now in the centre of the block. Sew block as 4-patch.

materials

- 4 remaining sqs from BE1

broken dishes

see other variations page 64

project: dish towel
[19 1/2in x 29 1/2in (49.5cm x 74.9cm)]

1   Make 12 BD3 blocks pairing print with cream sqs. Sew 2 rows of 6 blocks.

2   Sew each row to top and bottom of linen centre panel then add linen end strips to the top and bottom.

3   Make hanging loop pressing fabric in half long ways, bring long edges to centre fold, press again to make double fold strip and stitch along edges. Add to centre front of one side of dish towel. Place backing panel over towel front RS tog.

4   Stitch around edge leaving 5in (12.7cm) gap for turning. Close opening with slip stitch. Press and top stitch through all layers around outer edge and 1/4in (6mm) above each seam line between linen and blocks.

broken dishes main block [BD1 — 6in (15cm) block]

1   Pair sqs grey/print RS together. Make 4 HST units. Trim each to 3 1/2in (8.9cm) sq.

2   Arrange as block photograph. Join as 4-patch.

see variations page 65

brick wall

materials

- 16 x 2 1/2in x 4 1/2in (6.3cm x 11.4cm) rects, each of 2 colours

main block [BWA1 — 16in (40.6cm) block]

1 Sew the rects into rows and then join the rows together to make the block. Refer to the photograph for placement.

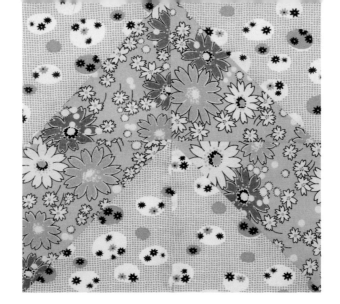

chevron

see variations page 66

main block [CH1 — 8in (20.3cm) block]

1   Pair A/B sqs. Make 4 HST units, trim to 4 1/2in (11.4cm) sq.

2   Sew tog using photograph for reference. Join rows.

materials

■ **col A (blue):**
    2 x 5in (12.7cm) sqs
■ **col B (yellow):**
    2 x 5in (12.7cm) sqs

see variations page 67

checkerboard

materials

- ■ **col A (red):**
  13 x 2 1/2in (6.3cm) sqs
- ■ **col B (pale):**
  12 x 2 1/2in (6.3cm) sqs

main block [CB1 — 10in (25.4cm) block]

1   Sew into rows alternating colours. Join rows following the layout in the photograph.

cheyenne

see variations page 68

main block [CY1 — 8in (20.3cm) block]

1   Pair 2 x A/BKG 3in (7.6cm) sqs. Make 4 HST units. Trim to 2 1/2in
    (6.3cm) sq. Repeat with B/BKG sqs.

2   Join HST units and 2 1/2in (6.3cm) sqs into 4 rows using block
    photograph for reference. Join rows.

materials

- ■ **col A (white):** 4 x 2 1/2in
  (6.3cm) sqs, 2 x 3in (7.6cm) sqs
- ■ **col B (grey):** 4 x 2 1/2in
  (6.3cm) sqs, 2 x 3in (7.6cm) sqs
- ■ **BKG:** 4 x 3in (7.6cm) sqs

courthouse steps

see other variations page 69

main block [CST1 — 6in (15.2cm) block]

1 Starting with centre sq, sew 1 of each of the smallest grey strips to both side edges. Repeat with smallest yellow strips to top edges.

2 Repeat for next border using the next size of strips and alternating yellow/grey. Add a third border in the same way.

materials

- **centre sq (black):** 2in (5.1cm) sq
- **col A (grey):** 1 1/4in x 2in (3.2cm x 5.1cm), 1 1/4in x 3 1/2in (3.2cm x 8.9cm), 1 1/4in x 5in (3.2cm x 12.7cm)
- **col B (grey):** 1 1/4in x 2in (3.2cm x 5.1cm), 1 1/4in x 3 1/2in (3.2cm x 8.9cm), 1 1/4in x 5in (3.2cm x 12.7cm)
- **col C (yellow):** 1 1/4in x 3 1/2in (3.2cm x 8.9cm), 1 1/4in x 5in (3.2cm x 12.7cm), 1 1/4in x 6 1/2in (3.2cm x 16.5cm)
- **col D (yellow):** 1 1/4in x 3 1/2in (3.2cm x 8.9cm), 1 1/4in x 5in (3.2cm x 12.7cm), 1 1/4in x 6 1/2in (3.2cm x 16.5cm)

variation 1 [CST2 — 10in (25.4cm) block]

1 Starting with centre sq, sew sqs to both side edges. Add dark sml rects to top and bottom edges.

2 Repeat for outer border alternating light and dark.

materials

- **centre sq (pink):** 2 1/2in (6.3cm) sq
- **light:** 2 x 2 1/2in sqs (6.3cm), 2 x 2 1/2in x 6 1/2in (6.3cm x 16.5cm) sml rects
- **dark:** 2 x 2 1/2in x 6 1/2in (6.3cm x 16.5cm) sml rects, 2 x 2 1/2in x 10 1/2in (6.3cm x 26.7cm)

cracker

main block [CR1 — 8 1/2in (21.6cm) block]

1   Sew dark rect either side of light rect along 6 1/2in (16.5cm) edges to make centre sq.

2   Cut the light/dark 5 1/4in (13.3cm) sqs in half along diagonal.

3   Find centre of each centre sq edge, mark with pins. Find centre of bias edge of each light triangle. Join diagonal of light triangles to dark sides of centre sq matching centre points. Repeat with dark triangles to remaining sides. Trim block to approx 9in (22.9cm) sq.

materials

- **light print A:** 2 1/2in x 6 1/2in (6.3cm x 16.5cm) rect
- **light print B:** 5 1/4in (13.3cm) sq
- **dark:** 2 x 2 1/2in x 6 1/2in (6.3cm x 16.5cm) rects, 5 1/4in (13.3cm) sq

---

variation 1 [CR2 — 8 1/2in (21.6cm) block]

1   As for CR2, using 2 colours instead of 3.

see other variations page 70

materials

- **col A (brown):** 2 x 1 1/2in x 6 1/2in (3.8cm x 16.5cm) rect, 5 1/4in (13.3cm) sq
- **col B (green/multi):** 4 1/2in x 6 1/2in (11.4cm x 16.5cm) rect, 5 1/4in (13.3cm) sq

economy square

main block [ES1 — 8in (20.3cm) block]

1   Add 4 CSTs to the corners of the 8 1/2in (21.6cm) sq using the
    4 1/2in (11.4cm) sqs.

materials
■ **BKG:**
   8 1/2in (21.25cm) sq
■ **col A:**
   4 x 4 1/2in (11.25cm) sqs for
   CSTs

---

variation 1 [ES2 — 12in (30.5cm) block]

1   Cut the 5in (12.7cm) sqs into 4 x 2 1/2in
    (6.3cm) sqs each.

2   Add 4 CSTs to each of the 4 1/2in (11.4cm)
    sqs using the 2 1/2in (6.3cm) sqs, adding
    dark CSTs to light sqs and light CSTs to
    dark sqs.

3   Sew the 9 sqs into a 9-patch.

see other variations page 71

materials
■ 9 x 4 1/2in (11.4cm) sqs
   (4 dark, 5 light)
■ 9 x 5in (12.7cm) sqs
   (5 dark, 4 light)

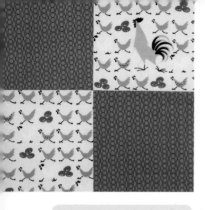

four square

main block [FO1 — 10in (25.4cm) block]

1   Arrange sqs as block photograph. Join pairs of sqs to make 2 rows. Join rows. This method is also known as 4-patch.

materials
■ **dark:**
2 x 5 1/2in (14cm) sqs
■ **light:**
2 x 5 1/2in (14cm) sqs

---

variation 1 [FO2 — 7in (17.8cm) block]

see other variations page 72

1   Join sqs tog as for FO1. Sash with sml rects on the side edges and lrg rects top and bottom.

materials
■ 4 x 2 1/4in (5.7cm) sqs, 2 each in 2 colours
■ **BKG:**
2 x 2 1/4 x 4in (5.7cm x 10.2cm) sml rects, 2 x 2 1/4in x 7 1/2in (5.7cm x 19cm) lrg rects

nine-patch

main block [NP1 — 6in (15.2cm) block]

1   Sew the sqs into rows and then into the finished block following
    the layout in the photograph.

materials

■ **col A (light):**
    5 x 2 1/2in (6.3cm) sqs
■ **col B (dark):**
    4 x 2 1/2in (6.3cm) sqs

variation 1 [NP2 — 12in (30.5cm) block]

see other variations page 73

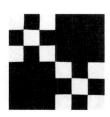

1   Make 2 9-patches as for NP1.

2   Sew into a 4-patch with the 2 x 6 1/2in
    (16.5cm) sqs.

materials

■ 2 x requirements
    for NP1, plus:
■ 2 x 6 1/2in (16.5cm) sqs

see variations page 74

frame

materials

- **centre sq:**
  8 1/2in (21.6cm) sq
- **border sqs (mixed colours):**
  20 x 2 1/2in (6.3cm) sqs

main block [FR1 — 12in (30.5cm) block]

1   Join 4 sqs in a row. Repeat. Sew rows to centre sq side edges.

2   Join 6 sqs in a row. Repeat. Sew rows to centre sq top/bottom edges.

log cabin

main block [LC1 — 9in (22.9cm) block]

1 Sew cream sq to right edge of centre sq. Sew cream 1 1/2in x 2 1/2in (3.8cm x 6.3cm) rect to bottom edge of the two starting sqs. Continue adding in a clockwise direction, each border will be made up of 2 colours and the fabrics get darker as the block gets bigger.

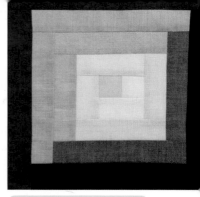

materials

- **yellow centre**: 1 1/2in (3.8cm) sq
- **border 1 cream**: 1 1/2in (3.8cm) sq, 1 1/2in x 2 1/2in (3.8cm x 6.3cm)
- **border 1 light blue**: 1 1/2in x 2 1/2in (3.8cm x 6.3cm), 1 1/2in x 3 1/2in (3.8cm x 8.9cm)
- **border 2 beige**: 1 1/2in x 3 1/2in (3.8cm x 8.9cm), 1 1/2in x 4 1/2in (3.8cm x 11.4cm)
- **border 2 medium blue**: 1 1/2in x 4 1/2in (3.8cm x 11.4cm), 1 1/2in x 5 1/2in (3.8cm x 14cm)
- **border 3 light brown**: 1 1/2in x 5 1/2in (3.8cm x 14cm), 1 1/2in x 6 1/2in (3.8cm x 16.5cm)
- **border 3 lilac**: 1 1/2in x 6 1/2in (3.8cm x 16.5cm), 1 1/2in x 7 1/2in (3.8cm x 19cm)
- **border 4 brown**: 1 1/2in x 7 1/2in (3.8cm x 19cm), 1 1/2in x 8 1/2in (3.8cm x 21.6cm)
- **border 4 dark blue**: 1 1/2in x 8 1/2in (3.8cm x 21.6cm), 1 1/2in x 9 1/2in (3.8cm x 24.1cm)

variation 1 [LC2 — 10 1/2in (26.7cm) block]

see other variations page 75

1 Sew light sq to right edge of centre sq. Sew light 1 1/2in x 2 1/2in (3.8cm x 6.3cm) rect to bottom edge of the two starting sqs. Continue adding in a clockwise direction, each border will be made up of 2 light strips and 2 dark.

materials

- **yellow centre**: 2in (5.1cm) sq
- **border 1 light**: 2in sq (5.1cm), 2in x 3 1/2in (5.1cm x 8.9cm)
- **border 1 dark**: 2in x 3 1/2in (5.1cm x 8.9cm), 2in x 5in (5.1cm x 12.7cm)
- **border 2 light**: 2in x 5in (5.1cm x 12.7cm), 1 1/2in x 6 1/2in (3.8cm x 16.5cm)
- **border 2 dark**: 1 1/2in x 6 1/2in (3.8cm x 16.5cm), 1 1/2in x 8in (3.8cm x 20.3cm)
- **border 3 light**: 1 1/2in x 8in (3.8cm x 20.3cm), 1 1/2in x 9 1/2in (3.8cm x 24.1cm)
- **border 3 dark**: 1 1/2in x 9 1/2in (3.8cm x 24.1cm), 1 1/2in x 11in (3.8cm x 27.9cm)

hourglass

main block [HG1 — 4in (10.2cm) square]

1   On WS light sq draw a diagonal line from corner to corner in pencil. Pair dark/light sqs, sew 2 x HST units. Cut each pair in half diagonally along pencil line, select 2 triangles to get opposing colour pattern, and discard 2. Join along diagonal seam. Trim block to 4 1/2in (11.4cm) sq.

materials

■ **dark:**
5 1/2in (14cm) sq
■ **light:**
5 1/2in (14cm) sq

note: this makes 2 blocks

variation 1 [HG2 — 4in (10.2cm) square]

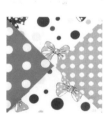

1   Pair light sqs with A and B. Continue as HG1.

see other variations page 76

materials

■ **col A:**
5 1/2in (14cm) sq
■ **col B:**
5 1/2in (14cm) sq
■ **light:**
2 x 5 1/2in (14cm) sqs

note: this makes 4 blocks

maple leaf

main block [ML1 — 6in (15.2cm) block]

1. Cut lrg BKG sq in half along diagonal. Sew the stalk strip to the long bias side of one of the resulting triangles and then to the other. Trim to 2 1/2in (6.3cm) sq.

2. Make 4 HST units pairing the lrg 3in (7.6cm) sqs and trimming to 2 1/2in (6.3cm) sq.

3. Using photograph for ref, sew block tog as 9-patch.

materials

- **green scraps:** 3 x 2 1/2in (6.3cm) sml sqs, 2 x 3in (7.6cm) lrg sqs
- **stalk:** 3/4in x 5in (1.9cm x 12.7cm) strip
- **BKG:** 2 1/2in (6.3cm) sml sq, 3 x 3in (7.6cm) lrg sqs

variation 1 [ML2 — 9in (22.9cm) block]

1. As for ML1, trimming sqs to 3 1/2in (8.9cm).

see other variations page 77

materials

- **leaf:** 3 x 3 1/2in (8.25cm) sml sqs, 2 x 4in (10cm) lrg sqs
- **stalk:** 1in x 6in (2.5cm x 15cm) strip
- **BKG:** 3 1/2in (8.25cm) sml sq, 3 x 4in (10cm) sqs

kaleidoscope

see other variations page 78

main block [KAL1 — 10in (25.4cm) block]

1 Sew the triangles into pairs, 1 of each colour, and then sew those pairs into two halves of the octagon. Sew the two halves together to make the octagon.

2 Sew the four HSTs onto four corners and trim to 10 1/2in (26.7cm).

materials

- 2 x 5 1/2in x 15in (14cm x 38.1cm) rects of 2 different fabrics each cut into 4 triangles using the 10in (25.4cm) line on the Kaleido Ruler
- 2 x 4in (10.2cm) sqs cut in half along the diag

note: for these blocks you will need a large Marti Mitchell Kaleido Ruler

variation 1 [KAL2 — 12in (30.5cm) block]

1 Make as for KAL1 then sash the sides using the shorter strips, and the top and bottom using the longer strips.

materials

- as for KAL1, plus:
- 2 x 1 1/2in x 10 1/2in (3.8cm x 26.7cm) strips, 2 x 1 1/2in x 12 1/2in (3.8cm x 31.7cm) strips

octagon snowball

main block [OS1 — 7in (17.8cm) block]

1   Add 4 CSTs to the 5 1/2in (14cm) sq using 4 x B 2in (5.1cm) sqs.

2   Sash the sides using the shorter and then the top and bottom using the longer strips.

materials

- ■ col A (black):
    5 1/2in (14cm) sq
- ■ col B (white):
    4 x 2in (5.1cm) sqs,
    2 x 1 1/2in x 5 1/2in (3.8cm
    x 14cm) strips, 2 x 1 1/2in
    x 7 1/2in (3.8cm x 19cm)
    strips

variation 1 [OS2 — 6in (15.2cm) block]

see other variations page 79

1   Make as for OS1 step 1.

2   Cut the octagon in half vertically and sash back tog using 1 of the 1in x 5 1/2in (2.5cm x 14cm) strips.

3   Cut the octagon in half horizontally and sash back tog using 1 more of the 1in x 5 1/2in (2.5cm x 14cm) strips.

4   Follow step 2 of OS1.

materials

- ■ as for OS1, replacing the
    1 1/2in (3.8cm) strips with:
    4 x 1in x 5 1/2in (2.5cm x
    14cm) strips, 2 x 1in x
    6 1/2in (2.5cm x 16.5cm)
    strips

pinwheel

main block [PW1 — 8 1/2in (21.6cm) block]

1   Make 4 HST units pairing the 4 1/2in (11.4cm) sqs. Trim to 4in (10.2cm) sq.

2   Sew into a 4-patch following the layout in the photograph.

3   Add the shorter sashing strips onto the top and bottom, then the longer onto the two sides of the block.

materials

■   2 x 4 1/2in (11.4cm) sqs of each of 2 different colours
■   **sashing:**
    2 x 1 1/4in x 7 1/2in (3.2cm x 19cm) strips, 2 x 1 1/4in x 9in (3.2cm x 22.9cm) strips

---

variation 1 [PW2 — 10in (25.4cm) block]

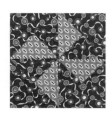

1   Make as for PW1 steps 1 and 2.

2   Add the 6in (15.2cm) HSTs onto top and bottom then two sides of the block and trim to 10 1/2in (26.7cm).

see other variations page 80

materials

■   2 x 4 1/2in (11.25cm) sqs of each of 2 different colours
■   2 x 6in (15cm) sqs cut in half along the diag

scots plaid

see other variations page 81

main block [SP1 – 13in (33cm) block]

1   Join D rect to top edge of A lrg sq. Join A sml sq to 4in (10.2cm) edge B sml rect. Add to right side of lrg A sq.

2   Repeat with B lrg rect and A sml sq/C lrg rect.

materials

- ■ **col A (grey):** 2 x 4in (10.2cm) sml sqs, 6 1/2in (16.5cm) lrg sq
- ■ **col B (navy):** 4in x 6 1/2in (10.2cm x 16.5cm) sml rect, 4in x 10in (10.2cm x 25.4cm) lrg rect
- ■ **col C (red):** 4in x 10in (10.2cm x 25.4cm) lrg rect
- ■ **col D (green):** 4in x 6 1/2in (10.2cm x 16.5cm) sml rect

variation 1 [SP2 – 6in (15.2cm) block]

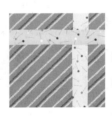

1   Sew A rect to right edge of BKG lrg sq. Add BKG rect to far right edge.

2   Sew B rect to top edge of step 1 section.

3   Sew A sq to right edge of BKG rect. Add BKG sml sq to far right edge. Join to top of steps 1/2 section.

materials

- ■ **BKG (pink):** 1 1/2in (3.8cm) sml sq, 4 1/2in (11.4cm) lrg sq, 2 x 1 1/2in x 4 1/2in (3.8cm x 11.4cm) rects
- ■ **col A (aqua):** 1 1/2in (3.8cm) sml sq, 1 1/2in x 4 1/2in (3.8cm x 11.4cm) rect
- ■ **col B (green):** 1 1/2in x 6 1/2in (3.8cm x 16.5cm) rect

see variations page 82

shoofly

materials

- **BKG:** 2 x 3in (7.6cm) sqs, 4 x 2 1/2in (6.3cm) sqs
- **shoofly:** 2 x 3in (7.6cm) sqs, 2 1/2in (6.3cm) sq

main block [SF1 — 6in (15.2cm) block]

1   Make 4 HST units pairing the 3in (7.6cm) sqs. Trim to 2 1/2in (6.3cm).

2   Assemble block following the layout in the photograph.

tumblers

see variations page 83

main block [TMB1 — 12in (30.5cm) block]

1 Mark 1/2in (1.3cm) in from both top corners of each sq. Trim sq to tumbler shape by cutting from each bottom corner up to its matching mark.

2 Sew the tumblers into 6 rows of 9 and then into the block following the layout in the photograph. Trim block to 12 1/2in (31.7cm) wide.

materials

■ 54 x 2 1/2in (6.3cm) sqs

windows

see other variations page 84

main block [WWS1 — 14 1/2in (36.8cm) block]

1   Make 9 pairs of QST units, pairing together 5in (12.7cm) sqs. Trim to 4in (10.2cm) sq. 9 of these units will be discarded but can be used for WWS2.

2   Sash the 9 QST sqs together using the 4in (10.2cm) strips, then the 13in (33cm) strips, and then the 15in (38.1cm) strips.

materials

■ **prints:** 18 x 5in (12.7cm) squares of different colours

■ **white:** 6 x 1 1/2in x 4in (3.8cm x 10.7cm) strips, 4 x 1 1/2in x 13in (3.8cm x 33cm) strips, 2 x 1 1/2in x 15in (3.8cm x 38.1cm) strips

variation 1 [WWS2 — 12 1/2in (31.7cm) block]

1   Make 9 pairs of QSTs as in step 1 of WWS1, or use the spare QSTs made in WWS1. Sew together in a 9-patch.

2   Sash using the 1 1/2in (3.8cm) sqs and 1 1/2in (3.8cm) strips following the layout in the photograph.

materials

■ **prints:**
    18 x 5in (12.7cm) squares of different colours (or use those left over from WWS1), 4 x 1 1/2in (3.8cm) sqs

■ **black:**
    4 x 1 1/2in x 11in (3.8cm x 27.9cm) strips

variations

basket weave

see base design page 33

variation 2
[BWE3 — 8in (20.3cm) block]

materials
light:
2 1/2in x 19in (6.3cm x 48.3cm) strip
med:
1 1/2in x 19in (3.8 x 48.3cm) strip
dark:
1 1/2in x 19in (3.8cm x 48.3cm) strip

1. As for BWE1 but arranging set of strips med/light/dark and cutting into 4 x 4 1/2in (11.4cm) sqs.

variation 3
[BWE4 — 7in (17cm) block]

materials
light A:
1 1/4in x 19in (3.2cm x 48.3cm) strip
col B:
1 1/2in x 19in (3.8cm x 48.3cm) strip
light C:
1 1/4in x 19in (3.2cm x 48.3cm) strip
col D:
1 1/2in x 19in (3.8cm x 48.3cm) strip

1. Arrange strips A/B/C/D. Continue as for BWE2 but cutting into 4 x 4in (10.2cm) sqs.

variation 4
[BWE5 — 8in (20.3cm) block]

materials
light:
2 x 1 1/2in x 19in (3.8cm x 48.3cm) strips
col A:
1 1/2in x 19in (3.8cm x 48.3cm) strip
col B:
1 1/2in x 19in (3.8cm x 48.3cm) strip

1. Arrange strips light/A/B/light. Continue as for BWE2, instead cutting into 4 x 4 1/2in (11.4cm) sqs.

bento

see base design page 34

variation 2
[BE3 — 12in (30.5cm) block]

materials for block A
centre sq dark: 5 1/2in (14cm) sq. **inner border light:** 2 x 1 1/2in x 5 1/2in (3.8cm x 14cm), 2 x 1 1/2in x 7 1/2in (3.8cm x 19cm). **outer border med:** 2 x 3 1/2in x 7 1/2in (8.9cm x 19cm), 2 x 3 1/2in x 13 1/2in (8.9cm x 34.3cm)

materials for block B
centre sq light: 5 1/2in (14cm) sq. **inner border med:** 2 x 1 1/2in x 5 1/2in (3.8cm x 14cm), 2 x 1 1/2in x 7 1/2in (3.8cm x 19cm). **outer border dark:** 2 x 3 1/2in x 7 1/2in (8.9cm x 19cm), 2 x 3 1/2in x 13 1/2in (8.9cm x 34.3cm)

1. Make as for BE1.

variation 3
[BE4 — 12in (30.5cm) block]

materials
4 remaining sqs from BE3

1. As for BE2.

variation 4
[BE5 — 12in (30.5cm) block]

materials
from each of col A (white) and col B (aqua): 4 x 2 1/2in (6.3cm) sqs, 4 x 2 1/2in x 4 1/2in (6.3 x 11.4cm) sml rects, 2 x 2 1/2in x 6 1/2in (6.3cm x 16.5cm) lrg rects

1. Make 4 CST3 blocks. Two of these will start with aqua corner sqs and two will start with white corner sqs. Use photograph for reference when adding the rects.
2. Join blocks as 4-patch, corner sqs in the centre of the block.

variations

broken dishes

see base design page 37

variation 1
[BD2 — 6in (15cm) block]

materials
dark:
2 x 4in (10cm) sqs
light:
2 x 4in (10cm) sqs

1. Complete as BRD1 arranging sqs as block photograph before joining rows.

variation 2
[BD3 — 6in (15cm) block]

materials
col A (cream):
8 x 2 1/2in (6.25cm) sqs
col B (scraps):
8 x 2 1/2in (6.25cm) sqs, each in a different print

1. Pair sqs A and B RS tog. Sew HST units. Trim each to 2in (5cm) sq.
2. Arrange as block photograph, sew into rows of 4, nesting seams. Join rows together.

variation 3
[BD4 — 6in (15cm) block]

materials
col A (red cross-weaves):
4 x 4in (10cm) sqs, each a different shade
col B (blue):
4 x 4in (10cm) sqs

note: BRD4 will make 2 blocks

1. Complete as BRD2.

variation 4
[BD5 — 6in (15cm) block]

materials
dark:
2 x 4in (10cm) sqs
light:
2 x 4in (10cm) sqs

1. Complete as BRD2.

variations
brick wall

see base design page 38

variation 1
[BWA2 — 16in (40cm) block]

materials
16 x 2 1/2in x 4 1/2in (6.25cm x 11.25cm) rect scraps.

1. As for BWA1.

variation 2
[BWA3 — 16in (40cm) block]

materials
col A (orange/yellow):
5 1/2in (13.25cm) sq,
10 x 2 1/2in x 4 1/2in (6.25cm x 11.25cm) rects
col B (grey):
5 1/2in (13.25cm) sq,
20 x 2 1/2in x 4 1/2in (6.25cm x 11.25cm) rects

1. Make a QST pairing the 5 1/2in (13.25cm) sqs and trimming to 4 1/2in (11.25cm) sq.
2. Sash the sides and then top of the QST using grey rects.
3. Sash again using yellow/orange rects and then again using grey rects.

variation 3
[BWA4 — 12in (30cm) block]

materials
col A (black):
8 x 2 1/2in x 4 1/2in (6.25cm x 11.25cm) rects,
3 x 2 1/2in (6.25cm) sqs
col B (white):
7 x 2 1/2in x 4 1/2in (6.25cm x 11.25cm) rects,
3 x 2 1/2in (6.25cm) sqs

1. Sew the rects and sqs into rows and then join the rows together to make the block. Refer to the photograph for placement.

variation 4
[BWA5 — 12in (30cm) block]

materials
15 x 2 1/2in x 4 1/2in (6.25cm x 11.25cm) rect scraps, 6 x 2 1/2in (6.25cm) sq scraps

1. Sew the rects into rows and then join the rows together to make the block. Refer to the photograph for placement.

chevron

see base design page 39

variation 1
[CH2 — 8in (20.3cm) block]

materials
col A (light):
2 x 5in (12.7cm) sqs in different prints
col B (dark):
2 x 5in (12.7cm) sqs

1. Make as for CH1.

variation 2
[CH3 — 8in (20.3cm) block]

materials
col A (pink):
1 x 5in (12.7cm) sq
col B (floral):
2 x 5in (12.7cm) sqs
col C (green):
1 x 5in (12.7cm) sq

1. Pair A/B sqs. Make 2 HST units, trim to 4 1/2in (11.4cm) sqs. Join into row.
2. Make as for step 1 with B/C sqs.
3. Join as for CH1.

variation 3
[CH4 — 8in (20.3cm) block]

materials
(this makes 2 blocks)
col A (light):
4 x 5in (12.7cm) sqs in different prints
col B (dark):
4 x 5in (12.7cm) sqs in different prints

1. Pair A and B sqs. Make 4 HST units, trim to 4 1/2in (11.4cm) sq.
2. Arrange to make 2 scrappy blocks. Join as for CH1.

variation 4
[CH5 — 8in (20.3cm) block]

materials
col A (light): 2 x 3in (7.6cm) sqs
col B (dark): 4 x 3in (7.6cm) sqs
col C (light): 4 x 3in (7.6cm) sqs
col D (dark): 4 x 3in (7.6cm) sqs
col E (light): 2 x 3in (7.6cm) sqs

1. Pair 2 A/B sqs. Make 4 HST units, trim to 2 1/2in (6.3cm) sq. Sew tog as per photograph to make 1st row.
2. Pair 2 B/C sqs. Continue as for step 1.
3. Repeat steps 1 and 2 with C/D and D/E to make 4 rows. Join rows.

variations
checkerboard

see base design page 40

variation 1
[CB2 — 14in (35.6cm) block]

materials
col A (cream):
18 x 2 1/2in (6.3cm) sqs
col B (dark scraps):
18 x 2 1/2in (6.3cm) sqs,
2 x 1 1/2in x 12 1/2in
(3.8cm x 31.7cm) strips,
2 x 1 1/2in x 14 1/2in
(3.8cm x 36.8cm) strips

1. Sew sqs into
rows alternating
colours and then into
the checkerboard
following the layout
in the photograph.
2. Sash the sides and
then the top and bottom
using the shorter then
the longer strips.

variation 2
[CB3 — 14in (35.6cm) block]

materials
light:
16 x 2 1/2in (6.3cm) sqs
medium:
24 x 2 1/2in (6.3cm) sqs
dark:
9 x 2 1/2in (6.3cm) sqs

1. Sew into rows and
then into the block
following the layout in
the photograph.

variation 3
[CB4 — 12in (30.5cm) block]

materials
col A (purple)
light: 8 x 2 1/2in
(6.3cm) sqs
medium: 10 x 2 1/2in
(6.3cm) sqs
dark: 6 x 2 1/2in
(6.3cm) sqs
col B (pink)
light: 2 x 2 1/2in
(6.3cm) sqs
medium: 4 x 2 1/2in
(6.3cm) sqs
dark: 6 x 2 1/2in
(6.3cm) sqs

1. Sew into rows and
then into the block
following the layout in
the photograph.

variation 4
[CB5 — 10in (25.4cm) block]

materials
for each of dark
and light:
7 x 3 1/2in (8.9cm) sqs,
6 x 2 1/2in (6.3cm) sqs

1. Make 14 QST units
using the 3 1/2in (8.9cm)
sqs. Discard 1, and trim
to 2 1/2in (6.3cm) sq.
2. Sew into rows and
then into the block
following the layout
in the photograph.

variations

cheyenne

see base design page 41

variation 1
[CY2 — 8in (20.3cm) block]

materials
scraps in diff colours:
8 x 2 1/2in (6.3cm) sqs,
4 x 3in (7.6cm) sqs
BKG:
4 x 3in (7.6cm) sqs

1. Make as for CY1.

variation 2
[CY3 — 8in (20.3cm) block]

materials
col A (yellow):
2 x 2 1/2in x 8 1/2in
(6.3cm x 21.6cm) lrg rects,
4 x 2 1/2in x 4 1/2in (6.3cm
x 11.4cm) sml rects
BKG:
8 x 2 1/2in (6.25cm) sqs

1. Add BKG sqs to both
ends of A lrg rect as CSTs
using photograph for
placement. Repeat for 1
end of each sml rect. Join
CST ends of sml rects
together to make 2 rows.
2. Arrange rows as block
photograph. Join rows.

variation 3
[CY4 — 8in (20.3cm) block]

materials
col A:
2 1/2in x 8 1/2in (6.3cm
x 21.6cm) lrg rect
col B:
2 x 2 1/2in x 4 1/2in (6.3cm
x 11.4cm) sml rects
col C:
2 x 2 1/2in x 4 1/2in (6.3cm
x 11.4cm) sml rects
col D:
2 1/2in x 8 1/2in (6.3cm
x 21.6cm) lrg rect
BKG:
8 x 2 1/2in (6.3cm) sqs

1. Make as CY3,
each row will be a
contrasting colour.

variation 4
[CY5 — 12in (30cm) block]

materials
scraps in diff colours:
8 x 2 1/2in (6.3cm) sqs, 8
x 3in (7.6cm) sqs
BKG:
12 x 2 1/2in (6.3cm) sqs,
8 x 3in (7.6cm) sqs

1. Make as for CY1,
pairing 8 BKG/scrap
sqs and making 16 HST
units. Trim to 2 1/2in
(6.3cm) sq.
2. Arrange blocks into 6
rows using photograph
for ref, join rows.

variations

courthouse steps

see base design page 43

variation 2
[CST3 — 6in (15.2cm) block]

materials
corner sq (dark): 2in (5.1cm) sq
various light: 2in (5.1cm) sq, 2in x 3 1/2 in (5.1cm x 8.9cm) sml rect, 2in x 5in (5.1cm x 12.7cm) med rect
various dark: 2in x 3 1/2in (5.1cm x 8.9cm) sml rect, 2in x 5in (5.1cm x 12.7cm) med rect, 2 1/2in x 6 1/2in (6.3cm x 16.5cm) lrg rect

1. Starting with bottom right corner sq, sew light sq to top edge. Add dark sml rect to left side edge.
2. Repeat adding light for horizontal strips and dark for vertical, finishing with lrg dark rect.

variation 3
[CST4 — 13in (33cm) block]

materials
centre sq dark:
5 1/2in (14cm) sq
inner border light:
2 x 1 1/2in x 5 1/2in (3.8cm x 14cm),
2 x 1 1/2in x 7 1/2in (3.8cm x 19cm)
outer border med:
2 x 3 1/2in x 7 1/2in (8.9cm x 19cm),
2 x 3 1/2in x 13 1/2in (8.9cm x 34.3cm)

1. As for CST1 but making inner border from all 1 colour, followed by outer border all in 1 colour.

variation 4
[CST5 — 12in (30cm) block]

materials
(scraps in diff shades of one colour) centre 4 1/2in (11.4cm) sq, 6 x 2 1/2in x 4 1/2in (6.3cm x 11.4cm) sml rects, 4 x 2 1/2in x 6 1/2in (6.3cm x 16.5cm) med rects, 2 x 2 1/2in x 8 1/2in (6.3cm x 21.6cm) lrg rects

1. Starting with centre sq, sew 2 sml rects to top and bottom edges. Add 2 lrg rects to side edges.
2. Join short edges of 2 sml rects tog, sew to side of block. Repeat for other side to each side.
3. As for step 2, using med rects and adding to top and bottom edges.

cracker

see base design page 44

variation 2
[CR3 — 8 1/2in (21.6cm) block]

materials
col A (red):
2 x 2 1/2in x 6 1/2in (6.3cm x 16.5cm) rects, 5 1/4in (13.3cm) sq
col B (grey):
2 x 2 1/2in (6.3cm) sqs
col C (pink):
2 1/2in (6.3cm) sq
col D (white):
5 1/4in (13.3cm) sq

1. Sew col B/C 2 1/2in (6.3cm) sqs together in row of col 3. Add A rects to either side along 6 1/2in (16.5cm) edges to make centre sq.
2. Complete as for CR1.

variation 3
[CR4 — 8 1/2in (21.6cm) block]

materials
col A (pink): 3 1/2in x 6 1/2in (8.9cm x 16.5cm) rect, 5 1/4in (13.3cm) sq
col B (teal): 3 1/2in x 6 1/2in (8.9cm x 16.5cm) rect, 5 1/4in (13.3cm) sq
col C (floral): 5 1/4in (13.3cm) sq

1. Join light/dark rects along 6 1/2in (16.5cm) edges.
2. Cut the sqs in half diagonally. Discard 1 each of pink/teal triangles. Add remaining triangles at each corner following photo, using technique from CR1.

variation 4
[CR5 — 8 1/2in (21.6cm) block]

materials
col A (gingham):
2 x 3 1/2in (8.9cm) sqs, 5 1/4in (13.3cm) sq
col B (dots):
2 x 3 1/2in (8.9cm) sqs, 5 1/4in (13.3cm) sq

1. Join 3 1/2in (8.9cm) sqs as 4-patch.
2. As for CR4, step 2

variations
economy square

see base design page 45

variation 2
[ES3 — 8in (20.3cm) block]

materials
col A (red):
6 1/2in (16.5cm) sq,
2 x 2 1/2in x 6 1/2in
(6.3cm x 16.3cm) strips,
2 x 2 1/2in x 8 1/2in
(6.3cm x 21.6cm) strips
col B (cream striped):
4 x 3 1/2in (8.9cm) sqs
(cut on the bias)

1. Add 4 x B CTSs to the
corners of the col A sq.
2. Sash the sides using
the shorter col A strips,
and the top and bottom
using the longer ones.

variation 3
[ES4 — 10in (25.4cm) block]

materials
col A (print):
6 1/2in (16.5cm) lrg sq,
2 x 3 1/2in (8.9cm) sml
sqs
col B (blue):
6 x 3 1/2in (8.9cm) sqs,
4 x 2 1/2in x 6 1/2in
(6.3cm x 16.5cm) strips

1. Add 4 x B CSTs to the
A lrg sq using 4 x B sqs.
2. Make 4 QSTs pairing
A/B 3 1/2in (8.9cm) sqs.
Trim to 2 1/2in (6.3cm) sq.
3. Sew the 9 pieces
together into a 9-patch
following the layout in
the photograph.

variation 4
[ES5 — 8in (20.3cm) block]

materials
col A (gold):
4 x 4 1/2in (11.4cm) sqs
col B (stripes):
4 x 5in (12.7cm) sqs (cut
on the bias)

1. Cut the B sqs into
4 x 2 1/2in (6.3cm) sqs
each to make 4 CSTs.
2. Add 4 x B CSTs to each
of the A sqs.
3. Sew the 4 sqs into a
4-patch.

variations

four square

see base design page 46

variation 2
[FO3 — 13in (33cm) block]

materials
dark: 2 x 5 1/2in (14cm) sqs, 2 x 2in (5.1cm) sqs
light: 2 x 5 1/2in (14cm) sqs, 2 x 2in (5.1cm) sqs
white: 4 x 10 1/2in x 2in (26.7cm x 5.1cm) rects

1. Arrange 5 1/2in (14cm) sqs as for FO1. Join as for FO1. Sew white rects to either side of block along 10 1/2in (26.7cm) edges.
2. Sew dark/light 1 1/2in (3.8cm) sqs to either side of 1 white rect. Repeat with the other rect but alternating the sqs light/ dark. Sew these strips to top and bottom edges of block using photograph for reference.

variation 3
[FO4 — 12in (30.5cm) block]

materials
col A (yellow):
2 x 2 1/2in (6.3cm) sqs
col B (pink):
2 x 2 1/2in (6.3cm) sqs, 2 x 2 1/2in x 6 1/2in (6.3cm x 16.5cm) rects
col C (white):
2 x 3in (7.6cm) sqs
col D (grey):
2 x 2 1/4in x 3in (5.7cm x 7.6cm) rects, 2 x 2 1/4in x 6 1/2in (5.7cm x 16.5cm) rects

1. Sew B sqs either side of each A sq. Add B rects to top and bottom.
2. Repeat step 1 with C sqs and D rects.
3. Arrange and sew as 4-patch.

variation 4
[FO5 — 8in (20.3cm) block]

materials
dark:
2 x 2 1/2in (6.3cm) sqs, 2 x 2 1/2in x 4 1/2in (6.3cm x 11.4cm) rects
medium:
2 x 4 1/2in (11.4cm) sqs
light:
2 x 2 1/2in (6.3cm) sqs

1. Sew dark sq to right edge of light sq, add dark rect to top. Repeat with other light/dark pieces but on opposite edges.
2. Arrange and sew sqs as for FO1.

variations

nine-patch

see base design page 47

variation 2
[NP3 — 8 1/2in (21.6cm) block]

materials
as for NP1, plus:
2 x 5 1/2in (14cm) sqs
BKG fabric cut in half
along the diag.

1. Make the 9-patch then
sew the 4 HSTs to the
corners to turn block on
point and trim to 9in
(22.9cm) sq.

variation 3
[NP4 — 6in (15.2cm) block]

materials
col A (dark):
2 x 2 1/2in (6.3cm) sqs,
3 1/2in (8.9cm) sq
col B (medium):
2 x 2 1/2in (6.3cm) sqs,
3 1/2in (8.9cm) sq
BKG:
4 x 2 1/2in (6.3cm) sqs

1. Make a QST unit
from the dark and
medium 3 1/2in (8.9cm)
sqs, and trim to 2 1/2in
(6.3cm) sq.
2. Finish as for NP1
following the layout in
the photograph.

variation 4
[NP5 — 6in (15.2cm) block]

materials
as for NP4 omitting
BKG 2 1/2in (6.25cm) sqs,
with an additional 3in
(7.6cm) sq of each of the
print fabrics and
2 x 3in (7.6cm) sqs
of BKG.

1. As for NP4.
2. Make 4 HST units
pairing the print and
BKG 3in (7.6cm) sqs,
and trim to 2 1/2in
(6.3cm) sq.
3. Finish as for NP1
following the layout in
the photograph.

variations

frame

see base design page 48

variation 1
[FR2 — 12in (30.5cm) block]

materials
centre sq:
8 1/2in (21.6cm) sq
border:
10 x 2 1/2in x 4 1/2in (6.3cm x 11.4cm) rects, 5 dark, 5 light

1. Join 2 dark/light rects. Repeat. Sew to centre sq side edges.
2. Join 3 dark/light/dark rects. Repeat light/dark/ light. Sew to centre sq top/bottom edges.

variation 2
[FR3 — 12in (30.5cm) block]

materials
centre sq:
8 1/2in (21.6cm) sq
col A (orange):
4 x 2 1/2in x 4 1/2in (6.3cm x 11.4cm) rects
col B (yellow):
4 x 2 1/2in x 4 1/2in (6.3cm x 11.4cm) rects
col C (blue):
4 x 2 1/2in (6.3cm) sqs

1. As for FR2 step 1, changing colour A/B for light/dark.
2. Join C/A/B/C. Repeat, reversing A/B. Sew to centre sq top/bottom edges.

variation 3
[FR4 — 12in (30.5cm) block]

materials
centre sq:
8 1/2in (21.6cm) sq
col A (cream):
7 x 3in (7.6cm) sqs
col B (purple):
7 x 3in (7.6cm) sqs
col C (pink):
4 x 3in (7.6cm) sqs
col D (brown):
2 x 3in (7.6cm) sqs

1. Pair 20 A/B/C/D sqs randomly. Sew tog to make 20 HST units. Trim to 2 1/2in (6.3cm) sq.
2. Arrange direction of sqs as in photograph (colours are random). Join tog as FR1.

variation 4
[FR5 — 12in (30.5cm) block]

materials
centre sq: 8 1/2in (21.6cm) sq
dark: 2 x 3in (7.6cm) sqs, 8 x 2 1/2in x 4 1/2in (6.3cm x 11.4cm) rects
light: 2 x 3in (7.6cm) sqs, 16 x 2 1/2in (6.3cm) sqs

1. Sew 8 light/dark sqs tog to make 4 HST units. Trim to 2 1/2in (6.3cm) sq.
2. Add 2 x 2 1/2in (6.3cm) sqs as CSTs to each dark rect to make 8 flying geese.
3. Join pairs of geese tog along 2 1/2in (6.3cm) edges. Add to centre sq. Arrange remaining geese and HST to make top and bottom rows. Join; add to centre sq.

variations

log cabin

see base design page 49

variation 2
[LC3 — 12 1/2in (31.7cm) block]

materials
orange centre: 5in (12.7cm) sq
border 1 blue: 1 1/2in x 5in (3.8cm x 12.7cm), 2 x 1 1/2in x 6in (3.8cm x 15.2cm), 1 1/2in x 7in (3.8cm x 17.8cm)
border 2 striped: 2 1/2in x 7in (6.3cm x 17.8cm), 2 x 2 1/2in x 9in (6.3cm x 22cm), 2in x 11 1/2in (5.1cm x 29.2cm)
border 3 blue floral: 1 1/2in x 11 1/2in (3.8cm x 29.2cm), 2 x 1 1/2in x 12in (3.8cm x 30.5cm), 1 1/2in x 13in (3.8cm x 33cm)

1. Make as for LC1 but each colour creates a border around the previous sq.

variation 3
[LC4 — 12 1/4in (31.1cm) block]

materials
floral centre: 4in (10.2cm) sq; **border 1 pink:** 1 1/4in x 4in (3.2cm x 10.2cm), 1 1/4in x 4 3/4in (3.2cm x 12.1cm); **border 1 green:** 1 3/4in x 4 3/4in (4.4cm x 12.1cm), 1 3/4in x 6in (4.4cm x 15.2cm); **border 2 pink:** 2 1/2in x 6in (6.3cm x 15.2cm), 2 1/2in x 8in (6.3cm x 20.3cm); **border 2 green:** 2in x 8in (5.1cm x 20.3cm), 2in x 9 1/2in (5.1cm x 24.1cm); **border 3 pink:** 1 3/4in x 9 1/2in (4.4cm x 24.1cm), 1 3/4in x 10 3/4in (4.4cm x 27.3cm); **border 3 green:** 2 1/2in x 10 3/4in (6.3cm x 27.3cm), 2 1/2in x 12 3/4in (6.3cm x 32.4cm)

1. Make as for LC1, each border with 2 colours.

variation 4
[LC5 — any size block]

materials
centre sq any size assorted strips ranging from 1in to 3in (2.5cm to 7.6cm) wide

1. Starting with centre sq, sew strip of desired width to right edge of sq. Trim the excess strip beyond the length of the sq at the end of the seam. Add next strip in the same way working clockwise. Continue adding strips, trimming the excess strip at the end of the seam each time and working clockwise around centre sq until you get to desired size.

variations

hourglass

see base design page 50

variation 2
[HG3 — 4in (10.2cm) block]

materials
col A:
5 1/2in (14cm) sq
col B:
5 1/2in (14cm) sq
col C:
5 1/2in (14cm) sq
col D:
5 1/2in (14cm) sq

note: this makes 4 blocks

1. Pair sqs: A/B and C/D. Continue as HG1.

variation 3
[HG4 — 6in (15.2cm) block]

materials
dark:
2 x 2 1/2in x 7 1/2in (6.3cm x 19cm) rects, 7 1/2in (19cm) sq **light:** 3 1/2in x 7 1/2in (8.9cm x 19cm) rect

1. Sew dark/light/dark rects tog along 7 1/2in (19cm) edges to make 7 1/2in (19cm) sq.
2. Pair sq from step 1 with dark 7 1/2in (19cm) sq and continue as HG1. Trim block to 6 1/2in (16.5cm).

variation 4
[HG5 — 4in (10.2cm) block]

materials
light:
2 x 2 1/2in (6.3cm) sqs, 3in (7.6cm) sq
dark:
3in (7.6cm) sq

1. Pair light/dark 3in (7.6cm) sqs. Sew 2 HST units. Trim to 2 1/2in (6.3cm) sq.
2. Arrange sqs as photograph in 4-patch. Join as 4-patch.

variations

maple leaf

see base design page 51

variation 2
[ML3 — 6in (15.2cm) block]

materials
col A (orange):
2 x 3in (7.6cm) sqs
col B (yellow):
2 1/2in (6.3cm) sml sq, 3in (7.6cm) lrg sq
stalk:
3/4in x 5in (1.9cm x 12.7cm) strip
BKG:
2 1/2in (6.3cm) sml sq, 4 x 3in (7.6cm) lrg sqs

1. As ML1 step 1.
2. Make 4 HST units with A/BKG 3in (7.6cm) sqs. Trim to 2 1/2in (6.3cm) sq. Repeat to make 2 HST units with B/BKG 3in (7.6cm) sqs. Complete block as for ML1.

variation 3
[ML4 — 6in (15.2cm) block]

materials
col A (green):
4 x 3in (7.6cm) lrg sqs
col B (beige):
2 x 3in (7.6cm) lrg sq
stalk:
3/4in x 5in (1.9cm x 12.7cm) strip
BKG:
2 1/2in (6.3cm) sml sq, 3 x 3in (7.6cm) lrg sqs

1. As for ML1, making 7 HST units: 4 x A/BKG and 3 x B/C.

variation 4
[ML5 — 8in (20.3cm) block]

materials
cols A/B/C:
3 x 2 1/2in (6.3cm) sml sqs (1 in each colour), 3 x 3in (7.6cm) lrg sqs (1 in each colour)
stalk:
1in x 7 1/2in (2.5cm x 19cm) strip
BKG:
3 x 2 1/2in (6.3cm) sml sqs, 3 x 3in (7.6cm) med sqs, 5in (12.7cm) lrg sq

1. Pair A/BKG 3in (7.6cm) sqs. Make 2 HST units. Trim to 2 1/2in (6.3cm) sq. Arrange and sew 4-patch of BKG sml sq, 2 x HSTs and A sq. Repeat for colours B and C with BKG.
2. As for ML1 step 1, trimming sq to 4 1/2in (11.4cm) sq. Complete as for ML1.

kaleidoscope

see base design page 53

variation 2
[KAL3 — 10in (25.4cm) block]

materials
light:
2 x 1 1/2in x 30in (3.8cm x 76.2cm) strips, 2 x 4in (10.2cm) sq cut in half along the diag
dark:
3 1/2in x 30in (8.9cm x 76.2cm) strip

1. Sew the 3 strips together along the long edges in order of light, dark, light.
2. Cut 8 triangles from the strips using the 10in (25.4cm) line on the Kaleido Ruler.
3. Finish as for KAL1.

variation 3
[KAL4 — 10in (25.4cm) block]

materials
2 x 3in x 30in (7.6cm x 76.2cm) strips of 2 different fabrics 2 x 4in (10.2cm) sqs cut in half along the diag

1. Sew the 2 strips together along the long edges.
2. Cut 8 triangles from the strips using the 10in (25.4cm) line on the Kaleido Ruler.
3. Finish as for KAL1.

variation 4
[KAL5 — 10in (25.4cm) block]

materials
dark:
8 x 2 1/2in (6.3cm) sqs cut in half along diag
medium and light:
4 x 3in x 10in (7.6cm x 25.4cm) rects each cut into 4 triangles using the 5in (12.7cm) line on the Kaleido Ruler

1. Make 4 units as for KAL1 and sew into a 4-patch following using the photograph for reference.

variations

octagon snowball

see base design page 54

variation 2
[OS3 — 6in (15.2cm) block]

materials
as for OS2, replacing 2 of the 1in x 5 1/2in (2.5cm x 14cm) strips with 1in x 8in (2.5cm x 20.3cm) strips

1. Cut the 5 1/2in (14cm) sq in half along the diag. Sash back together using 1 of the 1in x 8in (2.5cm x 20.3cm) strips.
2. Cut in half along the other diag and sash back together using the other 1in x 8in (2.5cm x 20.3cm) strip.
3. Make block as for OS1 but using thinner sashing strips as for OS2.

variation 3
[OS4 — 7in (17.8cm) block]

materials
as for OS1, replacing the strips with 4 x 1 1/2in x 5 1/2in (3.8cm x 14cm) strips and 4 x 1 1/2in (3.8cm) sqs

1. Make as for OS1 but sash using the cornerstones following the layout in the photograph.

variation 4
[OS5 — 6in (15.2cm) block]

materials
12 1/2in (31.7cm) sq main fabric, 4 x 4in (10.2cm) sqs background fabric

1. Add 4 CSTs to the 12 1/2in (31.7cm) sq using the 4 x 4in (10.2cm) sqs BKG fabric.

variations

pinwheel

see base design page 55

variation 2
[PW3 — 8in (20.3cm) block]

materials
8 x 3in (7.6cm) sqs of 2 different fabrics

1. Make 16 HST units pairing the BKG and pinwheel fabrics, and trim to 2 1/2in (6.3cm) sq.
2. Sew tog following the layout in the photograph.

variation 3
[PW4 — 8in (20.3cm) block]

materials
BKG:
8 x 3in (7.6cm) sqs
pinwheels:
2 x 3in (7.6cm) sqs of each of 4 different fabrics

1. Make as for PW3 but following the layout in the photograph.

variation 4
[PW5 — 11in (27.9cm) block]

materials
as for PW4, plus:
BKG:
2 x 1 1/2in x 4 1/2in (3.8cm x 11.4cm) strips,
3 x 1 1/2in x 9 1/2in (3.8cm x 24.1cm) strips,
2 x 1 1/2in x 11 1/2in (3.8cm x 29.2cm) strips

1. Make 16 HST units and sew into 4 pinwheels.
2. Sash into pairs using the 1 1/2in x 4 1/2in (3.8cm x 11.4cm) strips.
3. Sash the 2 halves of the block together using 1 of the 1 1/2in x 9 1/2in (3.8cm x 24.1cm) strips then add 2 more to each side of the block.
4. Sash the top and bottom of the block using the 1 1/2in x 11 1/2in (3.8cm x 29.2cm) strips.

variations

scots plaid

see base design page 56

variation 2
[SP3 — 6in (15.2cm) block]

materials
col A (yellow): 2 x 1in (2.5cm) sml sqs, 2 x 1 1/2in (3.8cm) med sqs, 2 x 2in (5.1cm) lrg sqs
col B (grey): 2 x 1in (2.5cm) sml sqs, 2 x 1 1/2 (3.8cm) med sqs, 2 x 1 1/2in x 2 1/2in (3.8cm x 6.3cm) sml rects, 2 x 2in x 3 1/2in (5.1cm x 8.9cm) med rects, 2 x 2in x 5in (5.1cm x 12.7cm) lrg rects

1. Sew 4 A/B sml sqs in 4-patch. Sew B med sq to right edge of 4 patch. Join med A sq to right edge of 2nd grey med sq. Join to top edge of section so far.
2. Continue as in step 2 with A med sq/B sml rects, then A lrg sq/B med rects, finishing with A lrg sq/B lrg rects.

variation 3
[SP4 — 6in (15.2cm) block]

materials
col A (orange): 3 x 1 1/2in (3.8cm) sqs
col B (pink): 2 x 2in (5.1cm) sqs
col C (grey): 2 x 1 1/2in x 3in (3.8cm x 7.6cm) sml rects, 2 x 1 1/2in x 5 1/2in (3.8cm x 14cm) lrg rects
col D (cream): 2 x 1 1/2in x 2in (3.8cm x 5.1cm) sml rects, 2in x 4in (5.1cm x 10.2cm) lrg rects

1. Sew sml D rect to right edge of A sq side. Join sml D rect to B sq. Sew to top edge of D sq.
2. As step 1 with D sq/C sml rects.
3. As step 1 with B sq/D lrg rects.
4. As step 1 with A sq/C lrg rects.

variation 4
[SP5 — 9in (22cm) block]

materials
col A (white): 4 x 1 1/2in (3.8cm) sqs, 4 x 1 1/2in x 6 1/2in (3.8cm x 16.5cm) strips
col B (multi): 5 x 1 1/2in (3.8cm) sqs, 6 1/2in (16.5cm) sq, 4 x 1 1/2in x 6 1/2in (3.8cm x 16.5cm) strips

1. Make 9-patch with A/B 1 1/2in (3.8cm) sqs.
2. Join A strips either side of each B strip. Join 1 strip set to left edge of B sq.
3. Join remaining strip set to right edge of 9-patch. Join to top of block.

variations
shoofly

see base design page 58

variation 1
[SF2 — 12in (30.5cm) block]

materials
as for SF1 x 4

1. Make four SF1 blocks and sew together following the layout in the photograph.

variation 2
[SF3 — 8 1/2in (21.6cm) block]

materials
as for SF1, plus:
2 x 5 1/2in (14cm) sqs BKG fabric cut in half on diag

1. Make as for SF1 then add triangles to 4 sides and trim to 9in (22.9cm) sq.

variation 3
[SF4 — 10in (25.4cm) block]

materials
BKG:
4 x 3in (7.6cm) sqs, 12 x 2 1/2in (6.3cm) sqs, 4 x 2 1/2in x 4 1/2in (6.3cm x 11.4cm) rects
shoofly:
4 x 3in (7.6cm) sqs, 2 1/2in (6.3cm) sq

1. Make 8 HST units pairing the 3in (7.6cm) sqs. Trim to 2 1/2in (6.3cm).
2. Assemble block following the layout in the photograph.

variation 4
[SF5 — 12in (30.5cm) block]

materials
as for SF1 x 4

1. Make the HSTs as for SF1 x 4 but assemble following the layout in the photograph.

variations

tumblers

see base design page 59

variation 1
[TMB2 – 9 1/2in x 10in
(24.1cm x 25.4cm) block]

materials
20 x 2 1/2in (6.3cm) sqs
BKG: 16 x 1in x 3in (2.5cm
x 7.6cm) strips, 5 x 1in x
9 1/2in (2.5cm x 24.1cm)
strips, 2 x 1in x 11in
(2.5cm x 27.9cm) strips

1. Cut 20 tumblers as
in TMB1.
2. Sash the tumblers
together in 4 rows of 5
using the short sashing
strips in between each.
3. Sash the rows together,
also adding sashing to top
and bottom using the 9
1/2in (24.1cm) strips.
4. Trim block down the
sides to 9 1/2in (24.1cm).
5. Add sashing to the 2 sides
using the 11in (27.9cm) strips.

variation 2
[TMB3 – 15in (38.1cm)
block]

materials
petals: 2 x 2 1/2in
(6.3cm) sqs
centre: 8in (20.3cm) sq
fusible web
BKG:
15 1/2in (39.4cm) sq

1. Fuse petal and centre
fabric to fusible web.
2. Cut 12 tumblers as in
TMB1 and a 7in (17.8cm)
circle.
3. Fuse then sew to BKG.

variation 3
[TMB4 – 8in (20.3cm)
block]

materials
12 x 2 1/2 (6.3cm) sqs
of each of dark and light
fabric

1. Make as for TMB1 but
following the layout in
the photograph and trim
to 8 1/2in (21.6cm) sq.

variation 4
[TMB5 – 12in (30.5cm)
block]

materials
BKG:
12 1/2in (31.7cm) sq
tumblers:
16 x 2 1/2in (6.3cm) sqs
fusible web

1. Fuse the 2 1/2in
(6.3cm) sqs to the fusible
web and cut out 16
tumblers following the
cutting instructions in
TMB1.
2. Fuse the tumblers to
the BKG following the
layout in the photograph.

variations

windows

see base design page 61

variation 2
[WWS3 – 9in (22.9cm) block]

materials
QSTs:
5 1/4in (13.3cm) sq of each of 2 prints, cut in half along the diag
sashing:
2 x 2in x 6 1/2in (5.1cm x 16.5cm) strips, 2 x 2in x 9 1/2in (5.1cm x 24.1cm) strips

1. Sew the 4 HSTs into a QST. Trim to 6 1/2in (16.5cm) sq.
2. Sash the sides and then the top and bottom using the shorter and then the longer strips.

variation 3
[WWS4 – 11in (27.9cm) block]

materials
QSTs: 5in (12.7cm) sq of each of 2 prints, cut in half along the diag
skinny strips: 2 x 1in x 5 1/2in (2.5cm x 14cm) strips, 2 x 1in x 7 1/4in (2.5cm x 18.4cm) strips, 2 x 1in x 8 1/4in (2.5cm x 21cm) strips, 1in x 11in (2.5cm x 27.9cm) strip
wide strips: 2 x 2 1/2in x 8 1/4in (6.3cm x 21cm) strips, 2 x 2 1/2in x 12 1/4in (6.3cm x 31.1cm) strips

1. Sash the HSTs into pairs using the 5 1/2in (14cm) skinny strips, then into a QST using the 11in (27.9cm) skinny strip.
2. Sash the sides using the 7 1/4in (18.4cm) skinny strips and the top and bottom using the 8 1/4in (21cm) skinny strips.
3. Sash the sides using the 8 1/4in (21cm) wide strips and the top and bottom using the 12 1/4in (31.1cm) wide strips.
4. Trim to 11 1/2in (29.2cm) sq.

variation 4
[WWS5 – 9in (22.9cm) block]

materials
QSTs:
2 x 5in (12.7cm) sqs cut in half along the diag
dark:
28 x 1 1/2in (3.8cm) sqs
light:
25 x 1 1/2in (3.8cm) sqs

1. Sew the dark and light sqs into the following strips, alternating dark and light: 2 strips of 5 with dark at each end; 1 strip of 11 with dark at each end; 2 strips of 7 with light at each end; and 2 strips of 9 with dark at each end.
2. Sash 2 of the HSTs tog using the strips of 5 sqs.
3. Sash those 2 tog using the strip of 11 sqs.
4. Sash the sides using the strips of 7 sqs and then the top and bottom using the strips of 9 sqs.

simple blocks:
squares and triangles

Squares and triangles are the basic components
of many classic and modern quilting blocks.
Here you will use half-square triangles, quarter-
square triangles, corner square triangles and
flying geese in a range of beginner friendly and
intermediate blocks. From these you can make
an almost infinite variety of designs. Projects
include: a handy doorstop, the delicate eye
pillow, a useful scissor-keeper pincushion, Ohio
Star coasters and the stunning Road to
Tennessee quilt.

attic window

see other variations page 114

main block [AW1 — 6in (15.2cm) block]

1 Sew red sq to vertical sides of centre sq. Add rects to top and bottom.

2 Draw diag line on WS of each C sq, place 1 sq over top right corner, check that centre of drawn line aligns with centre sq corner underneath and sew diagonally to make CST.

3 Repeat for bottom left corner.

Note: Block pictured left at top.

materials
- **centre:**
  2 1/2in (6.3cm) sq
- **col A (red):**
  2 x 2 1/2in (6.3cm) sqs
- **col B (cream):**
  2 x 2 1/2in x 6 1/2in (6.3cm x 16.5cm) rects
- **col C (green):**
  2 x 4 1/2in sqs

---

variation 1 [AW2 — 6in (15.2cm) block]

1 Make as for AW1

materials
- **centre:**
  2 1/2in (6.3cm) sq
- **col A (rust):**
  2 x 2 1/2in (6.3cm) sqs,
  2 x 2 1/2in x 6 1/2in (6.3cm x 16.5cm) rects
- **col B (floral):**
  2 x 4 1/2in (11.4cm) sqs

amish quilt block

see variations page 115

project: doorstop [6in x 6in (15.2cm x 15.2cm) cube]

1 Make 4 Amish quilt blocks AQB1.

2 Fold handle fabric in half lengthwise and press.

3 Bring long edges to centre fold, press to make double fold strip. Stitch 1/4in (6mm) from each edge along length.

4 Pin handle to one of the black squares and sew in place 1/8in (3mm) from the edges on two opposite sides.

5 Sew into a cube with the two 6 1/2in (16.5cm) black squares on the top and the bottom of the cube. Leave 3in (7.6cm) gap for turning. Clip corners.

6 Turn RS out, push corners out and press seams.

7 Sew the batting into a cube leaving 3in (7.6cm) turning gap.

8 Insert the batting cube into the sewn cube. Fill with heavy filling and slipstitch each opening to close.

materials
- **doorstop sides:**
  as for AQB1 x 4
- **doorstop base and top:**
  2 x 6 1/2in (16.5cm) sqs
- **for handle:**
  6in x 15in (15.2cm x 38.1cm) fabric strip
- **lining:**
  6 x 6 1/2in (16.25cm) batting sqs
- **stuffing:**
  crushed walnut shells, rice, or gravel

---

main block [AQB1 — 6in (15.2cm) block]

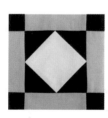

1 Make the centre following the instructions for making CSTs in the introduction using the 4 1/2in (11.4cm) central sq fabric and the 4 x 2 1/2in (6.3cm) sqs.

2 Sew the block together following the layout in the photograph.

note: block also featured in project at right.

materials
- **black fabric:**
  4 x 1 1/2in (3.8cm) sqs,
  4 x 2 1/2in (6.3cm) sqs
- **central square fabric:**
  1 x 4 1/2in (11.4cm) sq
- **side sashing strips:**
  4 x 1 1/2in x 4 1/2in (3.8cm x 11.4cm) strips

bear paw

main block [BP1 — 14in (35.6cm) block]

1 From each of the 4 colours, make 4 HST units using 3in (7.6cm) sqs of coloured and BGK fabric. Trim to 2 1/2in (6.3cm) sq.

2 Assemble each corner bearpaw block following the layout in the photograph.

3 Sew 2 corner bearpaw blocks to either side of a BKG 2 1/2in x 6 1/2in (6.3cm x 16.5cm) rect. Repeat.

4 Sew the 4 1 1/2in (3.8cm) sqs into a 4-patch and join to remaining BKG 2 1/2in x 6 1/2in (6.3cm x 16.5cm) rects.

5 Join the three rows following the layout in the photograph.

materials

■ **each of 4 coloured fabrics:**
4 1/2in (11.4cm) sq, 2 x 3in (7.6cm) sqs, 1 1/2in (3.8cm) sq

■ **BKG fabric:**
8 x 3in (7.6cm) sqs, 4 x 2 1/2in (6.3cm) sq, 4 x 2 1/2in x 6 1/2in (6.3cm x 16.5cm) rects

variation 1 [BP2 — 12in (30.5cm) block]

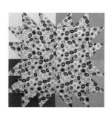

1 Make as per steps 1 and 2 of BP1 then sew together to make the block following the layout in the photograph.

see other variations page 116

materials

■ **col A (floral):**
4 x 4 1/2in (11.4cm) sqs, 8 x 3in (7.6cm) sqs

■ **BKG (1 of the following for each of 4 BKG colours):**
2 x 3in (7.6cm) sqs, 1 x 2 1/2in (6.3cm) sq

contrary wife

see variations page 117

main block [CW1 — 6in (15.2cm) block]

1   Pair dark/light 3in (7.6cm) sqs. Sew 4 HST units. Trim to 2 1/2in (6.3cm) sq.

2   Using photograph for reference, arrange sqs into 3 rows. Finish as 9-patch.

materials

■ **dark:**
2 x 3in (7.6cm) sqs
■ **light:**
2 x 3in (7.6cm) sqs
■ **med:**
5 x 2 1/2in (6.3cm) sqs

churn dash

see variations page 118

project: eye pillow [3in x 8 1/2in (7.6cm x 21.6cm)]

1 Following CD1 block instructions, make two churn dash blocks trimming HST units to 1 1/2in (3.8cm). Sew blocks to either side of centre sashing.

2 Add sashing strips at either side of pillow front.

3 Bring long edges of backing fabric together and press to make a folded double layer. Sew around edges and treat as one piece of fabric.

4 Place pillow front and backing RS together. Sew around edges leaving 2in (5.1cm) gap. Clip corners, turn through, press, and fill with rice. Close the opening with slip stitch.

materials

■ col A (grey lawn cotton):
4 x 2in x 2in (5.1cm x 5.1cm) sqs,
8 x 1in x 1 1/2in (2.5cm x 3.8cm) rects, 2 x 1 1/2in (3.8cm) sqs,
2 x 1in x 3 1/2in (2.5cm x 8.9cm) rects for side sashing
1 1/2in x 3 1/2in (3.8cm x 8.9cm) rect for centre sashing
■ col B (red lawn): 4 x 2in (5.1cm) sqs, 8 x 1in x 1 1/2in (2.5cm x 3.8cm) rects,
■ backing: 7in x 8 1/2in (17.8cm x 21.6cm) silk or lawn cotton
■ rice for stuffing

main block [CD1 — 6in (15.2cm) block]

1 Make four pairs of HST units from the 3in (7.6cm) squares using the HST instructions in the introduction section. Trim to 2 1/2in (6.3cm).

2 Sew the four pairs of 1 1/2in x 2 1/2in (3.8cm x 6.3cm) rectangles together — pairing one col A with one col B each time.

3 Assemble the block by sewing into rows and then joining the rows following the layout in the photograph.

materials

■ col A (cream):
2 x 3in (7.6cm) sq, 4 x 1 1/2in x 2 1/2in (3.8cm x 6.3cm) rects,
2 1/2in (6.3cm) sq
■ col B (black):
2 x 3in (7.6cm) sq, 4 x 1 1/2in x 2 1/2in (3.8cm x 6.3cm) rects

double hourglass

see other variations page 119

main block [DH1 — 7 1/2in (19cm) block]

1   Sew the 2 strips together along the long edges and press.

2   Using the marks on the cutting mat, cut a 45 degree line removing the end of the strips. Cut four more 45 degree lines to make 4 triangles.

3   Sew the triangles into pairs so that the fabrics alternate dark/light. Sew two halves together to make finished block and trim to 8in (20.3cm).

materials

■ 2 x 2 1/2in x 18in (6.3cm x 45.7cm) strips of contrasting fabric

variation 1 [DH2 — 8 1/2in (21.6cm) block]

1   Sew the 3 strips together along the long edges and press.

2   Cut 7 triangles following DH1 directions; use the 4 where the dark fabric is at the point of the triangle.

3   Sew together as for DH1 but without alternating the colours.

materials

■ 3 x 2in (5.1cm) x WOF strips of 3 different fabrics

see variations page 120

flying geese

main block [FG1 — 12in (30.5cm) block]

materials

- **geese:**
  6 x 2 1/2in x 4 1/2in (6.3cm x 11.4cm) rects of each of 3 colours
- **BKG:**
  36 x 2 1/2in (6.3cm) sqs

1 Make 18 flying geese units.

2 Assemble into the finished block following the layout in the photograph.

friendship

main block
[FS1 — 6in (15.2cm) block]

1 Pair light sqs with ABCD lrg sqs.
   Sew along diagonal, trim excess
   and open out to make HST unit.
   Use photos for placement.

2 On inner corner of each sq
   that meets in the centre of the
   block, add same colour sml sq,
   sewing diagonally to make
   a CST.

3 Join as 4-patch.

materials

- **light:** 4 x 3 1/2in (8.9cm) sq
  (diagonal print or bias cut)
- **col A:** 2 1/2in (6.3cm) sml sq,
  3 1/2in (8.9cm) lrg sq
- **col B:** 2 1/2in (6.3cm) sml sq,
  3 1/2in (8.9cm) lrg sq
- **col C:** 2 1/2in (6.3cm) sml sq,
  3 1/2in (8.9cm) lrg sq
- **col D:** 2 1/2in (6.3cm) sml sq,
  3 1/2in (8.9cm) lrg sq

---

variation 1 [FS2 — 6in (15.2cm) block]

see other variations page 121

1 As for FS1, using 2 colours for the sml/lrg
   sqs to make each sq in the 4-patch.

materials

- **light:**
  4 x 3 1/2in (8.9cm) sqs
- **col A:**
  2 x 2 1/2in (6.3cm) sml sqs,
  2 x 3 1/2in (8.9cm) lrg sqs
- **col B:**
  2 x 2 1/2in (6.3cm) sml sqs,
  2 x 3 1/2in (8.9cm) lrg sqs

saint john's pavement

see other variations page 122

project: pincushion [3 1/4in x 7 1/4in (8.3cm x 18.4cm)]

1 Make block as for SJP2. Join front rect to right edge of block. Add lace trim along seam line between blocks and front rect. Attach twill tape by stitching in SA of front rect, 2in (5.1cm) away from lace trim.

2 Place front and back RS tog. Stitch around edge leaving 2 1/2in (6.3cm) gap for turning. Clip corners, turn through, press. Fill. Slip stitch opening closed.

materials

- as for SJP2, plus:
- **front rect:** 3 3/4in x 4 1/2in (9.5cm x 11.4cm) pink/green
- **backing fabric:** 3 3/4in x 7 3/4in (9.5cm x 19.7cm)
- **lace trim:** 1 1/4in x 3 3/4in (3.2cm x 9.5cm)
- **twill tape:** 1/2in x 3 3/4in (1.3cm x 9.5cm)
- polyester filling

main block [SJP1 — 8in (20.3cm) block]

1 Place centre sq on point, join 2 rects to top right and lower left side edges to make centre row. Placing right angles together, join 2 1/2in (6.3cm) side of BKG sml triangles to 1 3/4in (4.4cm) ends of remaining rects. Sew rect/triangle strips to top left and lower right edges of centre sq.

2 Add BKG lrg triangles bias edges to outer rects 5in (12.7cm) edges to make block corners. Trim block to approx 8in (20.3cm) sq, cutting 1/4in (6mm) away from outer rectangle corner points.

materials

- **centre sq:** 5in (12.7cm) sq
- **red:** 4 x 1 3/4in x 5in (4.4cm x 12.7cm) rects
- **BKG:** 2 x 2 1/2in (6.3cm) sml sqs cut in half diagonally, 2 x 5in (12.7cm) lrg sqs cut in half diagonally

double 9-patch

see variations page 123

main block [DNP1 — 9in (22.9cm) block]

materials

- **light:**
  4in x 1 1/2in (10.2cm x 3.8cm) sqs, 4 x 3 1/2in (8.9cm) sqs
- **dark:**
  5in x 1 1/2in (12.7cm x 3.8cm) sqs, 4 x 3 1/2in (8.9cm) sqs

1   Sew light/dark 1 1/2in (3.8cm) sqs as 9-patch.

2   Arrange sqs as block photograph. Sew tog as 9-patch.

granny squares

main block [GS1 — 8 1/2in (21.6cm) block]

1 Using diagonal block construction, arrange colours as in photograph.

2 Sew into rows. Row 1 = 1 square, Row 2 = 3 squares, etc. Join rows.

3 Trim to 9in (22.9cm) sq.

materials

■ 4 colours of 2 1/2in (6.3cm) sqs:
12 BKG, 8 outer sq, 4 inner sq, 1 centre

---

variation 1 [GS2 — 12in (30.5cm) block]

1 Make as for GS1 but placing 4 outer sqs in the corner positions instead of 4 BKG sqs. Trim to 9in (22.9cm) sq.

2 Sash sides using the shorter strips followed by the top and bottom using the longer.

see other variations page 124

materials

■ 4 colours of 2 1/2in (6.3cm) sqs:
8 BKG, 12 outer sq, 4 inner sq, 1 centre
■ BKG:
2 x 2 1/4in x 9in (5.7cm x 22.9cm) strips, 2 x 2 1/4in x 12 1/2in (5.7cm x 31.7cm) strips

half-square triangles

see variations page 125

materials

- **col A (white):**
  16 x 4in (10.2cm) sqs
- **col B (assorted scraps):**
  16 x 4in (10.2cm) sqs

main block [HST1 — 12in (30.5cm) block]

1   Make 16 HST units from pairs of 4in (10.2cm) sqs. Trim to 3 1/2in (8.9cm) sq.

2   Sew together following the layout in the photograph.

propeller

see variations page 126

main block [PR1 — 10in (25.4cm) block]

1   Pair A/C lrg sqs. Join diagonally to make 4 HST units.
    Trim to 4 1/2in (11.4cm) sq.

2   Pair B/D sml sqs. Join. Repeat x3.

3   Arrange sqs/rect as block photo, sew in rows, join rows.

materials
- col A (white):
  2 1/2in (6.3cm) sml sq, 2 x 5in
  (12.7cm) lrg sqs
- col B (aqua):
  4 x 2 1/2in (6.3cm) sml sqs
- col C (lime):
  2 x 5in (12.7cm) lrg sqs
- col D (orange):
  4 x 2 1/2in (6.3cm) sml sqs

ohio star

see other variations page 127

project: coasters [4 1/2in (11.4cm) square set of 4]

1 Make 4 OHS5 blocks.

2 Glue or sew the batting to the backing fabric leaving a gap around the edges for the seams.

3 Sew the blocks made in step 1 to the 4 sq of backing fabric, RST, using a 1/4in (6mm) seam and leaving a 3in (7.6cm) section of 1 edge unsewn.

4 Turn inside out, press, and hand-sew the open seam closed.

materials

- as for OHS5 x 4, plus:
- **backing:** 4 x 4 1/2in (11.4cm) sq
- **batting:** 4 x 4 1/4in (11.4cm) sq

---

main block [OHS1 — 7 1/2in (19cm) block]

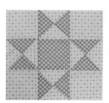

1 Make the 4 QST blocks pairing A/BKG 4in (10.2cm) sqs. Trim to 3in (7.6cm) sq.

2 Sew into rows and then into the block following the layout in the photograph.

materials

- **BKG:**
  4 x 3in (7.6cm) sqs, 2 x 4in (10.2cm) sqs
- **col A (pink):**
  3in (7.6cm) sq, 2 x 4in (10.2cm) sqs

mother's dream

see other variations page 128

main block [MDR1 — 8 1/2in (21.6cm) block]

1 Pair A/B rects, join along 3 1/2in (8.9cm) edges to make sqs. Using photograph for reference arrange sqs in 3 diagonal rows to make an X. Join top right and lower left A/B sqs to centre sq to make centre row.

2 Add BKG lrg HSTs to sides of top left and bottom left A/B sqs. The bias edges of these triangles will form part of the block outer edges

3 Add BKG sml HSTs joining bias edges to A/B sq edges to make block corners. Join rows, trim block to 9in (22.9cm) approx allowing 1/4in (6mm) SA around edge beyond square points.

materials
■ **centre sq:**
  3 1/2in (8.9cm) sq
■ **col A:** 4 x 2in x 3 1/2in (5.1cm x 8.9cm) rects
■ **col B:** 4 x 2in x 3 1/2in (5.1cm x 8.9cm) rects
■ **BKG:** 2 x 4in (10.2cm) sml sqs cut in half diagonally, 2 x 4 1/2in (11.4cm) lrg sqs cut in half diagonally

variation 1 [MDR2 — 8 1/2in (21.6cm) block]

1 Make as MDR1 but rotate AB sqs 90 degrees when arranging block.

materials
■ as for MDR1

sheep fold

main block [SHF1 — 8in (20.3cm) block]

1 Sew 2 rects either side of med sq.

2 Sew small sqs either side of rect. Repeat. Sew rows to top and bottom of block.

materials

- **light:** 4 x 2 1/2in x 4 1/2in (6.3cm x 11.4cm) rects
- **dark:** 4 x 2 1/2in (6.3cm) sml sqs, 4 1/2in (11.4cm) med sq

---

variation 1 [SHF2 — 8in (20.3cm) block]

see other variations page 129

1 Make as for SHF1 using 2 colours for rects, arrange as in photograph.

materials

- **light:** 2 x 2 1/2in x 4 1/2in (6.3cm x 11.4cm) rects
- **dark:** 4 x 2 1/2in (6.3cm) sml sqs, 4 1/2in (11.4cm) med sq
- **medium:** 2 x 2 1/2in (6.3cm) sqs, 2 x 2 1/2in x 4 1/2in (6.3cm x 11.4cm) rects

formal garden

main block [FGA1 — 6in (15.2cm) block]

1 Pair light/dark sqs. Make 8 HST units. Trim to 2 1/2in (6.3cm) sq.

2 Arrange HST units and centre sq as in photograph. Sew tog as 9-patch.

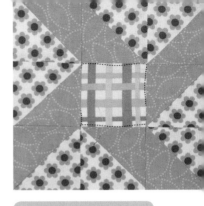

materials
- **dark:**
  4 x 3in (7.6cm) sqs
- **light:**
  4 x 3in (7.6cm) sqs
- **centre sq:**
  2 1/2in (6.3cm) sq

---

variation 1 [FGA2 — 6in (15.2cm) block]

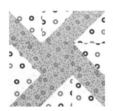

1 Make as for FGA1, centre sq is dark 2 1/2in (6.3cm) sq.

see other variations page 130

materials
- **dark:**
  4 x 3in (7.6cm) sqs, 2 1/2in (6.3cm) sq
- **light:**
  4 x 3in (7.6cm) sqs

windmill

see other variations page 131

main block [WM1 — 8in (20.3cm) block]

1   Make 4 HST units pairing the A/BKG and B/BKG 3 1/2in (8.9cm) sqs. Trim to 3in (7.6cm) sq.

2   Place each HST RS tog with a matching A or B 3in (7.6cm) sq. Sew tog along the diagonal making sure the diag lines are sewn perpendicular to the HST diag.

3   Trim off the excess seam allowance making sure to trim each one so that the triangles fall in the same pattern (following the layout in the photograph).

4   Sew the 4 sqs together following the layout in the photograph.

5   Sash the sides of the block using the shorter strips and the top and bottom using the longer strips.

materials

■ **BKG:** 2 x 3 1/2in (8.9cm) sqs, 2 x 2in x 5 1/2in (5.1cm x 14cm) strips, 2 x 2in x 8 1/2in (5.1cm x 21.6cm) strips
■ **col A (black):** 3 1/2in (8.9cm) sq, 2 x 3in (7.6cm) sqs
■ **col B (grey):** 3 1/2in (8.9cm) sq, 2 x 3in (7.6cm) sqs

variation 1 [WM2 — 10in (25.4cm) block]

1   Make 4 x WM1 (steps 1–4) taking care to follow the layout of each quarter of the finished block as 2 of the blocks are a mirror image of the other 2.

2   Assemble the block following the layout in the photograph.

materials

■ WM1 x 4 without the sashing strips

road to tennessee

see other variations page 132

project: Sashiko quilt [68in x 68in (173cm x 173cm)]

1   Make 13 of block RTT4 and 12 of block RTT5.

2   Sew into 5 rows of 5, alternating the blocks. Sew the rows into the quilt top following the layout in the photograph.

3   Sew the WOF strips into a long piece and sash the sides and the top and bottom of the quilt top. Make the backing by cutting the 4 yds into 2 equal lengths and sewing back together along the long edges.

4   Back, quilt and bind as desired.

materials

- **print fabrics:**
  400 x 3in (7.6cm) sq scraps
- **BKG:** 25 x 13in (33cm) sqs
  7 x 3in (7.6cm) WOF strips
- **binding:** 1/2 yd (0.46m)
- **backing:** 4 yds (3.66m)
- **batting:** 76in (193cm) sq
- **template:** RTTi

main block [RTT1 — 16in (40.6cm) block]

1   Sew 2 CSTs to opposite corners of each 4 1/2in (11.4cm) sq using 2 x 2 1/2in (6.3cm) sqs.

2   Sew tog following the layout in the photograph.

materials

- 8 x 4 1/2in (11.4cm) sqs of each of dark and light fabric
- 16 x 2 1/2in (6.3cm) sqs of each of dark and light fabric

see templates page 280

variations

attic window

see base design page 87

variation 2
[AW3 — 6in (15.2cm) block]

materials
centre: 2 1/2in (6.3cm) sq
col A (blue): 2 x 2 7/8in (7.3cm) sqs halved diagonally to make 4 sml HSTs. **col B (black/cream):** 2 x 2 1/2in (6.3cm) sqs, 4 7/8in (12.4cm) sq cut in half diagonally to make 2 lrg HSTs

1. Sew 2 sml HSTs to vertical sides of centre sq.
2. Starting seam at right angles of sq and HST, sew 1 sml HST to left vertical side of 1 B sq. Repeat sewing HST to right edge of other B sq. Join to top and bottom edge of centre. Add lrg HST to each corner.

variation 3
[AW4 — 6in (15.2cm) block]

materials
centre: 2 1/2in (6.3cm) sq
col A (yellow): 2 x 2 7/8in (7.3cm) sqs cut in half diagonally to make 4 sml HSTs, 3in (7.6cm) lrg sq
col B (brown): 4 7/8in (12.4cm) sq cut in half diagonally to make 2 lrg HSTs, 3in (7.6cm) lrg sq

1. Pair A/B 3in (7.6cm) sqs and make 2 HST units. Trim to 2 1/2in (6.3cm) sq.
2. Continue as for AW3 with the HST units replacing the 2 1/2in (6.3cm) sqs.

variation 4
[AW5 — 6in (15.2cm) block]

materials
centre: 2 1/2in (6.3cm) sq
col A (lilac): 2 x 2 7/8in (7.3cm) sqs cut in half diagonally to make 4 sml HSTs, 3in (7.6cm) lrg sq
col B (blue): 4 7/8in (12.4cm) sq cut in half diagonally to make 2 lrg HSTs, 3in (7.6cm) lrg sq

1. As AW4, rotating HSTs 180 degrees to make an on-point rect in the centre of the block.

variations
amish quilt block

see base design page 88

variation 1
[AQB2 — 6in (15.2cm) block]

materials
as for AQB1 replacing 4 1/2in (11.4cm) sq and 4 x 2 1/2in (6.3cm) sqs with 4 x 3in (7.6cm) sqs

1. Make 4 HST units pairing the black and coloured 3in (7.6cm) sqs. Trim to 2 1/2in (6.3cm) sq. Sew into a 4 patch.
2. Make block following layout in photograph.

variation 2
[AQB3 — 8 1/2in (21.6cm) block]

materials
as for AQB1 plus 2 x 5 1/2in (14cm) sqs cut in half along the diag

1. Make as for AQB1.
2. Add half squares to the corners to set on point.
3. Trim to 9in (22.9cm) sq.

variation 3
[AQB4 — 6in (15.2cm) block]

materials
as for AQB1 replacing 4 1/2in (11.4cm) sq and 4 x 2 1/2in (6.3cm) sqs with 2 x 5 1/2in (14cm) sqs

1. Make a QST block using the 5 1/2in (14cm) sqs. You will have enough fabrics to make a spare QST block which can be discarded. Trim to 4 1/2in (11.4cm) sq.
2. Finish as for AQB1.

variation 4
[AQB5 — 8in (20.3cm) block]

materials
as for AQB1 plus 4 x 1 1/2in x 4 1/2in (3.8cm x 11.4cm) strips and 12 x 1 1/2in (3.8cm) sqs

1. Make centre as in AQB1 step 1.
2. Make 4 corner 4-patches using the 1 1/2in (3.8cm) sqs.
3. Sew the 1 1/2in x 4 1/2in (3.8cm x 11.4cm) strips into pairs.
4. Assemble the block following the layout in the photograph.

variations

bear paw

see base design page 90

variation 2
[BP3 — 12in (30.5cm) block]

materials
from each of 4 prints:
2 x 3in (7.6cm) sqs,
3 x 2 1/2in (6.3cm) sqs
BKG:
8 x 3in (7.6cm) sqs,
8 x 2 1/2in (6.3cm) sqs

1. For each of the four prints, make a 4-patch using 3 x 2 1/2in (6.3cm) print sqs and 1 x 2 1/2in (6.3cm) BKG sq.
2. Make the rest of the block as per steps 1 and 2 of BP1. Then sew together to make the block following the layout in the photograph.

variation 3
[BP4 — 12in (30.5cm) block]

materials
BKG:
8 x 3in (7.6cm) sqs,
4 x 2 1/2in (6.3cm) sqs
col A (dark blue):
8 x 3in (7.6cm) sqs,
2 x 1 1/2in x 6 1/2in (3.8cm x 16.5cm) strips,
2 x 1 1/2in x 8 1/2in (3.8cm x 21.6cm) strips
col B (floral):
6 1/2in (16.5cm) sq

1. Sash the B square using first the 6 1/2in (16.5cm) and then the 8 1/2in (21.6cm) strips.
2. Make 16 HST units pairing A/BKG 3in (7.6cm) sqs and trim to 2 1/2in (6.3cm) sq.
3. Sew together the strips of HSTs for the sides of the block then sew these to the central square.
4. Repeat for the top adding BKG 2 1/2 (6.3cm) sqs at each end. Sew the block together following the layout in the photograph.

variation 4
[BP5 — 12in (30.5cm) block]

materials
col A (floral):
8 x 3in (7.6cm) sqs
BKG:
8 x 3in (7.6cm) sqs,
4 x 2 1/2in (6.3cm) sqs,
8 1/2in (21.6cm) sq

1. Make 16 HST units pairing A/BKG 3in (7.6cm) sqs and trim to 2 1/2in (6.3cm) sq.
2. Finish the block as per steps 3–4 of block BP4.

variations

contrary wife

see base design page 91

variation 1
[CW2 — 6in (15.2cm) block]

materials
col A (green):
2 x 3in (7.6cm) sqs
col B (pink):
2 x 3in (7.6cm) sqs
col C (white):
5 x 2 1/2in (6.3cm) sqs

1. Make as for CW1, using photograph for reference when arranging sqs.

variation 2
[CW3 — 6in (15.2cm) block]

materials
col A (brown):
2 x 3in (7.6cm) sqs
col B (aqua):
2 x 3in (7.6cm) sqs,
2 1/2in (6.3cm) sq
col C (yellow):
4 x 2 1/2in (6.3cm) sqs

1. Make as for CW1, using photograph for reference when arranging sqs.

variation 3
[CW4 — 6in (15.2cm) block]

materials
col A (yellow):
2 x 2 1/2in (6.3cm) sqs,
2 x 3in (7.6cm) sqs
col B (light grey):
2 x 3in (7.6cm) sqs
col C (dark grey):
3 x 2 1/2in (6.3cm) sqs

1. Make as for CW1, using photograph for reference when arranging sqs.

variation 4
[CW5 — 6in (15.2cm) block]

materials
col A (aqua):
3 x 3in (7.6cm) sqs
col B (light brown):
3 x 3in (7.6cm) sqs
col C (dark brown):
4 x 2 1/2in (6.3cm) sqs

1. Make as for CW1, discarding 1 HST unit, and using photograph for reference when arranging sqs.

churn dash

see base design page 92

variation 1
[CD2 — 6in (15.2cm) block]

materials
col A (white):
2 x 3in (7.6cm) sqs,
4 x 1 1/2in x 2 1/2in
(3.8cm x 6.3cm) rects,
4 x 1 1/2in (3.8cm) sqs
col B (green):
2 x 3in (7.6cm) sqs,
2 1/2in (6.3cm) sq,
4 x 1 1/2in x 2 1/2in
(3.8cm x 6.3cm) rects

1. Add 4 CSTs to the
2 1/2in (6.3cm) sq B fabric
using the four 1 1/2in
(3.8cm) sqs of B fabric.
2. Make the rest of the
block as for CD1 and
assemble following the
layout in the photograph.

variation 2
[CD3 — 6in (15.2cm) block]

materials
col A (striped fabric):
2 x 3in (7.6cm) sqs (cut on
the bias) 4 x 1 1/2in x
2 1/2in (3.8cm x 6.3cm)
rects
col B (BKG):
2 x 3in (7.6cm) sqs,
4 x 1 1/2in x 2 1/2in
(3.8cm x 6.3cm) rects,
2 1/2in (6.3cm) sq

1. Make as for CD1 but
assemble following the
layout in the photograph.

variation 3
[CD4 — 6in (15.2cm) block]

materials
col A (floral):
2 x 3in (7.6cm) sqs,
4 x 2 1/2in (6.3cm) sqs
col B (red):
2 x 3in (7.6cm) sqs,
2 1/2in (6.3cm) sq

1. As in CD1 step 1.
2. Assemble the block
following the layout in
the photograph.

variation 4
[CD5 — 12in (30.5cm) block]

materials
col A (scraps):
4 x 3in (7.6cm) sqs,
12 x 2 1/2in (6.3cm) sqs
BKG:
4 x 3in (7.6cm) sqs,
4 x 2 1/2in (6.3cm) sqs,
1 x 4 1/2in (11.4cm) sq,
4 x 2 1/2in x 4 1/2in
(6.3cm x 11.4cm) rects

1. Make 8 HSTs pairing
the 3in (7.6cm) A/BKG
sqs. Trim to 2 1/2in
(6.3cm) sq.
2. Assemble the top 2
and bottom 2 rows.
Sew each pair of
rows together (continued
on page 119).

variations
double hourglass

see base design page 95

variation 2
[DH3 — 7 1/2in (18.25cm) block]

materials
4 x 1 1/2in x 22in (3.8cm x 55.9cm) strips of 4 different fabrics

1. Sew the 4 strips together along the long edges and press.
2. Cut 4 x 45 degree triangles and piece as for DH1 following the colour placement in the photograph above.

variation 3
[DH4 — 7in (17.8cm) block]

materials
2 x 1 1/2in (3.8cm) x WOF strips of 2 different fabrics

1. Piece as for DH1 four times.
2. Piece into a 4-patch taking care to alternate colours as in the photograph.

variation 4
[DH5 — 7in (17.8cm) block]

materials
fabrics and piecing: as for DH4 but following colour placement in photograph.

variations
flying geese

see base design page 96

variation 1
[FG2 — 8in (20.3cm) block]

materials
geese:
2 x 2 1/2in x 4 1/2in
(6.3cm x 11.4cm) rects
of each of 4 colours
BKG:
16 x 2 1/2in (6.3cm) sqs

1. Make 8 flying
geese units.
2. Sew into pairs and
then assemble into the
finished block following
the layout in the
photograph.

variation 2
[FG3 — 8in (20.3cm) block]

materials
geese:
2 x 2 1/2in x 4 1/2in
(6.3cm x 11.4cm) rects
of each of 4 colours
BKG:
8 x 2 1/2in (6.3cm) sqs
of each of 2 colours

1. Make as for FG2
assembling the block
following the
photograph.

variation 3
[FG4 — 12in (30.5cm) block]

materials
geese:
4 x 2 1/2in x 4 1/2in
(6.3cm x 11.4cm) rects
of each of 4 colours
BKG:
32 x 2 1/2in (6.3cm) sqs,
4 1/2in (11.4cm) sq

1. Make 16 flying
geese units.
2. Sew into pairs and
then assemble into the
finished block following
the layout in the
photograph as if making
a 9-patch.

variation 4
[FG5 — 12in (30.5cm) block]

materials
tree tops:
12 x 2 1/2in x 4 1/2in
(6.3cm x 11.4cm) rects
tree trunks:
3 x 1 1/2in x 4 1/2in
(3.8cm x 11.4cm) rects
BKG:
24 x 2 1/2in (6.3cm) sqs,
6 x 2in x 4 1/2in (5.1cm x
11.4cm) rects

1. Make 12 flying geese
units.
2. Sew the BKG rects to
either side of the tree
trunk rects.
3. Sew geese in pairs and
assemble with tree trunks
into finished block as per
the photograph as if
making a 9-patch.

variations

friendship

see base design page 97

variation 2
[FS3 — 6in (15.2cm) block]

materials
light:
4 x 3 1/2in (8.9cm) sqs (diagonal print or bias cut)
col A:
2 x 2 3/4in (7cm) sqs
col B:
2 x 2 3/4in (7cm) sqs
col C:
2 x 2 3/4in (7cm) sqs
col D:
2 x 2 3/4in (7cm) sqs

1. Add 2 A sqs as CSTs to opposite corners of 1 light 3 1/2in (8.9cm) sq. Repeat with B/C/D sqs using photograph for ref.
2. Join as 4-patch.

variation 3
[FS4 — 10in (25.4cm) block]

materials
light:
16 x 3in (7.6cm) sqs
assorted scraps:
32 x 2 1/2in (6.3cm) sqs (16 fabrics, 2 of each)

1. Make as for FS3 using 2 sqs of same colour for CSTs. Join finished sqs into 4 rows of 4. Join rows.

variation 4
[FS5 — 6in (15.2cm) block]

materials
col A:
2 x 3 1/2in (8.9cm) sqs
col B:
2 x 3 1/2in (8.9cm) sqs
col C (BKG):
8 x 2 3/4in (7cm) sqs

1. As for FS4, but arranging squares as in the photograph.

saint john's pavement

see base design page 99

variation 1
[SJP2 — 3 1/4in (8.3cm) block]

materials
centre sq:
2in (5.1cm) sq
red/green:
4 x 1 1/4in x 2in (3.2cm x 5.1cm) rects, 2 in each colour
BKG:
2 x 2in (5.1cm) sml sqs cut in half diagonally, 2 x 2 1/2in (6.3cm) sqs cut in half diagonally

1. Make as for SJP1, alternating pink/cream rects.

variation 2
[SJP3 — 8in (20.3cm) block]

materials
centre sq:
5in (12.7cm) sq (print cut on point)
4 colours:
4 x 1 3/4in x 5in (4.4cm x 12.7cm) rects, 1 in each colour
BKG:
2 x 2 1/2in (6.3cm) sml sqs cut in half diagonally, 2 x 5in (12.7cm) lrg sqs cut in half diagonally

1. Make as for SJP1.

variation 3
[SJP4 — 8in (20.3cm) block]

materials
centre sq:
5in (12.7cm) sq
aqua:
4 x 1 3/4in x 5in (4.4cm x 12.7cm) rects
BKG (green) B:
2 x 2 1/2in (6.3cm) sml sqs cut in half diagonally
BKG (red):
2 x 5in (12.7cm) lrg sqs cut in half diagonally

1. Make as for SJP1.

variation 4
[SJP5 — 8in (20.3cm) block]

materials
centre sq:
5in (12.7cm) sq
col A:
4 x 1 3/4in x 2 3/4in (4.4cm x 7cm) rects
col B:
4 x 1 3/4in x 2 3/4in (4.4cm x 7cm) rects
BKG:
2 x 2 1/2in (6.3cm) sml sqs cut in half diagonally, 2 x 5in (12.7cm) lrg sqs cut in half diagonally

1. Make as for SJP1, joining A/B rects along 1 3/4in (4.4cm) edges before sewing to centre sq.

variations
double 9-patch

see base design page 100

variation 1
[DNP2 — 9in (22.9cm) block]

materials
light:
4in x 1 1/2in (10.2cm x 3.8cm) sqs
med:
5in x 1 1/2in (12.7cm x 3.8cm) sqs, 4 x 3 1/2in (8.9cm) sqs
dark:
4in x 3 1/2in (10.2cm x 8.9cm) sqs

1. Make as for DPN1, using photograph to help arrange different colours.

variation 2
[DNP3 — 13 1/2in (34.3cm) block]

materials
col A (cream):
4in x 2in (10.2cm x 5.1cm) sqs, 4in x 5in (10.2cm x 12.7cm) sqs
assorted scraps:
5in x 2in (12.7cm x 5.1cm) sqs, 4in x 5in (10.2cm x 12.7cm) sqs

1. Make as for DNP1.

variation 3
[DNP4 — 9in (22.9cm) block]

materials
light:
2 x 1 1/2in x 8in (3.8cm x 20.3cm) sml rects, 1 1/2in x 14in (3.8cm x 35.6cm) lrg rect, 5in x 3 1/2in (12.7cm x 8.9cm) sqs
dark: 1 1/2in x 8in (3.8cm x 20.3cm) sml rect, 2 x 1 1/2in x 14in (3.8cm x 35.6cm) lrg rect

1. Strip piece 2 light sml rects and 1 dark. Rotary cut into 4 x 1 1/2in x 3 1/2in (3.8cm x 8.9cm) strips — light sq/dark sq/light sq. Repeat with 2 dark lrg rects and 1 light. Rotary cut into 8 x 1 1/2in x 3 1/2in (3.8cm x 8.9cm) strips — dark sq/light sq/dark sq. Using strips, make 4 x 9-patch sqs.
2. Arrange 9-patch sqs and light 3 1/2in (8.9cm) sqs to make block, as per photograph. Join as 9-patch.

variation 4
[DNP5 — 9in (22.9cm) block]

materials
dark:
2 x 1 1/2in x 9in (3.8cm x 22.9cm) sml rects, 1 1/2in x 18in (3.8cm x 45.7cm) lrg rect, 4 x 3 1/2in (8.9cm) sqs
light:
1 1/2in x 9in (3.8cm x 22.9cm) sml rect, 2 x 1 1/2in x 18in (3.8cm x 45.7cm) lrg rect

1. Make as for DNP4 but cutting 5 strips from the pieced sml rects, 10 strips from the lrg rects and making 5 9-patch sqs, as in step 1.

granny squares

see base design page 101

variation 2
[GS3 — 11 1/2in (29.2cm) block]

materials
5 colours of 2 1/2in (6.3cm) sqs:
16 outer BKG, 12 outer sqs, 8 middle sqs, 4 inner sqs, 1 centre

1. Make as for GS1. Trim to 12in (30.5cm) sq.

variation 3
[GS4 — 14in (35.6cm) block]

materials
col A (red):
9 x 2 1/2in (6.3cm) sqs
col B (light red):
4 x 2 1/2in (6.3cm) sqs, 8 x 2 1/2in x 4 1/2in (6.3cm x 11.4cm) rects
col C (pink):
8 x 2 1/2in (6.3cm) sqs
col D (cream):
4 x 2 1/2in x 4 1/2in (6.3cm x 11.4cm) rects, 4 x 2 1/2in (6.3cm) sqs

1. Sew 4 col C sqs to 4 col D sqs then sew those to 4 col D 2 1/2in x 4 1/2in (6.3cm x 11.4cm) rects.
2. Sew 2 col B sqs to 2 col C sqs. Sew 2 sqs made at step 1 on each side of each of those following the layout in the photograph.
3. Sew 2 x 2 1/2in x 4 1/2in (6.3cm x 11.4cm) col B rects to either end of the units made at step 2.
4. Assemble the remaining rows and then sew into the block following the layout in the photograph.

variation 4
[GS5 — 14in (35.6cm) block]

materials
col A (dark blue floral):
2 1/2in (6.3cm) sq
col B (blue dot):
4 x 2 1/2in (6.3cm) sqs, 4 x 2 1/2in x 6 1/2in (6.3cm x 16.5cm) rects, 4 x 2 1/2in x 4 1/2in (6.3cm x 11.4cm) rects
col C (red):
4 x 2 1/2in (6.3cm) sqs
col D (lt. blue):
8 x 2 1/2in (6.3cm) sqs
col E (cream):
12 x 2 1/2in (6.3cm) sqs

1. Assemble the block in rows and then into the finished block following the layout in the photograph.

variations
half–square triangles

see base design page 102

variation 1
[HST2 — 12in (30.5cm) block]

materials
col A (dark pink):
8 x 2 1/2in x 4 1/2in
(6.3cm x 11.4cm) rects,
8 x 3in (7.6cm) sqs
col B (light pink):
8 x 3in (7.6cm) sqs

1. Make 16 HSTs from
pairs of 3in (7.6cm) sqs,
and trim to 2 1/2in
(6.3cm) sq.
2. Assemble HSTs and
rects into 9 x 4 1/2in
(11.4cm) sqs following
the layout in the
photograph then sew
into one block.

variation 2
[HST3 — 12in (30.5cm) block]

materials
col A (blue):
4 x 2 1/2in x 4 1/2in
(6.3cm x 11.4cm) rects,
4 x 3in (7.6cm) sqs
col B (yellow):
5 x 4 1/2in (11.4cm) sqs,
4 x 3in (7.6cm) sqs

1. Make 8 HSTs from
pairs of 3in (7.6cm) sqs,
and trim to 2 1/2in
(6.3cm) sq.
2. Assemble HSTs and
rects into 4 1/2in
(11.4cm) sqs following
the layout in the
photograph then sew
into one block.

variation 3
[HST4 — 12in (30.5cm) block]

materials
col A (light grey):
8 x 2 1/2in x 4 1/2in
(6.3cm x 11.4cm) rects,
4 x 2 1/2in (6.3cm) sqs,
8 x 3in (7.6cm) sqs
col B (dark grey):
8 x 3in (7.6cm) sqs

1. Make 16 HSTs from
pairs of 3in (7.6cm) sqs,
and trim to 2 1/2in
(6.3cm) sq.
2. Assemble HSTs and
rects into 9 x 4 1/2in
(11.4cm) sqs following
the layout in the
photograph then sew
into one block.

variation 4
[HST5 — 12in (30.5cm) block]

materials
col A (white):
8 x 2 1/2in x 4 1/2in
(6.3cm x 11.4cm) rects,
6 x 3in (7.6cm) sqs
col B (blue):
4 1/2in (11.4cm) sq,
6 x 3in (7.6cm) sqs

1. Make 12 HSTs from
pairs of 3in (7.6cm) sqs,
and trim to 2 1/2in
(6.3cm) sq.
2. Assemble HSTs and
rects into 4 1/2in
(11.4cm) sqs following
the layout in the
photograph then sew
into one block.

variations

propeller

see base design page 103

variation 1
[PR2 — 10in (25.4cm) block]

materials
as PR1, with changes below:
col A (cream)
col B (solid colour scraps)
col C/D (light scraps)

1. Make as for PR1.

variation 2
[PR3 — 10in (25.4cm) block]

materials
col A (light):
2 1/2in (6.3cm) sml sq,
2 x 5in (12.7cm) lrg sqs
col B (blue):
4 x 2 1/2in (6.3cm) sml sqs, 2 x 5in (12.7cm) lrg sqs
col C (multi):
4 x 2 1/2in (6.3cm) sml sqs

1. Make as for PR1, pairing A/B lrg sqs for HSTs.
2. As for PR1 Pair B/C sml sqs. Complete as for PR1.

variation 3
[PR4 — 10in (25.4cm) block]

materials
col A (coral):
2 1/2in (6.3cm) sml sq,
2 x 5in (12.7cm) lrg sqs
col B (lilac):
2 x 5in (12.7cm) lrg sqs
col C (green):
4 x 2 1/2in x 4 1/2in (6.3cm x 11.4cm) rects

1. Make as for PR1, substituting rects for pairs of sml sqs in step 2.

variation 4
[PR5 — 10in (25.4cm) block]

materials
col A (cream):
2 x 2 1/2in x 4 1/2in (6.3cm x 11.4cm) sml rects, 2 1/2in x 10 1/2in (6.3cm x 26.7cm) lrg rect
col B (grey):
2 x 5in (12.7cm) lrg sqs
col C (red):
2 x 5in (12.7cm) lrg sqs

1–2. Make as for PR4, pairing B/C lrg sqs for HST units.
3. As for PR1, all of row 2 will be col A, large rect.

ohio star

see base design page 104

variation 1
[OHS2 — 7 1/2in (19cm) block]

materials
as for OHS1, swapping 1 x 4in (10.2cm) BKG sq for 1 x 4in (10.2cm) light sq

1. Make 4 HST units pairing A/BKG and A/light 4in (10.2cm) sqs.
2. Make QSTs as for OHS1 pairing the A/BKG with the A/light HSTs. Trim to 3in (7.6cm) sq.
3. Make the block following the layout in the photograph.

variation 2
[OHS3 — 7 1/2in (19cm) block]

materials
as for OHS1 but replacing the 4 3in (7.6cm) BKG sqs with 4 BKG 3 1/2in (8.9cm) sqs and 4 star fabric 3 1/2in (8.9cm) sqs, and replacing the star fabric 3in (7.6cm) sq with a BKG 3in (7.6cm) sq

1. Make the 4 HST units pairing the 3 1/2in (8.9cm) sqs.
2. Finish as for OHS1.

variation 3
[OHS4 — 7 1/2in (19cm) block]

materials
as for OHS1 with an additional 4 x 1 3/4in (4.4cm) sqs BKG fabric

1. Make the centre sq by adding 4 CSTs to the A 3in (7.6cm) sq using the 4 x 1 3/4in (4.4cm) sqs BKG fabric.
2. Finish as for OHS1.

variation 4
[OHS5 — 4 1/2in (11.4cm) block]

materials
BKG:
4 x 2in (5.1cm) sqs, 2 x 3in (7.6cm) sqs
col A (blue):
2in (5.1cm) sq, 2 x 3in (7.6cm) sqs

1. Make as per OHS1 but pairing the 3in (7.6cm) sqs to make the QSTs, and trimming to 2in (5.1cm) sq.

mother's dream

see base design page 107

variation 2
[MDR3 — 8 1/2in
(21.6cm) block]

materials
centre sq:
3 1/2in (8.9cm) sq
col A:
4 x 2in x 3 1/2in (5.1cm
x 8.9cm) rects
col B:
4 x 2in (5.1cm) sqs
col C:
4 x 2in (5.1cm) sqs
BKG:
2 x 4in (10.2cm) sml sqs
cut in half diagonally, 2 x
4 1/2in (11.4cm) lrg sqs
cut in half diagonally

1. Pair B/C sqs. Join to A
rects. Continue as MDR1.

variation 3
[MDR4 — 8 1/2in
(21.6cm) block]

materials
centre sq:
3 1/2in (8.9cm) sq
col A:
8 x 2in (5.1cm) sqs
col B:
8 x 2in (5.1cm) sqs
BKG:
2 x 4in (10.2cm) sml sqs
cut in half diagonally, 2 x
4 1/2in (11.4cm) lrg sqs
cut in half diagonally

1. Pair A/B sqs. Join pairs
tog as 4-patch 3 1/2in
(8.9cm) sqs. Continue as
MDR1.

variation 4
[MDR5 — 9in (22.9cm)
block]

materials
centre sq:
3 1/2in (8.9cm) sq
col A/col B:
rects as MDR1
BKG:
4 x 3 1/2in (8.9cm) sqs

1. Sew A/B rects together
as MDR1. Arrange and
sew sqs as 9-patch.

variations
sheep fold

see base design page 108

variation 2
[SHF3 — 16in (40.6cm) block]

materials
as for SHF1 x 2
light:
2 x 8 1/2in (21.6cm) sqs

1. Make 2 SHF1 blocks.
2. Arrange and sew blocks 8 1/2in (21.6cm) squares as 4-patch.

variation 3
[SHF4 — 16in (40.6cm) block]

materials
as for SHF1 x 2 with coral for dark and grey for light
dark (coral):
6 x 2 1/2in (6.3cm) sml sqs, 2 x 6 1/2in (16.5cm) lrg sqs
light (assorted grey):
4 x 2 1/2in x 4 1/2in (6.3cm x 11.4cm) rects

1. Make 2 SHF1 blocks.
2. Join sml sq to rect. Add to one side of lrg sq. Sew sml sqs to each end of rect. Join to base of lrg sq. Repeat joining sml sq/ rect to opp side of lrg sq.
3. Arrange and sew as 4-patch.

variation 4
[SHF5 — 12in (30.5cm) block]

materials
as for SHF1 with citron as dark and floral as light
outer border:
citron: 4 x 2 1/2in (6.3cm) sqs, floral: 4 x 2 1/2in x 8 1/2in (6.3cm x 21.6cm) rects

1. Make SHF1 block.
2. As for SHF1 steps 1 and 2 using outer border sqs/rects.

variations
formal garden

see base design page 109

variation 2
[FGA 3 — 12in (30.5cm) block]

materials
col A (pink):
2 x 5in (12.7cm) sqs, 2 x
2 1/2in (6.3cm) sqs
col B (aqua):
2 x 5in (12.7cm) sqs, 2 x
2 1/2in (6.3cm) sqs
BKG:
4 x 5in (12.7cm) sqs

1. Join 2 1/2in (6.3cm)
sqs as 4-patch to make
centre sq.
2. Pair BKG with colour
sqs making 8 HST units.
Trim to 4 1/2in (11.4cm)
sq. Finish as for FGA1.

variation 3
[FGA 4 — 6in (15.2cm) block]

materials
col A (yellow): 2 1/2in
(6.3cm) sq, 2 x 3in (7.6cm)
sqs
col B (white): 2 1/2in
(6.3cm) sq, 2 x 3in (7.6cm)
sqs
BKG: 4 x 3in (7.6cm) sqs

1. Pair A/B 2 1/2in (6.3cm)
sqs, sew tog with diagonal
seam corner to corner.
Trim away one side 1/4in
(6mm) from seam and
open out to make centre
2 1/2in (6.3cm) sq.
2. Pair 2 x A/BKG sqs to
make 4 HST, trim to
2 1/2in (6.3cm) sq.
Repeat B/BKG sqs.
Complete as for FGA1.

variation 4
[FGA 5 — 6in (15.2cm) block]

materials
col A (blue):
5 x 3in (7.6cm) sqs
col B (red):
5 x 3in (7.6cm) sqs

1. Pair A/B sqs and make
10 HST units. Discard 1.
Trim 9 to 2 1/2in
(6.3cm) sqs.
2. Arrange HST units into
diagonal lines as in
photograph. Join as
9-patch.

variations
windmill

see base design page 111

variation 2
[WM3 — 7in (17.8cm) block]

materials
as for WM1 without
the sashing strips, plus:
2 x 4 1/2in (11.4cm) sqs
BKG fabric cut in half
along diag

1. Make as for WM1
steps 1–4.
2. Add 4 1/2in (11.4cm)
HSTs to sides then top
and bottom to set on
point.
3. Trim to 7 1/2in
(19cm) sq.

variation 3
[WM4 — 5in (12.7cm) block]

materials
as for WM1 without
the sashing strips

1. Make as for WM1
steps 1–4 but assemble
following the layout in
the photograph.

variation 4
[WM5 — 6in (15.2cm) block]

materials
as for WM1 without
the sashing strips, plus:
4 x 1 1/2in x 3in (3.8cm x
7.6cm) strips BKG fabric,
1 1/2in (3.8cm) sq of 1 of
the windmill fabrics

1. Make as for WM1
steps 1–3.
2. Sew into rows using
the BKG 1 1/2in (3.8cm)
strips and the print fabric
1 1/2in (3.8cm) sq to sash
and conerstone between
the 4 windmills.
3. Assemble into the
finished block following
the layout in the
photograph.

road to tennessee

see base design page 112

variation 1
[RTT2 — 16in (40.6cm) block]

materials
16 x 4 1/2in (11.4cm) sqs BKG fabric, 32 x 2 1/2in (6.3cm) sqs of scraps

1. Make as for RTT1 and sew tog following the layout in the photograph.

variation 2
[RTT3 — 8in (20.3cm) block]

materials
grey print:
4 x 4 1/2in (11.4cm) sqs
grey solid:
8 x 2 1/2in (6.3cm) sqs

1. Make as for RTT1 but only making 4 units and sew tog following the layout in the photograph.

variation 3
[RTT4 — 12 1/2in (31.7cm) block]

materials
13in (33cm) sq BKG fabric, 16 x 3in (7.6cm) sq scraps
template: RTTi

1. EPP the 16 lozenges using template RTTi.
2. Sew together as per the layout in the photograph.
3. Appliqué the shape to the background fabric.
4. Trim excess fabric from the back; remove EPP papers.

variation 4
[RTT5 — 12 1/2in (31.7cm) block]

materials
as for RTT4

1. Make as for RTT4 but follow the layout in the photograph.

intermediate blocks: squares and triangles

Get ready for more blocks made from squares and triangles. These designs are increasingly complex and often feature a greater number of pieces, giving you the opportunity to practice techniques from chapter 2 in a wider range of designs. The projects vary in size from a tiny pincushion to a jumbo floor cushion. The padded tablet case provides an opportunity to practice hand quilting on a small scale and the tree themed table runner is ideal for those who want to dip their toe into machine quilting.

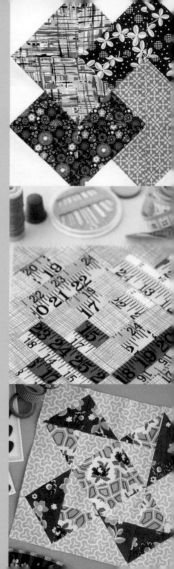

card trick

see variations page 162

main block [CTK1 — 6in (15.2cm) block]

1 Pair BKG/A 5in (12.7cm) sqs. Make 2 HST units, trim to 4 1/2in (11.4cm) sq. Discard 1 HST. Repeat with BKG and B/C/D. These are the corner sqs of the block.

2 Take A 5 1/2in (14cm) sq, cut in half diagonally, and halve one half again to make 1 HST and 2 QSTs. Repeat with B/C/D 5 1/2in (14cm) sqs. Cut BKG 5 1/2in (14cm) sq to make 4 QSTs.

3 Pair A/BKG QSTs, with A on left and BKG on the right and placing right angles together, start seam at right angle to make HST. Repeat with B/C/D and BKG. Pair each col/BKG HST with the next colour HST working clockwise around the block A with B and so on, using photograph for reference. Join along diagonal, trim to 4 1/2in (11.4cm) sq.

4 Pair A/BKG HST with B HST, join, trim to 4 1/2in (11.4cm) sq. Repeat for B/BKG HST with C HST, etc.

5 Pair remaining QSTs A/B, C/D to make HSTs, then join to make the centre sq. Trim to 4 1/2in (11.4cm) sq.

6 Using photograph for reference, sew tog as 9-patch.

Note: Block pictured left at top.

materials

(colours clockwise around block starting top left)

- col A: 5in (12.7cm) sq, 5 1/2in (14cm) sq
- col B: 5in (12.7cm) sq, 5 1/2in (14cm) sq
- col C: 5in (12.7cm) sq, 5 1/2in (14cm) sq
- col D: 5in (12.7cm) sq, 5 1/2in (14cm) sq
- BKG: 4 x 5in (12.7cm) sqs, 5 1/2in (14cm) sq

broken wheel

see variations page 163

project: pincushion [3 1/2in (8.9cm) square]

1   Make as for BW1.

2   Add C strips to sides and then to top and bottom, starting with the shorter length strips.

3   Sew the front of the pincushion to the back leaving a small section of seam unsewn.

4   Turn inside out, trim corners, stuff, and hand sew the opening closed using a whip stitch.

materials

- **col A (white):** 4 x 1in x 1 1/2in (2.5cm x 3.8cm) rect, 16 x 1in (2.5cm) sq, 1 1/2in (3.8cm) sq
- **col B (rainbow scraps):** 4 x 1 1/2in (3.8cm) sq, 4 x 1in x 1 1/2in (2.5cm x 3.8cm) rect
- **fabric C (B+W dot):** 2 x 3/4in x 3 1/2in (1.9cm x 8.9cm) strips, 2 x 3/4in x 4in (1.9cm x 10.2cm) strips, 4in (10.2cm) sq
- **stuffing**

main block [BW1 — 9in (22.9cm) block]

1   Make each of the four corner sqs by sewing the 2in (5.1cm) A sqs to each corner of 4 of the 3 1/2in (8.9cm) B sqs to make 4 CSTs on each square.

2   Sew the four pairs of rects together — pairing one fabric A with one fabric B each time.

3   Assemble the block following the layout in the photograph.

materials

- **col A (cream):** 4 x 2in x 3 1/2in (5.1cm x 8.9cm) rects, 16 x 2in (5.1cm) sqs
- **col B (orange):** 5 x 3 1/2in (8.9cm) sqs, 4 x 2in x 3 1/2in (5.1cm x 8.9cm) rects

chubby star

see other variations page 164

main block [CS1 — 12in (30.5cm) block]

1   Sew the A lrg sqs to the corners of the 9in (22.9cm) BKG sq to make CSTs.

2   Sew the A sml sqs to one end of each of the BKG rects to make CSTs. Make sure to alternate the direction of the seams so that half are sewn top left to bottom right and the other half are top right to bottom left.

3   Sew the BKG rects into pairs joining at the CST ends to make triangles.

4   Sew the shorter BKG rects to the sides and the longer BKG rects to the top and bottom.

materials

■   **BKG:** 9in (22.9cm) sq, 4 x 2 1/4in x 4 3/4in (5.7cm x 12.1cm) rects, 4 x 2 1/4in x 6 1/2in (5.7cm x 16.5cm) rects

■   **col A (brown):** 4 x 3in (7.6cm) lrg sqs, 8 x 2 1/4in (5.7cm) sml sqs

variation 1 [CS2 — 12in (30.5cm) block]

1   Make 4 HST units pairing the 3 1/2in (8.9cm) sqs. Trim to 3in (7.6cm)

2   Sew 1 onto each end of each of the 3in x 4in (7.6cm x 10.2cm) rects following the layout in the photograph.

3   Sew the two pieces made in step 2 to the top and bottom of the 4in x 9in (10.2cm x 22.9cm) rect.

4   Continue as from step 2 of CS1.

materials

■   **BKG as for CS1 omitting the 9in (22.9cm) sq, plus:** 2 x 3 1/2in (8.9cm) sqs, 2 x 3in x 4in (7.6cm x 10.2cm) rects, 4in x 9in (10.2cm x 22.9cm) rect

■   **col A (pink) as for CS1, omitting the 4 x 3in (7.6cm) sqs, plus:** 2 x 3 1/2in (8.9cm) sqs

see variations page 165

crown of thorns

materials

- **col A (orange):**
  8 x 3in (7.6cm) sqs, 4 x 2 1/2in
  (6.3cm) sqs
- **BKG:**
  8 x 3in (7.6cm) sqs, 5 x 2 1/2in
  (6.3cm) sqs

main block [COT1 — 10in (25.4cm) block]

1   Make 8 pairs of HST units from the 3in (7.6cm) sqs. Trim to 2 1/2in (6.3cm).

2   Sew into rows and then into the finished block following the layout in the photograph.

diamond square

see variations page 166

main block [DM1 — 12in (30.5cm) block]

1   Make 28 HST units pairing the following 3in (7.6cm) sqs: 4 x B/BKG, 8 x A/BKG and 2 x A/B. Trim all to 2 1/2in (6.3cm) sq.

2   Sew the sqs into rows and then into the finished block following the layout in the photograph.

materials

■ **BKG:**
8 x 2 1/2in (6.3cm) sqs, 12 x 3in (7.6cm) sqs

■ **col A (yellow):**
10 x 3in (7.6cm) sqs

■ **col B (white):**
6 x 3in (7.6cm) sqs

gem stone

main block [GST1 — 8in (20.3cm) block]

1   Cut 4 of the 3in (7.6cm) BKG sqs and the 4 1/4in (10.8cm) sqs in half along the diag.

2   Make 4 HST units pairing 2 x A/BKG 3in (7.6cm) sqs. Trim to 2 1/2in (6.3cm) sq.

3   Sew 2 of the BKG triangles cut from the 3in (7.6cm) sqs onto the sides of the HSTs following the layout in the block photograph. Trim.

4   Sew the 1in x 8in (2.5cm x 20.3cm) strips along the long edges of the triangles cut from the 4 1/4in (10.8cm) sqs. Trim.

5   Sew the 2 halves of each quadrant together. Trim to 4 1/2in (11.4cm) sq.

6   Sew the 4 quadrants together following the photograph.

materials

■ **BKG:**
6 x 3in (7.6cm) sqs, 2 x 4 1/4in (10.8cm) sqs

■ **col A (pink):**
2 x 3in (7.6cm) sqs, 4 x 1in x 8in (2.5cm x 20.3cm) strips

---

variation 1 [GST2 — 8in (20.3cm) block]

see other variations page 167

1   Cut the BKG 5in (12.7cm) sqs in half along the diag.

2   Continue as from step 4 of GS1, alternating the colours of the HSTs when making the block.

materials

■ **BKG:**
4 1/4in (10.8cm) sq, 2 x 5in (12.7cm) sqs

■ **col A (yellow):**
4 1/4in (10.8cm) sq, 4 x 1in x 8in (2.5cm x 20.3cm) strips

follow the leader

main block [FTL1 — 10in (25.4cm) block]

1   Print 4 FLTi templates. Place medium/light rects vertically, cut in half diagonally on RS from top left to lower right corner. Foundation paper piece FLTi sections, trim (remembering to leave 1/4in (6mm) SA around the edge) and remove paper.

2   Sew light triangle to medium sq by pairing right angles at start of seam. Repeat on adjacent square edge following photograph to make a large triangle. Pair with dark triangle, join along diagonal with scant 1/4in (6mm) seam. So should measure 4 1/2in (11.4cm) sq.

3   Arrange sections and sew tog as 9-patch using photograph for reference.

materials

- **dark (red):** 2 x 4 7/8in (12.4cm) sqs cut in half diag
- **medium (aqua):** 4 x 2 1/2in (6.3cm) sqs, 2 x 3 1/2in x 7in (8.9cm x 17.8cm) rects cut in half diag
- **light (cream):** 2 1/2in (6.3cm) sq, 4 x 2 7/8in (7.3cm) sqs cut in half diag, 2 x 3 1/2in x 7in (8.9cm x 17.8cm) rects
- **template:** FTLi

see other variations page 168

....

variation 1 [FTL2 — 10in (25.4cm)

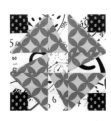

1   Make as for FTL1.

see templates page 280

materials

- **dark (navy):** 4 x 2 1/2in (6.3cm) sqs
- **medium (blue):** 2 x 4 7/8in (12.4cm) sqs cut in half diag, 2 x 3 1/2in x 7in (8.9cm x 17.8cm) rect cut in half diag
- **light (cream):** 2 1/2in (6.3cm) sq, 4 x 2 7/8in (7.3cm) sqs cut in half diag, 2 x 3 1/2in x7in (8.9cm x 17.8cm) rects
- **template:** FTLi

father's choice

see other variations page 169

main block [FC1 — 10in (25.4cm) block]

1. Make 8 HST units from 4 x A/B 3in (7.6cm) sqs. Trim to 2 1/2in (6.3cm) sq.

2. Assemble the block in rows and then into the block following the layout in the photograph.

materials
- ■ **col A (light):**
  8 x 2 1/2in (6.3cm) sqs,
  4 x 3in (7.6cm) sqs
- ■ **col B (dark):**
  9 x 2 1/2in (6.3cm) sqs,
  4 x 3in (7.6cm) sqs

---

variation 1 [FC2 — 10in (25.4cm) block]

1. Make 12 HST units pairing 6 x A/BKG 3in (7.6cm) sqs. Trim to 2 1/2in (6.3cm) sq.

2. Assemble the block in rows and then into the block following the layout in the photograph.

materials
- ■ **BKG:**
  8 x 2 1/2in (6.3cm) sqs,
  6 x 3in (7.6cm) sqs
- ■ **col A (grey):**
  5 x 2 1/2in (6.3cm) sqs,
  6 x 3in (7.6cm) sqs

christmas tree

see variations page 170

project: table runner [18in x 38in (45.7cm x 96.5cm)]

1   Make 12 CT1 Christmas tree blocks.

2   Sash them into 2 rows of 6, using 10 x 6 1/2in (16.5cm) strips cut from the 2 1/2in (6.3cm) WOF BKG strips in between each block.

3   Sash the 2 strips of trees together, then sash the top and bottom using 2 1/2in (6.3cm) WOF BKG strips 34in (86.4cm) long.

4   Sash the ends using 2 1/2in (6.3cm) WOF BKG strips 18in (45.7cm) long.

5   Back, quilt and bind as desired.

materials

- as for CT1 x 12, plus:
- **BKG:** 6 x 2 1/2in (6.3cm) x WOF strips
- **batting:** 20in x 40in (50.8cm x 102cm)
- **backing:** 20in x 40in (50.8cm x 102cm)
- **binding:** 3 x 2 1/2in (6.3cm) x WOF strips

....

main block [CT1 — 4in x 6in (10.2cm x 15.2cm)]

1   Place the 2 lrg BKG rect right sides together and cut them in half along one of the diagonals.

2   Fold the tree fabric in half and cut a triangle by cutting in half along the diagonal.

3   Sew one of each of the triangles from step 1 to each side of the tree. Press and trim the sides and bottom to give a block measuring 4 1/2in (11.4cm) sq.

4   Sew the tree trunk fabric to the two small rectangles of BKG fabric, press, and then sew to the bottom of the tree.

materials

- **col A (tree):** 1 x 5in (12.7cm) sq
- **col B (trunk):** 1 1/2in x 2 1/2in (3.8cm x 6.3cm) rect
- **BKG:** 2 x 3in x 6in (7.6cm x 15.2cm) lrg rects, 2 x 2in x 2 1/2in (5.1cm x 6.3cm) sml rects

jacob's ladder

main block [JL1 — 12in (30.5cm) block]

1   Make 4 HSTs pairing A/BKG 5in (12.7cm) sq. Trim to 4 1/2in (11.4cm) sq.

2   Make 5 4-patches using the 2 1/2in (6.3cm) sqs.

3   Assemble the block following the layout in the photograph.

materials
- **BKG:**
  2 x 5in (12.7cm) sqs, 10 x 2 1/2in (6.3cm) sqs
- **col A (red flower):**
  2 x 5in (12.7cm) sqs
- **col B (red dot):**
  10 x 2 1/2in (6.3cm) sqs

- -

variation 1 [JL2 — 12in (30.5cm) block]

1   Make as for JC1 but assemble following the layout in the photograph.

see other variations page 171

materials
- **col A (red):**
  2 x 5in (12.7cm) sqs, 10 x 2 1/2in (6.3cm) sqs
- **col B (blue):**
  2 x 5in (12.7cm) sqs
- **col C (cream floral):**
  10 x 2 1/2in (6.3cm) sqs

open window

main block [OW1 — 8in (20.3cm) block]

1 Make 16 HST units pairing the 3in (7.6cm) sqs as follows: 2 x A/B;
   2 xA/C; 4 x B/C. Trim to 2 1/2in (6.3cm) sq.

2 Assemble the block following the layout in the photograph.

materials
- col A (white):
  4 x 3in (7.6cm) sqs
- col B (pink):
  6 x 3in (7.6cm) sqs
- col C (black):
  6 x 3in (7.6cm) sqs

variation 1 [OW2 — 8in (20cm) block]

see other variations page 172

1 Make 16 HST units pairing the BKG
   3in (7.6cm) sqs with the blue fabric 3in
   (7.6cm) sqs.

2 Assemble the block following the layout in
   the photograph.

materials
- BKG:
  8 x 3in (7.6cm) sqs
- from each of 2 blue fabrics:
  4 x 3in (7.6cm) sqs

amish cross

see other variations page 173

project: padded tablet case [9in x 11in (22.9cm x 27.9cm)]

1   Make block as for AC1. Add black sml rect to top of block and lrg rect to bottom to make the case outer. Baste/spray smaller batting to lining and larger batting to case outer. Quilt as desired.

2   Bring top and bottom edges of the case outer RS together as a pocket. Stitch side seams. Press open, trim corners. Repeat with lining using a 3/8in (9mm) SA, leaving a 4in (10.2cm) opening along one edge for turning.

3   Find centre point of top edge on case outer back. Pin top of elastic loop to this point with loop facing downwards. Test with button to check size, adjust and stitch top of loop in SA.

4   Turn case outer RS out, place inside lining RS together, match side seams, pin and stitch around top. Turn case through lining side opening. Close with slip stitch. Press. Add button to front.

main block [AC1 — 6in (15.2cm) block]

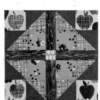

1   Pair B/D 3in (7.6cm) sqs. Sew 8 HST units. Trim to 2 1/2in (6.3cm) sq.

2   Join 4 HST units with D 2 1/2in (6.3cm) sqs using photograph for reference. Repeat with HST units/E sqs.

3   Using photograph for ref, join each HST/D sq with HST/E sq to make 4 x 4-patch sections.

4   Arrange 4-patch sections with remaining pieces as per photograph. Sew to make 3 rows. Join rows.

materials

- col A (aqua): 4 x 1 1/2in x 4 1/2in (3.8cm x 11.4cm) rects
- col B/C (red): 1 1/2in (3.8cm) sml sq, 4 x 3in (7.6cm) sqs
- col D (navy/white): 4 x 2 1/2in (6.3cm) sqs (n), 4 x 3in (7.6cm) sqs (w)
- col E (multi): 4 x 2 1/2in (6.3cm) sqs
- BKG (black): 1 1/2in x 9 1/2in (3.8cm x 24.1cm) rect, 9 1/2in x 12 1/2in (24.1cm x 31.7cm) rect
- lining: 9 1/2in x 22in (24.1cm x 55.9cm)
- batting: 9in x 21 1/2in (22.9cm x 54.6cm) for lining, 9in x 22in (22.9cm x 55.9cm) for case outer
- ponytail elastic band, large button and thicker thread

materials

- col A (brown): 4 x 1 1/2in x 4 1/2in (3.8cm x 11.4cm) rects
- col B (rust): 4 x 3in (7.6cm) sqs
- col C (gold): 1 1/2in (3.8cm) sq
- col D (cream): 4 x 2 1/2in (6.3cm) sqs, 4 x 3in (7.6cm) sqs
- col E (grey): 4 x 2 1/2in (6.3cm) sqs

mill wheel

see other variations page 174

main block [MW1 — 8in (20.3cm) block]

1 Pair 4 A/BKG 3in (7.6cm) sqs and make 8 HST units. Trim to 2 1/2in (6.3cm) sq.

2 Pair 2 B/BKG 3in (7.6cm) sqs and make 4 HST units. Trim to 2 1/2in (6.3cm) sq.

3 Add 4 BKG 2 1/2in (6.3cm) sqs to B lrg sq as CSTs to make block centre sq.

4 Using photograph for ref, arrange HST units around centre sq. Join side HST units and sew to centre sq sides. Join top and bottom sqs to make rows and add to centre sq.

materials

- col A (navy): 4 x 3in (7.6cm) sqs
- col B (aqua): 2 x 3in (7.6cm) sml sqs, 4 1/2in (11.4cm) lrg sq
- BKG (yellow): 4 x 2 1/2in (6.3cm) sml sqs, 6 x 3in (7.6cm) sqs

---

variation 1 [MW2 — 8in (20.3cm) block]

1 Pair A/BKG 3in (7.6cm) sqs and C/BKG and make 4 HST units with each. Repeat B/D making 4 HST units. Trim all to 2 1/2in (6.3cm) sq. Continue as MW1 using C 4 1/2in (11.4cm) lrg sq with D sml sqs as CSTs to make centre sq.

materials

- col A (dark grey): 2 x 3in (7.6cm) sqs
- col B (citron): 2 x 3in (7.6cm) sqs
- col C (light citron): 2 x 3in (7.6cm) sqs, 4 1/2 (11.4cm) lrg sq
- col D (light grey): 4 x 2 1/2in (6.3cm) sml sqs, 2 x 3in (7.6cm) sqs
- BKG (cream): 4 x 3in (7.6cm) sqs

swing in the centre

main block [STC1 – 12in (30.5cm) block]

1 Sew 2 A sqs to B rect to make flying geese unit. Make 4. Repeat with B sqs and A rects. Join pairs, 1 from each set of flying geese, together to make 4 sqs.

2 Sew 3 A sqs to 3 corners of C sq to make CSTS. Make 4. Sew 4 A sqs as CSTS to all corners of remaining C sq to make centre sq.

3 Arrange and sew as 9-patch.

materials:

■ **col A (light):** 24 x 2 1/2in (6.3cm) sqs, 4 x 2 1/2in x 4 1/2in (6.3cm x 11.4cm) rects

■ **col B (pink):** 8 x 2 1/2in (6.3cm) sqs, 4 x 2 1/2in x 4 1/2in (6.3cm x 11.4cm) rects

■ **col C (blue):** 5 x 4 1/2in (11.4cm) sqs

variation 1 [STC2 – 12in (30.5cm) block]

1 As STC1 using A sqs and B rects to make 4 geese units. Join geese to A rects to make 4 sqs.

2 Continue block as STC1 replacing col C centre sq with col D.

see other variations page 175

materials

■ **col A (white):** 24 x 2 1/2in (6.3cm) sqs, 4 x 2 1/2in x 4 1/2in (6.3cm x 11.4cm) rects

■ **col B (green):** 4 x 2 1/2in x 4 1/2in (6.3cm x 11.4cm) rects

■ **col C (red):** 5 x 4 1/2in (11.4cm) sqs

■ **col D centre sq (grey):** 4 1/2in (11.4cm) sq

washington pavement

main block [WP1 — 5 3/4in (14.6cm) finished block]

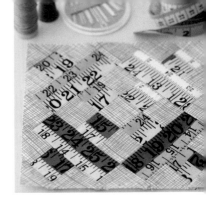

1   Use 4 X squares and 5 BKG sqs to make 9-patch (use photograph for reference if using directional prints). Place on point to make centre sq.

2   Sew BKG sqs either side of 1 X sq to make a row of 3. Join X rect underneath. Repeat. Join these sections to top left and bottom right edge of centre sq.

3   Repeat step 2 adding another 2 BKG sqs either side of X rect before joining together. Add to top right and bottom left edges of centre sq.

4   Add BKG sq on point to each corner. Trim block sq cutting 1/4in (6mm) away from outer square points to approx 6 1/4in (15.9cm) sq.

materials:
- **X (light):**
  4 x 1 1/2in x 3 1/2in (3.8cm x 8.9cm) rects,
  8 x 1 1/2in (3.8cm) sqs
- **BKG (dark):**
  21 x 1 1/2in (3.8cm) sqs

variation 1 [WP2 — 5 3/4in (14.6cm) block]

1   Make as for WP1 using a different colour for each X sq to make the centre sq 9-patch.

2   Continue as for WP1 using a different colour to complete each X.

see other variations page 176

materials
- **X (x 4 in 4 different colours):**
  1 1/2in x 3 1/2in (3.8cm x 8.9cm) rect, 2 x 1 1/2in (3.8cm) sqs
- **BKG:**
  21 x 1 1/2in (3.8cm) sqs

intermediate blocks: squares and triangles   155

weathervane

main block [WV1 — 12in (30.5cm) block]

1 Add CSTs to 2 adjacent corners of each of the 4 medium 4 1/2in (11.4cm) using light 2 1/2in (6.3cm) sqs.

2 Sew 2 of those to either side of the dark 4 1/2in (11.4cm) sq.

3 Sew together 4 pairs of dark and light 2 1/2in (6.3cm) sqs.

4 Sew each of those to 1 of the 2 1/2in x 4 1/2in (6.3cm x 11.4cm) rects.

5 Sew 2 of the sqs made at step 4 to either side of the spare CST units follo the layout in the photograph.

6 Assemble the block following the layout in the photograph.

materials

■ **dark:** 4 1/2in (11.4cm) sq,
4 x 2 1/2in (6.3cm) sqs
■ **medium:** 4 x 4 1/2in (11.4cm)
sqs
■ **light:** 12 x 2 1/2in (6.3cm)
sqs, 4 x 2 1/2in x 4 1/2in (6.3cm
x 11.4cm) rects

variation 1 [WV2 — 12in (30.5cm) block]

see other variations page 177

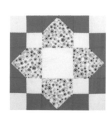

1 As for WV1 step 1.

2 As for WV1 step 2 but using the light 4 1/2in (11.4cm) sq.

3 As for WV1 but pairing 8 pairs of dark and light 2 1/2in (6.3cm) sqs.

4 Sew those into 4 4-patches.

5 Sew block together using layout in the photograph.

materials

■ **dark:**
16 x 2 1/2in (6.3cm) sqs
■ **medium:**
4 x 4 1/2in (11.4cm) sqs
■ **light:**
8 x 2 1/2in (6.3cm) sqs,
4 1/2in (11.4cm) sq

x and cross

main block [XAP1 — 10in (25.4cm) block]

1 Sew 2 BKG B sqs as CSTs to opposite corners of each X sq. Make 4.

2 Join cross sq and BKG A sq. Sew X sq from step 1 to either side of this using photograph for reference. Repeat.

3 Sew BKG A sqs to both 2 1/2in (6.3cm) edges of cross rect. Join X rows from step 2 above and below.

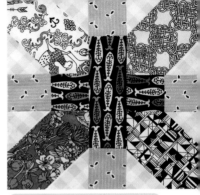

materials

- **X:** 4 x 4 1/2in (11.4cm) sqs in 4 diff colours
- **BKG col A (grey):** 4 x 2 1/2in (6.3cm) sqs
- **BKG col B (cream):** 8 x 2 1/2in (6.3cm) sqs
- **cross:** 2 x 2 1/2in (6.3cm) sqs, 2 1/2in x 6 1/2in (6.3cm x 16.5cm) rect

---

variation 1 [XAP2 — 10in (25.4cm) block]

1 1–2. As for XAP1.

2 Sew cross sqs either side of centre sq. Sew BKG sqs either side of this. Complete as for XAP1.

see other variations page 178

materials

- **X:** 4 x 4 1/2in (11.4cm) sqs in 4 diff colours
- **BKG:** 12 x 2 1/2in (6.4cm) sqs
- **centre sq:** 2 1/2in (6.4cm) sq
- **cross:** 4 x 2 1/2in (6.4cm) sqs

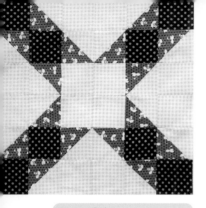

square cross

main block [SC1 — 12in (30.5cm) block]

1 Make 16 HST units pairing together the medium and light 3in (7.6cm) sqs. Trim to 2 1/2in (6.3cm) sq.

2 Assemble the block following the layout in the photograph.

materials

■ **dark:**
   8 x 2 1/2in (6.3cm) sqs
■ **medium:**
   8 x 3in (7.6cm) sqs
■ **light:**
   8 x 3in (7.6cm) sqs, 12 x 2 1/2in (6.3cm) sqs

---

variation 1 [SC2 — 12in (30.5cm) block]

see other variations page 179

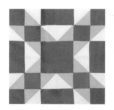

1 Make as for SC1 but following the layout in the photograph.

materials

■ as for SC1, swapping the 12 x light 2 1/2in (6.3cm) sqs for dark fabrics

wild goose chase

main block [WGC1 — 12in (30.5cm) block]

1   Add 4 CSTs to the 4 1/2in (11.4cm) sq using 2 1/2in (6.3cm) sqs.

2   Sash, using the 4 1/2in (11.4cm) and 6 1/2in (16.5cm) strips, then add 4 more CSTs.

3   Repeat, adding 3 more rounds of sashing and CSTs.

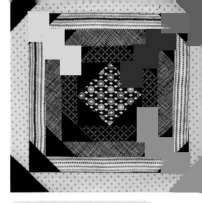

materials

- ▪ **dark:** 20 x 2 1/2in (6.3cm) sqs
- ▪ **coloured:** 4 1/2in (11.4cm) sq plus 1 1/2in (3.8cm) strips, lengths as follows: 2 x 4 1/2in (11.4cm), 4 x 6 1/2in (16.5cm), 4 x 8 1/2in (21.6cm), 4 x 10 1/2in (26.7cm), 2 x 12 1/2in (31.7cm)

---

variation 1 [WGC2 — 8in (20.3cm) block]

see other variations page 180

1   Make as for WGC1, adding just 1 round of sashing at step 3.

materials

- ▪ **dark:** 12 x 2 1/2in (6.3cm) sqs
- ▪ **BKG:** 4 1/2in (11.4cm) sq plus 1 1/2in (3.8cm) strips, lengths as follows: 2 x 4 1/2in (11.4cm), 4 x 6 1/2in (16.5cm), 2 x 8 1/2in (21.6cm)

windblown square

see other variations page 181

project: floor cushion [25in x 25in (63.5cm x 63.5cm)]

1 Make 4 WB3 blocks in 4 different colourways.

2 Add sml sashing strips to sides and lrg strips to top and bottom of each block using photograph for colour placement. Trim blocks to 13 1/4in (33.7cm) sq. Join blocks in 4 patch to make cushion front.

3 Apply fusible fleece to cushion front and both back sections. Quilt as desired. Bind 1 x 26in (66cm) edge on each back section using double-fold technique.

4 Place front and overlapping back pieces RS tog, placing bound edges at cushion opening. Stitch around edges. Turn through and press. Add cushion pad through envelope opening.

materials

- as for WB3 x 4 in 4 colour variations, plus:
- **sashing strips:** 2 x 3in x 8 1/2in (7.6cm x 21.6cm) sml, 2 x 3in x 13 1/2in (7.6cm x 34.3cm) lrg (x 4 — 1 set for each colour)
- **backing fabric:** 2 x 18in x 26in (45.7cm x 66cm) rects
- **binding strips:** 2 x 2 1/4in x 26in (5.7cm x 66cm) strips
- **fusible fleece:** 26in (66cm) sq, 2 x 18in x 26in (45.7cm x 66cm)
- **cushion pad:** 26in (66cm) sq

main square [WB1 — 12in (30.5cm) block]

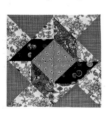

1 Pair 2 A/B triangles, place right angles together to start the seam. Sew tog to make large triangles for block corners. Use photograph for placement. Repeat x 3.

2 Pair C/E 4in (10.2cm) sqs and make 2 HST units. Trim to 3 1/2in (8.9cm) sq. Repeat with D/E sqs.

3 To each CE and DE HST unit, add 2 A, C or D triangles to each using photograph for colour placement to make lrg triangle.

4 Pair each lrg triangle with AB block corner triangles, match seam points at centre and sew along diagonal. Find centre point of sq on diag seam; trim outer edges evenly to make 6 1/2in (16.5cm) sq. Repeat x 3. Complete as 4-patch.

materials

- **col A (white):** 7 1/2in (19cm) sq quartered diag, 2 x 3 7/8in (9.8cm) sqs cut in half diag
- **col B (teal):** 7 1/2in (19cm) sq quartered diag
- **col C (black):** 3 7/8in (9.8cm) sq cut in half diag, 4in (10.2cm) sq
- **col D (brown):** 3 7/8in (9.8cm) sq cut in half diag, 4in (10.2cm) sq
- **col E (pink):** 2 x 4in (10.2cm) sqs

variations

card trick

see base design page 135

variation 1
[CTK2 – 12in (30.5cm) block]

materials
(colours clockwise around block starting top left)
col A:
5in (12.7cm) sq, 2 x 5 1/2in (14cm) sqs
col B:
5in (12.7cm) sq, 2 x 5 1/2in (14cm) sqs
BKG:
2 x 5in (12.7cm)sqs, 5 1/2in (14cm) sq

1. Make as for CTK1, alternating colours A/B instead of A/B/C/D. Use both HST units created in step 1.

variation 2
[CTK3 – 12in (30.5cm) block]

materials
as for CTK1

1. Make as for CTK1, rotating the centre QST sq 180°.

variation 3
[CTK4 – 12in (30.5cm) block]

materials
as for CTK2

1. Make as for CTK2, swapping each completed corner HST unit to the alternate colour.

variation 4
[CTK5 – 12in (30.5cm) block]

materials
As for CTK2

1. Make as for CTK2, rotating each corner HST unit by 180°.

variations

broken wheel

see base design page 136

variation 1
[BW2 — 9in (22.9cm) block]

materials
as for BW1 with only 4 x col B (green) 3 1/2in (8.9cm) sqs plus 1 additional col A (pale) 3 1/2in (8.9cm) sq

1. Make as for BW1, following the layout in the photograph.

variation 2
[BW3 — 9in (22.9cm) block]

materials
as for BW1 with additional 4 x col A (cream) 2in (5.1cm) sqs

1. As for BW1, making 5 CSTs sqs.
2. Assemble the block following the layout in the photograph.

variation 3
[BW4 — 9in (22.9cm) block]

materials
as for BW1 with only 12 x col A 2in (5.1cm) sqs, only 4 x col B 3 1/2in (8.9cm) sqs, plus 1 additional col A 3 1/2in (8.9cm) sq

1. Make as for BW1 but only add 3 CSTs to each B sq.
2. Assemble the block following the layout in the photograph.

variation 4
[BW5 — 9in (22.9cm) block]

materials
as for BW1 with only 12 x col A 2in (5.1cm) sqs and replacing 1 x col A (dark) 3 1/2in (8.9cm) sq with 1 x col A (pale) 3 1/2in (8.9cm) sq

1. Make as for BW1 but only add 3 CSTs to each corner square.
2. Assemble the block following the layout in the photograph.

variations

chubby star

see base design page 139

variation 2
[CS3 — 12in (30.5cm) block]

materials

BKG: as for CS1, omitting the 9in (22.9cm) sq, plus 2 x 3 1/2in (8.9cm) sqs, 4in (10.2cm) sq

col A (gingham): as for CS2, plus 4 x 3in x 4in (7.6cm x 10.2cm) rects

1. Make 4 HST units pairing the 3 1/2in (8.9cm) sqs. Trim to 3in (7.6cm).
2. Sew 1 onto each end of 2 of the 3in x 4in (7.6cm x 10.2cm) rects following the layout in the photograph.
3. Sew the 2 spare 3in x 4in (7.6cm x 10.2cm) rects onto 2 sides of the 4in (10.2cm) sq.
4. Sew the sections made in step 2 to the top and bottom of the section made in step 3.
5. Continue as from step 2 of CS1.

variation 3
[CS4 — 12in (30.5cm) block]

materials

as for CS3, replacing the BKG 4in (10.2cm) sq with a col B (red) 4in (10.2cm) sq and the col A (brown) 2 x 3in (7.6cm) sqs with col B (red) 2 x 3in (7.6cm) sqs

1. Make as for CS3 but assemble the block following the layout in the photograph.

variation 4
[CS5 — 12in (30.5cm) block]

materials

As for CS3, replacing the 4 x 3in x 4in (7.6cm x 10.2cm) col A rects with 8 x BKG 2 1/4in x 3in (5.7cm x 7.6cm) rects and 8 x col A 2 1/4in (5.7cm)

1. Add 1 CST to each of the 8 BKG 2 1/4in x 3in (5.7cm x 7.6cm) rects using the 8 x col A 2 1/4in (5.7cm) sqs, making sure to add half to the bottom left corner and half to the bottom right corner.
2. Sew into pairs along the longer side to make star triangles.
3. Make 4 HST units pairing the 3 1/2in (8.9cm) sqs. Trim to 3in (7.6cm) sq.
4. Sew HST units to each side of 2 of the units made in step 2.
5. Sew the remaining 2 units made in step 2 to 2 sides of the 4in (10.2cm) sq. BKG fabric.
6. Continue as from step 2 of CS1.

variations

crown of thorns

see base design page 140

variation 1
[COT2 – 10in (25.4cm) block]

materials
col A (dark):
as for COT1, with only 1 x 2 1/2in (6.3cm) sq plus an additional 4 x 3 1/2in (8.9cm) sqs
BKG (light): as for COT1, omitting the 2 1/2in (6.3cm) sqs, and plus an additional 4 x 3 1/2in (8.9cm) sqs

1. Make 8 QST units, pairing together the 3 1/2in (8.9cm) sqs. Trim to 2 1/2in (6.3cm) sq.
2. Finish and assemble block as for COT1 but following layout in photograph for COT2.

variation 2
[COT3 – 10in (25.4cm) block]

materials
col A (pale):
as for COT1 plus 2 x 3 1/2in (8.9cm) sqs
BKG (dark): as for COT1, omitting 4 x 2 1/2in (6.3cm) sqs, and plus an additional 2 x 3 1/2in (8.9cm) sqs

1. Make 4 QST units pairing together the 3 1/2in (8.9cm) sqs. Trim to 2 1/2in (6.3cm) sq.
2. Finish and assemble block as for COT1 but following layout in photograph for COT3.

variation 3
[COT4 – 10in (25.4cm) block]

materials
col A (from each of 4 colours):
2 x 3in (7.6cm) sqs
col B (black):
4 x 2 1/2in x 4 1/2in (6.3cm x 11.4cm) rects
BKG: as for COT1, with only 1 x 2 1/2in (6.3cm) sq

1. Make as for COT1 in step 1.
2. Sew HSTs into 4 x 4-patches.
3. Sew 2 of these onto either side of 2 of the B rects.
4. Assemble the block in a 9-patch following the layout in the photograph.

variation 4
[COT5 – 10in (25.4cm) block]

materials
col A (floral):
as for COT1, omitting the 2 1/2in (6.3cm) sqs
BKG: as for COT1, with only 1 x 2 1/2in (6.3cm) sq, plus an additional 4 x 2 1/2in x 4 1/2in (6.3cm x 11.4cm) rects

1. Make as for COT4.

diamond square

see base design page 141

variation 1
[DM2 — 12in (30.5cm) block]

materials
BKG:
16 x 2 1/2in (6.3cm) sqs,
4 x 3in (7.6cm) sqs
col A (green):
6 x 3in (7.6cm) sqs
col B (grey):
10 x 3in (7.6cm) sqs

1. Make 20 HST units pairing the following 3in (7.6cm) sqs: 6 x A/B, 4 x B/BKG. Trim all to 2 1/2in (6.3cm) sq.
2. Assemble block following layout in the photograph.

variation 2
[DM3 — 12in (30.5cm) block]

materials
BKG:
12 x 3in (7.6cm) sqs,
12 x 2 1/2in (6.3cm) sqs
col A (dark):
10 x 3in (7.6cm) sqs
col B (light):
2 x 3in (7.6cm) sqs

1. Make 24 HST units pairing the following 3in (7.6cm) sqs: 10 x A/BKG, 2 x B/BKG. Trim all to 2 1/2in (6.3cm) sq.
2. Assemble block following layout in the photograph.

variation 3
[DM4 — 12in (30.5cm) block]

materials
col A (dark):
10 x 3in (7.6cm) sqs
col B (medium):
6 x 3in (7.6cm) sqs,
12 x 2 1/2in (6.3cm) sqs
col C (light):
4 x 3in (7.6cm) sqs,
4 x 2 1/2in (6.3cm) sqs

1. Make 20 HST units pairing the following 3in (7.6cm) sqs: 6 x A/B, 4 x B/C. Trim all to 2 1/2in (6.3cm) sq.
2. Assemble block following layout in the photograph.

variation 4
[DM5 — 12in (30.5cm) block]

materials
BKG:
8 x 3in (7.6cm) sqs,
8 x 2 1/2in (6.3cm) sqs
col A (black):
8 x 3in (7.6cm) sqs
col B (light):
6 x 2 1/2in (6.3cm) sqs
col B (dark):
6 x 2 1/2in (6.3cm) sqs

1. Make 16 HST units pairing 8 x A/BKG 3in (7.6cm) sqs. Trim all to 2 1/2in (6.3cm) sq.
2. Assemble block following layout in the photograph.

variations

gem stone

see base design page 142

variation 2
[GST3 — 8in (20.3cm) block]

materials
BKG:
2 x 4 1/4in (10.8cm) sqs,
4 x 3in (7.6cm) sqs
col A (dark blue):
4 x 2 1/2in (6.3cm) sqs,
4 x 1in x 8in (2.5cm x 20.3cm) strips

1. Make as for GS1 but using the 4 x A 2 1/2in (6.3cm) sqs instead of step 2.

variation 3
[GST4 — 8in (20.3cm) block]

materials
BKG:
2 x 4 1/4in (10.8cm) sqs,
2 x 3 1/2in (8.9cm) sqs, 4 x 3in (7.6cm) sqs
col A (black):
2 x 3 1/2in (8.9cm) sqs,
4 x 1in x 8in (2.5cm x 20.3cm) strips

1. Make 4 HST units pairing the 3 1/2in (8.9cm) sqs. Trim to 2 1/2in (6.3cm) sq.
2. Make as for GS1, replacing the HST units with the QST units.

variation 4
[GST5 — 8in (20.3cm) block]

materials
col A (light dot):
2 x 4 1/4in (10.8cm) sqs,
4 x 1in x 8in (2.5cm x 20.3cm) strips
col B (check):
2 x 4 1/4in (10.8cm) sqs,
4 x 1in x 8in (2.5cm x 20.3cm) strips

1. Cut all sqs in half on the diag.
2. Sew the A strips onto the B triangles and the B strips onto the A triangles. Trim.
3. Sew the pairs of triangles together to make the 4 quadrants of the blocks and trim to 4 1/2in (11.4cm) sq.
4. Sew the 4 quadrants together following the layout in the photograph.

follow the leader

see base design page 143

variation 2
[FTL3 — 10in (25.4cm) block]

materials
dark:
2 x 3 1/2in x 7in (8.9cm x 17.8cm) rects cut in half diagonally
light:
2 1/2in (6.3cm) sq, 4 x 4 1/2in (11.4cm) sqs, 2 x 3 1/2in x 7in (8.9cm x 17.8cm) rects cut in half diagonally
template: FTLi

1. As for FTL1, then as for FTL1 step 3.

variation 3
[FTL4 — 10in (25.4cm) block]

materials
dark (brown): 2 x 3 1/2in x 7in (8.9cm x 17.8cm) rects cut in half diagonally
medium (orange): 2 1/2in (6.3cm) sq (centre sq)
medium (grey): 4 x 2 1/2in (6.3cm) sqs
light (BKG): 4 x 2 1/2in (6.3cm) sqs, 4 x 2 1/2in x 4 1/2in (6.3cm x 11.4cm) sml rects
template: FTLi

1. As for FTL1.
2. Join light/dark sqs. Add light sml rect to 4 1/2in (11.4cm) edge. Repeat x 3 using photograph to check placement.
3. Finish as for FTL1.

variation 4
[FTL5 — 10in (25.4cm) block]

materials
dark (peach): 2 x 5in (12.7cm) sqs
medium (green): 3 1/2in x 7in (8.9cm x 17.8cm) rects
light (white): 2 1/2in (6.3cm) sq, 2 x 5in (12.7cm) sqs, 2 x 3 1/2in x 7in (8.9cm x 17.8cm) rects
template: FTLi

1. As for FTL1.
2. Pair light/dark 5in (12.7cm) sqs. Make 4 HST units. Trim to 4 1/2in (11.4cm) sq.
3. Finish as for FTL1 step.

father's choice

see base design page 145

variation 2
[FC3 — 10in (25.4cm) block]

materials
BKG:
12 x 2 1/2in (6.3cm) sqs,
4 x 3in (7.6cm) sqs
col A (orange):
5 x 2 1/2in (6.3cm) sqs
col B (yellow):
4 x 3in (7.6cm) sqs

1. Make 8 HST units pairing 4 x B/BKG 3in (7.6cm) sqs. Trim to 2 1/2in (6.3cm) sq.
2. Assemble the block in rows and then into the block following the layout in the photograph.

variation 3
[FC4 — 10in (25.4cm) block]

materials
BKG:
9 x 2 1/2in (6.3cm) sqs,
4 x 3in (7.6cm) sqs, 2 x 3 1/2in (8.9cm) sqs
col A (green):
4 x 2 1/2in (6.3cm) sqs
col B (black):
4 x 3in (7.6cm) sqs
col C (red):
2 x 2 1/2in (6.3cm) sqs

1. Make 8 HST units pairing 4 x B/BKG 3in (7.6cm) sqs. Trim to 2 1/2in (6.3cm) sq.
2. Make 4 QST units pairing 2 x C/BKG 3 1/2in (8.9cm) sqs. Trim to 2 1/2in (6.3cm) sq.
3. Assemble the block in rows and then into block following photograph.

variation 4
[FC5 — 10in (25.4cm) block]

materials
BKG:
9 x 2 1/2in (6.3cm) sqs,
4 x 3in (7.6cm) sqs
col A (green):
8 x 2 1/2in (6.3cm) sqs
col B (pink):
4 x 3in (7.6cm) sqs

1. Make 8 HST units pairing 4 x B/BKG 3in (7.6cm) sqs. Trim to 2 1/2in (6.3cm) sq.
2. Assemble the block in rows and then into the block following the layout in the photograph.

variations

christmas tree

see base design page 146

variation 1
[CT2 — 6in (15.2cm) block]

materials
as for CT1 with an additional 2 x 1 1/2in x 6 1/2in (3.8cm x 16.5cm) BKG strips

1. Make as for CT1 then add a strip to either side of the block.

variation 2
[CT3 — 14in (35.6cm) block]

materials
4 x requirements for CT2
col B (trunk):
2 x 1 1/2in x 12 1/2in (3.8cm x 31.7cm) strips, 2 x 1 1/2in x 14 1/2in (3.8cm x 36.8cm) strips

1. Make 4 x CT2.
2. Sew into a 4-patch.
3. Sash left and right sides using the shorter col B strips.
4. Sash top and bottom using the longer col B strips.

variation 3
[CT4 — 17in (43.2cm) block]

materials
4 x requirements for CT2
BKG:
10in (25.4cm) sq, 6 1/2in (16.5cm) sq, 2 x 5 1/4in (13.3cm) sqs

1. Make 4 x CT2.
2. Cut the 10in (25.4cm) square into 4 QSTs and the 2 x 5 1/4in (13.3cm) sqs in half along the diag.
3. Assemble the block placing the smaller triangles at the corners and the larger on the sides. Piece together using the same method as for GS, piecing diag rows.
4. Trim to 17in (43.2cm) sq.

variation 4
[CT5 — 18in (45.7cm) block]

materials
4 x requirements for CT2
BKG:
4 x 6 1/2in (16.5cm) sqs, 4 x 3in (7.6cm) sqs
col B (trunk):
2 x 1 1/2in x 3in (3.8cm x 7.6cm) strips, 1 1/2in x 6 1/2in (3.8cm x 16.5cm) strip

1. Make 4 x CT2.
2. Make the cross block by sashing together pairs of 3in (7.6cm) sqs using the shorter B strips then sashing the 2 halves of the block using the longer strip.
3. Assemble the block following the layout in the photograph.

jacob's ladder

see base design page 148

variation 2
[JL3 — 12in (30.5cm) block]

materials
col A (cream):
2 x 5in (12.7cm) sqs,
2 x 4 1/2in (11.4cm) sqs,
6 x 2 1/2in (6.3cm) sqs
col B (light yellow):
2 x 5in (12.7cm) sqs
col C (dark yellow):
6 x 2 1/2in (6.3cm) sqs

1. Make as for JL1, only making 3 4-patches and then assemble following the layout in the photograph.

variation 3
[JL4 — 12in (30.5cm) block]

materials
col A (cream):
2 x 5in (12.7cm) sqs,
2 x 4 1/2in (11.4cm) sqs,
6 x 2 1/2in (6.3cm) sqs
col B (red):
2 x 5in (12.7cm) sqs
col C (pink):
6 x 2 1/2in (6.3cm) sqs

1. Make as for JL3 but assemble following the layout in the photograph.

variation 4
[JL5 — 12in (30.5cm) block]

materials
col A (cream):
3 x 5in (12.7cm) sqs,
6 x 2 1/2in (6.3cm) sqs
col B (dark black):
3 x 5in (12.7cm) sqs
col C (light black):
6 x 2 1/2in (6.3cm) sqs

1. Make as for JL3 but make 2 additional HST units from the 5in (12.7cm) sqs.
2. Assemble following the layout in the photograph.

open window

see base design page 149

variation 2
[OW3 – 8in (20.3cm) block]

materials
BKG:
8 x 3in (7.6cm) sqs
dark green fabric:
6 x 3in (7.6cm) sqs
light green fabric:
2 x 3in (7.6cm) sqs

1. Make 16 HST units pairing the BKG 3in (7.6cm) sqs with the green fabric 3in (7.6cm) sqs.
2. Assemble the block following the layout in the photograph.

variation 3
[OW4 – 8in (20.3cm) block]

materials
as for OW3

1. Make as for OW3 but assemble the block following the layout in the photograph.

variation 4
[OW5 – 8in (20.3cm) block]

materials
BKG:
8 x 3in (7.6cm) sqs,
4 x 2 1/2in (6.3cm) sqs
each of 4 red fabrics:
2 x 3in (7.6cm) sqs

1. Make 16 HST units pairing the BKG 3in (7.6cm) sqs with the red fabric 3in (7.6cm) sqs. Discard 1 of each print.
2. Assemble the block following the layout in the photograph.

variations

amish cross

see base design page 150

variation 1
[AC2 — 9in (22.9cm) block]

materials
col A (blue): 2 x 3in (7.6cm) sqs, 8 x 2 1/2in (6.3cm) sqs
col B (cream):
4 x 1 1/2in x 4 1/2in (3.8cm x 11.4cm) rects, 2 x 3in (7.6cm) sqs
col C (red): 1 1/2in (3.8cm) sml sq, 4 x 2 1/2in (6.3cm) sqs

1. Pair 2 A/B 3in (7.6cm) sqs. Sew 4 HST units. Trim to 2 1/2in (6.3cm) sq.
2. Join 4 HST units with A sqs using photograph for reference. Repeat with A/C sqs.
3. Using photograph for ref, join each HST/A sq with A/C sq to make 4 x 4-patch sections.
4. Complete as for AC1 step 4.

variation 2
[AC3 — 9in (22.9cm) block]

materials
col A (cream):
1 1/2in (3.8cm) sml sq, 8 x 2 1/2in (6.3cm)sqs, 2 x 3in (7.6cm) sqs
col B (green):
4 x 2 1/2in (6.3cm) sqs, 2 x 3in (7.6cm) sqs
col C (red):
4 x 1 1/2in x 4 1/2in (3.8cm x 11.4cm) rects

1. As AC2 pairing A/B sqs for step 2.

variation 3
[AC4 — 9in (22.9cm) block]

materials
col A (white): 4 x 3in (7.6cm) sqs
col B (pink): 4 x 3in (7.6cm) sqs
col C (black):
1 1/2in (3.8cm) sml sq, 8 x 2 1/2in (6.3cm) sqs
col D (orange):
4 x 1 1/2in x 4 1/2in (3.8cm x 11.4cm) rects

1. Pair 4 A/B sqs. Sew 8 HST units. Trim to 2 1/2in (6.3cm) sq.
2. Join 8 HST units with C sqs as AC2. Complete as AC1 step 4.

variation 4
[AC5 — 9in (22.9cm) block]

materials
col A (lilac):
8 x 2 1/2in (6.3cm) sqs
col B (green):
1 1/2in (3.8cm) sml sq, 4 x 2 1/2in (6.3cm) sqs
col C (peach):
4 x 2 1/2in (6.3cm) sqs
col D (yellow):
4 x 1 1/2in x 4 1/2in (3.8cm x 11.4cm) rects

1. Pair A/B sqs, join. Repeat with A/C sqs. Join units together to make 4 4-patch sqs. Complete as for AC1 step 4.

variations

mill wheel

see base design page 153

variation 2
[MW3 — 8in (20.3cm) block]

materials
cream/black: 8 x 3in (7.6cm) sqs, 4 1/2in (11.4cm) lrg sq
solid black: 4 x 2 1/2in (6.3cm) sml sqs
4 solid colours (red/ orange/green/teal): 3in (7.6cm) sq in each colour
4 cream/colour prints: 3in (7.6cm) sq in each colour

1. Make HST pairs using 3in (7.6cm) sqs as MW1 using photograph for colour pairs. There will be an excess of 4 HST units to discard.
2. Complete as MW1 using 4 1/2in (11.4cm) lrg sq with black sqs as CSTs to make centre sq.

variation 3
[MW4 — 8in (20.3cm) block]

materials
col A (dark): 4 x 3in (7.6cm) sqs, 4 1/2in (11.4cm) lrg sq
col B (teal): 2 x 2 1/2in (6.3 cm) sml sqs, 3in (7.6cm) sq
col C (pink): 2 x 2 1/2in (6.3cm) sml sqs, 3in (7.6cm) sq
BKG (cream): 6 x 3in (7.6cm) sqs

1–2. Make as MW1 pairing 4 x A/BKG sqs, B/BKG sq, C/BKG sq and making 8 x A/BKG, 2 x B/BKG and 2 C/ BKG HST units.
3. Complete as MW1 using A 4 1/2in (11.4cm) lrg sq and 2 x B and 2 x C sml sqs for CSTs to make centre sq.

variation 4
[MW5 — 8in (20.3cm) block]

materials
col A (green): 5 x 3in (7.6cm) sqs
col B (pink): 3 x 3in (7.6cm) sqs
BKG (grey): 8 x 3in (7.6cm) sqs

1. Pair 5 x A/BKG sqs. Make 10 x HST units. Repeat with B/BKG making 6 x HST units.
2. Arrange and sew HST units in 4 rows of 4 following photograph for reference. Join rows.

variations

swing in the centre

see base design page 154

variation 2
[STC3 — 12in (30.5cm) block]

materials
col A (light):
12 x 2 1/2in (6.3cm) sqs,
4 x 2 1/2in x 4 1/2in (6.3cm x 11.4cm) rects
col B (yellow):
8 x 2 1/2in (6.3cm) sqs,
4 x 2 1/2in x 4 1/2in (6.3cm x 11.4cm) rects
col C (blue):
5 x 4 1/2in (11.4cm) sqs
col D (cream):
16 x 2 1/2in (6.3cm) sqs

1. As STC1 step 1.
2. As STC1 step 2 but adding a 4th CST using D sq and using 4 D sqs for centre C sq CSTs. Continue as STC1.

variation 3
[STC4 — 12in (30.5cm) block]

materials
col A (purple):
4 x 4 1/2in (11.4cm) sqs
col B (green):
16 x 2 1/2in (6.3cm) sqs
col C (pink):
4 x 4 1/2in (11.4cm) sqs
col D centre sq (orange):
4 1/2in (11.4cm) sq

1. Sew 2 B sqs as CSTs to adjacent corners of A sq. Make 4.
2. Sew 1 B sq as CSTs to 1 corner of each C sq. Make 4.
3. Sew B sqs as CSTs to each corner of centre sq.
4. Sew as 9-patch.

variation 4
[STC5 — 12in (30.5cm) block]

materials
col A (pink):
8 x 2 1/2in (6.3cm) sqs,
4 x 2 1/2in x 4 1/2in (6.3cm x 11.4cm) rects
col B (cream):
16 x 2 1/2in (6.3cm) sqs
col C (grey):
4 x 4 1/2in (11.4cm) sqs
col D (orange):
4 1/2in (11.4cm) sq,
4 x 2 1/2in x 4 1/2in (6.3cm x 11.4cm) rects

1. As STC1 using B sqs/A rects to make 4 geese units and A sqs/D rects to make 4 further geese units. Join together as STC1.
2. As STC4 step 2.
3. As STC4 step 3, D is centre sq. Complete as STC4.

variations

washington pavement

see base design page 155

variation 2
[WP3 — 11in (27.9cm) block]

materials
X col A (blue):
4 x 2 1/2in x 6 1/2in
(6.3cm x 16.5cm) rects
X col B (lilac):
8 x 2 1/2in (6.3cm) sqs
BKG:
21 x 2 1/2in (6.3cm) sqs

1. Make as for WP1 using
B/BKG sqs to make the
centre sq 9-patch.
2. Continue as for WP1
using A and B to
complete each X and
trimming block to approx
11 1/2in (29.2cm) sq in
step 4.

variation 3
[WP4 — 11in (27.9cm) block]

materials
X col A (yellow):
2 x 2 1/2in x 6 1/2in
(6.3cm x 16.5cm) rects,
4 x 2 1/2in (6.3cm) sqs
X col B (white):
2 x 2 x 2 1/2in x 6 1/2in
(6.3cm x 16.5cm) rects,
4 x 2 1/2in (6.3cm) sqs
BKG col C (pink):
5 x 2 1/2in (6.3cm) sqs
BKG col D (green):
16 x 2 1/2in (6.3cm) sqs

1. Make as for WP1 using
2 x A and B X sqs with
BKG C sqs for centre sq.
2. Continue as for WP1
using different colour for
each X, trimming block
approx 11 1/2in (29.2cm)
sq in step 4.

variation 4
[WP5 — 11in (27.9cm) block]

materials
X:
2 x 2 1/2in x 6 1/2in (6.3cm x 16.5cm) rects,
4 x 2 1/2in (6.3cm) sqs
O:
4 x 2 1/2in x 6 1/2in (6.3cm x 16.5cm) rects,
4 x 2 1/2in (6.3cm) sqs
BKG:
19 x 2 1/2in (6.3cm) sqs

1. Place O rects diagonally. To make top of O shapes, add
BKG sq as CSTs to right end of 1 O rect using photograph for
diagonal placement. Repeat to left end of 2nd rect. Join the
CST rect ends to either side of X sq. Repeat with remaining
rects/X sq sewing diagonals in opposite direction to make
bottom of O shapes.
2. Using diagonal block construction, arrange and sew in
the same manner as GS1. Row 1 = 1 sq, row 2 = 1 sq,
1 rect, 1 sq, row 3 = rects from step 1, row 4 = 9 BKG/O
sqs etc.
3. Trim to approx 11 1/2in (29.2cm).

variations
weathervane

see base design page 156

variation 2
[WV3 – 12in (30.5cm) block]

materials
dark:
4 x 4 1/2in (11.4cm) sqs
medium:
4 x 4 1/2in (11.4cm) sqs
light:
8 x 2 1/2in (6.3cm) sqs,
4 1/2in (11.4cm) sq

1. As for WV1 but replacing the corner sections with dark 4 1/2in (11.4cm) sqs.

variation 3
[WV4 – 12in (30.5cm) block]

materials
dark:
5 x 4 1/2in (11.4cm) sqs
yellows:
6 x 2 1/2in (6.3cm) sqs of each of 2 fabrics
light:
16 x 2 1/2in (6.3cm) sqs

1. Make 4 4-patches using 8 yellow and 8 light 2 1/2in (6.3cm) sqs and 1 4-patch using 2 of each of the yellow fabrics.
2. Finish as for WV2 but replacing the centre 4 1/2in (11.4cm) sq with a yellow/yellow 4-patch and the corner squares with yellow/white 4 patches.

variation 4
[WV5 – 12in (30.5cm) block]

materials
dark:
4 1/2in (11.4cm) sq,
4 x 2 1/2in (6.3cm) sqs
medium:
4 x 2 1/2in x 4 1/2in (6.3cm x 11.4cm) rects
light:
12 x 2 1/2in (6.3cm) sqs,
8 x 2 1/2in x 4 1/2in (6.3cm x 11.4cm) rects

1. Make as for WV1 but first sewing 4 medium and 4 light 2 1/2in x 4 1/2in (6.3cm x 11.4cm) rects together along the longer sides to make the 4 1/2in (11.4cm) sqs used in step 1 of WV1.

x and cross

see base design page 157

variation 2
[XAP3 — 10in (25.4cm) block]

materials
cross:
2 x 2 1/2in (6.3cm) sqs,
2 1/2in x 6 1/2in (6.3cm
x 16.5cm) rect
BKG:
4 x 2 1/2in (6.3cm) sqs,
4 x 4 1/2in (11.4cm) sqs

1. As for XAP1 steps 2–3.

variation 3
[XAP4 — 10in (25.4cm) block]

materials
X:
4 x 4 1/2in (11.4cm) sqs
BKG:
8 x 2 1/2in (6.3cm) sqs
cross:
4 x 2 1/2in x 4 1/2in
(6.3cm x 11.4cm) rects
centre sq:
2 1/2in (6.3cm) sq

1. Make as in XAP2. The
centre row has horizontal
cross rects either side of
centre sq.

variation 4
[XAP5 — 10in (25.4cm) block]

materials
as for XAP1

note: each X sq has
contrasting colour CSTs

1. Make as in XAP1.

variations

square cross

see base design page 158

variation 2
[SC3 — 12in (30.5cm) block]

materials

as for SC1 but replacing 4 of the 2 1/2in (6.3cm) BKG squares with 1 x 4 1/2in (11.4cm) BKG sq and with 4 x 2 1/2in (6.3cm) sqs dark fabric

1. Add 4 CSTs to the 4 1/2in (11.4cm) sq using 4 x 2 1/2in (6.3cm) dark sqs.
2. Finish as for SC1.

variation 3
[SC4 — 12in (30.5cm) block]

materials

as for SC1 but swapping the 12 x 2 1/2in (6.3cm) light sqs for 4 x 3in (7.6cm) dark sqs, 4 x 3in (7.6cm) light sqs and 4 x 2 1/2in (6.3cm) medium sqs

1. Make as for SC1 step 1 but make 8 additional HST units pairing the 4 dark and 4 light 3in (7.6cm) sqs.
2. Assemble the block following the layout in the photograph.

variation 4
[SC5 — 12in (30.5cm) block]

materials

as for SC1 but swapping 8 of the 12 x 2 1/2in (6.3cm) light sqs for 4 x 3in (7.6cm) medium sqs and 4 x 3in (7.6cm) light sqs

1. Make as for SC4, pairing the 4 medium and 4 light 3in (7.6cm) sqs for 8 additional HST units.
2. Assemble following the layout in the photograph.

wild goose chase

see base design page 159

variation 2
[WGC3 — 11 1/2in (29.2cm) block]

materials
as for WGC2, plus:
2 x 7in (17.8cm) BKG sqs cut in half along the diag

1. Make as for WGC2 then add the HSTs to the sides, top and bottom to set on point. Trim to 12in (30.5cm) sq.

variation 3
[WGC4 — 9in (22.9cm) block]

materials
as for WGC2, plus:
2 x 1in x 8 1/2in (2.5cm x 21.6cm) strips, 2 x 1in x 9 1/2in (2.5cm x 24.1cm) strips

1. Make as for WGC2 then add the shorter sashing strips to the top and bottom and the longer to the sides.

variation 4
[WGC5 — 10in (25.4cm) block]

materials
as for WGC2 (alternating colour placement of strips and CSTs), plus:
2 x 1 1/2in x 8 1/2in (3.8cm x 21.6cm) strips, 2 x 1 1/2in x 10 1/2in (3.8cm x 26.7cm) strips

1. Make as for WGC2 then add the shorter sashing strips to the top and bottom and the longer to the sides.

variations
windblown square

see base design page 160

variation 1
[WB2 — 8in (20.3cm) block]

materials
col A (cream):
8 x 3in (7.6cm) sqs
col B (yellow):
4 x 3in (7.6cm) sqs
col C (aqua):
4 x 3in (7.6cm) sqs

1. Pair 4 A/B sqs.
Sew 8 HST units.
Trim to 2 1/2in
(6.3cm) sq. Repeat
with A/C.
2. Arrange as in
block photograph.
Sew tog in rows
of 4. Join rows.

variation 2
[WB3 — 8in
(20.3cm) block]

materials
col A (blue):
7 x 3in (7.6cm) sqs
col B (red):
4 x 3in (7.6cm) sqs
col C (white):
4 x 3in (7.6cm) sqs

1. As for WB2,
pairing 3 x A/B
sqs to make 6 HST
units, 4 x A/C sqs
to make 8 HST
units, and 1 x BC
sqs to make 2 HST
units. Complete as
for WB2.

variation 3
[WB4 — 8in (20.3cm) block]

materials
col A (grey): 2 x 3in (7.6cm) sqs,
2 7/8in (7.3cm) sq cut in half
diagonally, 6 1/4in (15.9cm) sq
quartered diagonally
col B (plum): 2 x 2 7/8in (7.3cm)
sqs cut in half diag, 6 1/4in
(15.9cm) sq quartered diag
(discard 2 triangles)
col C (orange): 2 x 3in (7.6cm) sqs,
2 7/8in (7.3cm) sq cut in half diag,
6 1/4in (15.9cm) sq quartered diag
(discard 2 triangles)

1. As for WB1 using A/B and A/C.
Make 2 lrg triangles with each.
2. Pair A/C sqs and make 4 HST
units. Trim to 2 1/2in (6.3cm) sq.
3. Continue as for WB1 using A,
B, or C triangles and photograph
for reference.
4. Continue as for WB1 trimming
sqs to 4 1/2in (11.4cm) sq.

variation 4
[WB5 — 8in (20.3cm) block]

materials
col A (green): 2 x 5in (12.7cm) sqs
cut in half diagonally, 3in (7.6cm) sq
col B (white): 2 x 2 7/8in (7.3cm)
sqs cut in half diagonally, 3in
(7.6cm) sq
col C (red): 2 7/8in (7.3cm) sq cut
in half diagonally, 3in (7.6cm) sq
col D (brown): 2 7/8in (7.3cm) sq
cut in half diagonally, 3in (7.6cm) sq

1. Pair A/D 3in (7.6cm) sqs and
make 2 HST units. Repeat with B/C
sqs. Trim to 2 1/2in (6.3cm) sq.
2. To each AD and BC unit, add B,
C, or D triangles as for WB1 step 3.
3. Pair each lrg triangle from step
2 with A triangle, sew along
diagonal, trim square to 4 1/2in
(11.4cm) sq and continue as WB1.

stars, circles, curves, flowers

This chapter focuses on more intricate shapes for quilt block motifs. Some are very simple to make, such as the raw edge appliqué Dresden. Others are more advanced, using more challenging techniques such as sewing curved seams with Drunkards Path blocks or foundation paper piecing with the Daisy block and quilt project. There are two pillow projects, a stylish Dresden Bolster and the English Paper Pieced Georgetown Carnival pillow, an ideal portable project to quilt on-the-go.

diamond star

see other variations page 210

main block [DS1 — 12in (30.5cm) block]

1 Sew the BKG sml triangles along the bottom of each A/B triangle.

2 Sew the BKG lrg triangles to the left and right side of each A/B triangle.

3 Trim to 6 1/2in (16.5cm) square ensuring the points of the triangle sit 1/4in (6mm) away from each seam edge.

4 Sew into a 4-patch following the layout in the photograph.

   Note: Block pictured left at top.

materials

■ **BKG:** 4 x 4in x 8in (10.2cm x 20.3cm) rects cut in half along the diag (making sure to cut 1/2 top left to bottom right and 1/2 top right to bottom left) — lrg triangles, 2 x 4in (10.2cm) sqs cut in half along the diag — sml triangles

■ **col A (orange):** 2 x 5in x 7 1/2in (12.7cm x 19cm) rects cut into isosceles triangles 7 1/2in (19cm) tall

■ **col B (grey):** 2 x 5in x 7 1/2in (12.7cm x 19cm) rects cut into isosceles triangles 7 1/2in (19cm) tall

variation 1 [DS2 — 12in (30.5cm) block]

1 Assemble as for DS1 following the layout in the photograph.

materials

■ as for DS1 but using 4 colours A/B/C/D for isosceles triangles and cutting the sml BKG triangles from each of those fabrics.

daisy

see other variations page 211
see template page 280

project: daisy quilt [50in x 70in (127cm x 178cm)]

1   Piece the 3 daisies as per DAI1.

2   Sew the stem strips between 2 x 5 1/2in (14cm) strips of same length BKG.

3   Sew 14 1/2in (36.8cm) BKG sections onto the tops of the daisy heads so that the 6 1/2in (16.5cm) strip goes on the tallest daisy and the 16 1/2in (41.9cm) strip on the shortest daisy.

4   Sew the quilt top together, sashing with the 7 1/2in (19cm) WOF strips in between each daisy and at either end.

5   Back, quilt, and bind as desired. Make the backing by cutting the 3 1/2 yds (3.2m) into 2 equal lengths and sewing back together along the long edges.

....

daisy main block [DAI1 — 14in (35.6cm) block]

1   Foundation paper piece four of template DAIi.

2   Trim fabric to dotted line and remove papers.

3   Sew together.

4   Cut out a 7 1/2in (19cm) circle and piece into the centre of the daisy block.

materials

■   **petals:** as for DAI1 x 3

■   **stem strips:** 4 1/2in x 20 1/2in (11.4cm x 52.1cm), 4 1/2in x 25 1/2in (11.4cm x 64.8cm), 4 1/2in x 30 1/2in (11.4cm x 77.5cm)

■   **BKG:** 1 yd (0.91m) for BKG to flowers, 2 yds (1.83m) sub-cut into: 5 x 7 1/2in (19cm) WOF strips sewn into 1 length and cut into 4 strips of 50 1/2in (128cm), 4 x 5 1/2in (14cm) WOF strips sewn into 1 length and cut into 2 strips of 20 1/2in (52.1cm), 2 strips of 25 1/2in (64.8cm), and 3 strips of 30 1/2in (77.5cm), 14 1/2in (36.8cm) WOF strip cut into lengths of 6 1/2in (16.5cm), 11 1/2in (29.2cm), and 16 1/2in (41.9cm)

■   **binding:** 1/2 yd (0.46m)

■   **backing:** 3 1/2 yds (3.20m)

■   **batting:** 58in x 78in (147cm x 198cm)

■   **template:** DAIi

materials

■   **petals:** 12 x 3in x 5in (7.6cm x 12.7cm) strips

■   **centre:** 7 1/2in (19cm) circle

■   **BKG:** approx 1/3 yd (0.30m)

■   **template:** DAIi

drunkard's path

see other variations page 212
see template page 280

main block [DPA1 — 8in (20.3cm) block]

1   On WS dark/light 5 1/2in (14cm) sqs draw round template DPAi in pencil, cut out adding 1/4in (6mm) SA all around.

2   As above for DPAii, with 4 1/2in (11.4cm) sqs.

3   Pair light/dark DPAi and DPAii pieces and join at curved edges to make sq. Repeat x 3. Arrange as in photograph. Join as 4-patch.

materials

- **dark:** 2 x 4 1/2in (11.4cm) sqs, 2 x 5 1/2in (14cm) sqs
- **light:** 2 x 4 1/2in (11.4cm) sqs, 2 x 5 1/2in (14cm) sqs
- **templates:** DPAi frame, DPAii 1/4 circle

---

variation 1 [DPA2 — 8in (20.3cm) block]

1   As for DPA1.

materials

- **assorted dark prints (1/4 circles):** 4 x 4 1/2in (11.4cm) sqs
- **assorted light prints (frames):** 4 x 5 1/2in (14cm) sqs
- **templates:** as for DPA1

electric fan

main block [EF1 — 8 1/2in (21.6cm) block]

1   Starch all quilt pieces. On BKG 5 1/2in (14cm) sqs draw round template DPAi in pencil, cut out adding 1/4in (6mm) SA on all edges. Repeat with EFii/B 3in (7.6cm) sqs and EFi/A 4 1/2in (11.4cm) sqs.

2   Pair A/B EFii and EFi pieces and sew tog to make 1/4 circle sections. Repeat x3. Join to white DPAi pieces. Trim sqs evenly to 4in (10.2cm); there should be 1/4in (6mm) SA from where the frame/1/4 circle seam curves at the corners of each sq.

3   Arrange sqs using diagram (see below) for reference. There will be a 1in (2.5cm) square gap in the centre. Join squares starting each seam at outside edge, sewing towards the centre and matching seam points. Work around the block.

4   On 3in (7.6cm) centre sq draw and cut out 2 3/4in (6.9cm) diameter circle. Using starch as you press, fold and press scant 1/4in (6mm) SA around edge. Appliqué by hand to centre of block. Trim/square block if needed.

materials

- **col A (grey):**
  4 x 4 1/2in (11.4cm) sqs
- **col B (yellow):**
  4 x 3in (7.6cm) sqs
- **BKG:**
  4 x 5 1/2in (14cm) sqs,
  4 x 2 1/4in x 4in (5.7cm x 10.2 cm) rects
- **centre:**
  3 1/2in (8.9cm) sq
- **templates:**
  DPAi frame, EFi whole arc,
  EFii 1/4 circle
- **starch:** use on all pieces
  before assembling

see variations page 213

see template page 280

friendship star

see variations page 214

main block [FST1 — 6in (15.2cm) block]

1   Make 4 HST units pairing A/B 3in (7.6cm) sqs. Trim to 2 1/2in (6.3cm).

2   Assemble the block following the layout in the photograph.

materials

■ **col A (white):**
   5 x 2 1/2in (6.3cm) sqs, 2 x 3in
   (7.6cm) sqs
■ **col B (red):**
   2 x 3in (7.6cm) sqs

dresden plate

see other variations page 215

see template page 281

project: Dresden plate bolster pillow [7in x 23in (17.8cm x 58.4cm)]

1 Make 4 x DP2.

2 Sew the 1 1/2in (3.8cm) sqs into 2 strips of 10, 3 strips of 21 and 2 strips of 23 and use to sash the 4 DP2 blocks following the layout shown in the photograph. Back the pillow top and ends with fusible fleece.

4 Sew the pillow ends to the pillow top using a 1/2in (1.3cm) SA. Sew the long seam using a 1/4in SA, adding a zipper if desired.

materials
- as for DP2 x 4, plus:
- **borders:** 129 x 1 1/2in (3.8cm) sqs
- **pillow ends:** 2 x 7 5/8in (19.4cm) circs
- fusible fleece
- 23in (58.4cm) zipper (optional)
- bolster pillow form 7in x 23in (17.8cm x 58.4cm)

main block [DP1 — 18in (45.7cm) block]

1 Cut out 2 petals from 10 of the 6in (15.2cm) sqs. Use Easy Dresden Ruler with top and bottom of the 6in (15.2cm) sqs aligned with the 1in (2.5cm) and 7in (17.8cm) lines.

2 Fold the tops of the petals RS tog; sew a seam along fold. Turn RS out, push out, press.

3 Sew leaves together in a circle. Baste to 18 1/2in (47cm) BKG, machine sew along edges of the petals.

4 Draw 5 1/2in (14cm) circle on back of fusible web, fuse to the back of remaining 6in (15.2cm) sq. Cut out, fuse to the plate, secure with blanket or zigzag stitch.

materials
- **BKG:**
  18 1/2in (47cm) sq
- **petals and centre:**
  11 x 6in (15.2cm) sqs
- Darlene Zimmerman Easy Dresden Ruler
- fusible web

variation 1 [DP2 — 10in (25.4cm) block]

1 Sew 4 BKG sqs together to make a 10 1/2in (26.7cm) sq BKG.

2 Using 12 DPi templates and 1 DPii, EPP the leaves and centre using the fabric scrap rects and sq. Sew together to make the Dresden plate.

3 Appliqué the Dresden plate to BKG.

materials
- **BKG:**
  4 x 5 1/2in (14cm) sqs
- **leaves and centre:**
  12 x 3in x 4in (7.6cm x 10.2cm) scrap rects, 3 1/2in (8.9cm) scrap sq
- **templates:** DPi, DPii

octagon flower

see other variations page 216

main block [OF1 — 22in (55.9cm) block]

1 Make 8 flying geese units using 8 of col A 3in x 5 1/2in (7.6cm x 14cm) rects and 16 x 3in (7.6cm) BKG sqs.

2 Sew the 8 col B rects to the flying geese units.

3 Sew 2 of these to the 2 ends of the 5 1/2in x 12 1/2in (14cm x 31.7cm) BKG rect.

4 Sew 2 x 4in x 5 1/2in (10.2cm x 14cm) rects to bottoms of 2 more flying geese units.

5 Sew 4 x 2 3/4in x 5 1/2in (6.9cm x 14cm) rects BKG fabric to tops of remaining 4 flying geese units.

6 Sew the 8 4 1/2in (11.4cm) BKG HSTs to the top and bottom of the 4 flying geese units made at step 5 and trim triangle corners.

7 Sew the 8 x 6in (15.2cm) BKG HSTs to each side of the 4 flying geese units made at step 6 to make 4 corner units. Trim to 9in square.

materials

- **col A (pink):** 8 x 3in x 5 1/2in (7.6cm x 14cm) rects
- **col B (blue):** 8 x 3in x 5 1/2in (7.6cm x 14cm) rects
- **BKG:** 16 x 3in (7.6cm) sqs, 5 1/2in x 12 1/2in (14cm x 31.7cm) rect, 2 x 4in x 5 1/2in (10.2cm x 14cm) rects, 4 x 2 3/4in x 5 1/2in (6.9cm x 14cm) rects, 4 x 4 1/2in (11.4cm sqs cut in half along the diag, 4 x 6in sqs cut in half along the diag

8 Sew 2 corner units to the 2 sides of each of the flying geese units made at step 4.

9 Sew the 3 sections tog to finish the block, following the photograph.

variation 1 [OF2 — 22in (55.9cm) block]

1 Make as for OF1 from step 3 using the 5 1/2in sqs in place of the flying geese and rect units.

materials

- **assorted prints** 8 x 5 1/2in (14cm) sqs
- **BKG:** as for OF1, omitting 16 x 3in (7.6cm) sqs

grandma's fan

main block [GF1 — 5in (12.7cm) block]

1 Draw around DPi onto WS of each petal fabric (3 petals). Cut out, allowing extra 1/4in (6mm) SA around template line. Starting seam inwards from outer corner as marked by the pencil template outline, sew petals tog.

2 Turn and press 1/4in (6mm) on petal outer edges. Appliqué along petal edges on to BKG sq.

3 Draw around DPii on to 3 1/2in (8.9cm) sq. Fold and press 1/4in (6mm) seam around half the circle edge, arrange at inner corner of petal curve to make 1/4in (6mm) circle shape allowing 1/4in (6mm) in SA of BKG sq. Hand-appliqué onto petal curve/BKG. Trim away excess layers of fabric on reverse, if desired.

see templates page 281

materials:

- **petals:** 3 x 3in x 4in (7.6cm x 10.2c) rects
- **circle:** 3 1/2in (8.9cm) sq
- **BKG:** 5 1/2in (14cm) sq
- **templates:** DPi, DPii

---

variation 1 [GF2 — 5in (12.7cm) block]

see other variations page 217

1 Apply fusible web to WS of petal rects. Draw around DPi onto fusible web paper backing and cut out 3 petals. No SA is needed. Arrange in corner of BKG sq, the outer petals need to be placed 1/4in (6mm) inwards from the outer edge to allow for SA. Press to fuse. Machine-appliqué petal edges to BKG.

2 Repeat step 1 with DPii and 3 1/2in (8.9cm) sq. Arrange DPii so the outer curve just covers raw edges of inner petal curve. Press to fuse. Trim excess circle. Machine-appliqué 1/4 circle curve.

materials:

- **BKG:** as GF1
- **petals:** 3 x 2 1/4in x 3 1/2in (5.7cm x 8.9cm) rects
- **circle:** 3in sq
- **fusible web:** 3 x 2 1/4in x 3 1/2in (5.7cm x 8.9cm) rects, 3in (7.6cm) sq
- **templates:** DPi, DPii

lemoyne star

main block [LS1 — 9 1/2in (24.1cm) block]

1. Cut 4 x 45° diamonds from each 2 1/2in x 20in (6.3cm x 50.8cm) strip by making 1 x 45° cut at one end then 4 more parallel cuts 2 1/2in (6.3cm) wide to make 4 diamonds per strip.

2. Lay out all cut pieces so that the larger BKG triangles are in the corners and the smaller triangles on the sides of the block.

3. Sew each of the 3 1/2in (8.9cm) triangles to 1 of the edges of each of the diamonds, press, and trim all but the outside edge of the finished block. Sew each of the 4in (10.2cm) triangles to the adjacent edge of each of the diamonds, press, and trim all but the outside edge of the finished block.

4. Sew two diamonds together along the long diagonal of the triangles.

5. Make the remaining four quadrants and sew together to make the finished block, following the layout in the photograph.

6. Trim to 10in (25.4cm) sq.

materials:

- **diamonds:**
  2 x 2 1/2in x 20in (6.3cm x 50.8cm strips (1 of each colour)
- **BKG:**
  4 x 4in (10.2cm) sqs cut in half along diag, 4 x 3 1/2in (8.9cm) sqs cut in half along diag

variation 1 [LS2 — 9 1/2in (24.1cm) block]

see other variations page 218

1. Make as for LS1 but following colour placement in photograph.

materials:

- **from each of 2 fabrics:**
  2 x 2 1/2in x 10in (25.4cm) strips, 2 x 4in (10.2cm) sqs cut in half along diag, 2 x 3 1/2in (8.9cm) sqs cut in half along diag

georgetown carnival

see variations page 219

see template page 281

project: Georgetown carnival pillow [17 1/2in (44.4cm) square]

1   Make block GC1.

2   Fuse pillow top and backing pieces to batting and trim.

3   Bind one 18in (45.7cm) side of each piece of backing.

4   Place pillow top and overlapping backing pieces WS tog and zigzag around edges.

5   Bind.

materials

- as for GC1, plus:
- **binding:** 3 x 2in (5.1cm) WOF strips
- **backing:** 2 x 18in x 11in (45.7cm x 27.9cm) rect
- **fusible batting:** 20in (50.8cm) sq, 2 x 20in x 12in (50.8cm x 30.5cm)
- **15-16in (38–41cm) sq pillow form**
- **templates:** GCi, ii, and iii

main block [GC1 — 17 1/2in (44.4cm) block]

1   EPP the hexagon, sqs and triangles using templates GCi, ii, and iii, and sew together.

2   Applique to the BKG.

materials

- 18in (45.7cm) sq BKG
- **scraps:** 5in (12.7cm) sq, 36 x 3in (7.6cm) sq
- **templates:** GCi, ii, and iii

pictures in the stairwell

main block [PS1 — 8in (20.3cm) block]

1 On A 5 1/2in (14cm) sqs WS draw round template DPAi in pencil, cut out adding 1/4in (6mm) SA all round.

2 As above for DPAii with B 4 1/2in (11.4cm) sqs.

3 Pair A/B DPAi and DPAii pieces and join at curved edges to make sq. Repeat.

4 Using C/D sqs make 2 x 4-patch blocks.

5 Arrange as photograph. Join as 4-patch.

see other variations page 220
see templates page 280

materials

■ **col A (navy):**
2 x 5 1/2in (14cm) sqs

■ **col B (white):**
2 x 4 1/2in (11.4cm) sqs

■ **col C (orange):**
4 x 2 1/2in (6.3cm) sqs

■ **col D (aqua):**
4 x 2 1/2in (6.3cm) sqs

■ **templates:**
DPAi frame, DPAii 1/4 circle

variation 1 [PS2 — 8in (20.3cm) block]

1 Cut 2 DPAi frames from 5 1/2in (14cm) sqs and 2 DPAii 1/4 circles from 2 x 4 1/2in (11.4cm) sqs. Join DPAi/DPAii sections and arrange and assemble block as photograph.

materials

■ **dark (aqua):**
2 x 5 1/2in (14cm) sqs

■ **light (multi):**
4 x 4 1/2in (11.4cm) sqs

■ **templates:**
as for PS1

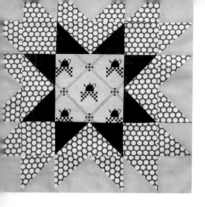

memory

main block [ME1 — 12in (30.5cm) block]

1   Using A sqs and B rects, make 4 flying geese units. Repeat with B sqs and C rects. Join each AB unit below BC unit.

2   Pair B/C 3in (7.6cm) sqs to make 8 HST units. Trim to 2 1/2in (6.3cm) sq. Join B sqs to B edge of unit — repeat to make 4 using photograph for HST diagonal direction. Join C sqs to B edges of remaining unit, making 4 as before. Join together to make block corner sqs.

3   Arrange and sew as 9-patch.

materials

- **centre sq:**
  4 1/2in (11.4cm) lrg sq
- **col A (navy):**
  8 x 2 1/2in (6.3cm) sqs
- **col B (orange):**
  12 x 2 1/2in (6.3cm) sqs,
  4 x 3in (7.6cm) sqs,
  4 x 2 1/2in x 4 1/2in
  (6.3cm x 11.4cm) rects
- **col C (beige):** 4 x 2 1/2in
  (6.3cm) sqs, 4 x 3in (7.6cm)
  sqs, 4 x 2 1/2in x 4 1/2in
  (6.3cm x 11.4cm) rects

variation 1 [ME2 — 24in (61cm) block)]

see other variations page 221

1   As ME1 step 1 with A/B only. Sew geese to B rects along long edges.

2   As ME1 using A/C 5in sqs to make HST units, trimming to 4 1/2in (11.4cm) sq and joining to A sqs and B sqs. Complete as for ME1.

materials

- **centre sq:**
  8 1/2in (21.6cm) lrg sq
- **col A (yellow):** 12 x 4 1/2in
  (11.4cm) sqs, 4 x 5in (12.7cm) sqs
- **col B (navy):** 4 x 4 1/2in
  (11.4cm) sqs, 4 x 4 1/2in x
  8 1/2in (11.4cm x 21.6cm) rects
- **col C (aqua):** 4 x 5in (12.7cm)
  sqs, 4 x 4 1/2in x 8 1/2in (11.4cm
  x 21.6cm) rects

lone star

main block [LST1 – 9 1/2in (21.4cm) block]

1 Sew the 1 1/2in (3.8cm) strips into two pairs. Make a 45° cut at one end of each of the strips, then 8 cuts parallel to that cut 1 1/2in (3.8cm) apart.

2 Take two of the pieces made at step 1 and sew together to make a 2 1/2in (6.3cm) diamond following the layout of the fabrics in the photograph. Repeat to make 7 more diamonds.

3 Finish as for the LeMoyne Star, LS1, from step 2 onwards.

materials

- **diamonds:** 4 x 1 1/2in x 22in (3.8cm x 55.9cm) strips (1 of each end fabric and 2 of the middle fabric)
- **BKG:** 4 x 4in (10.2cm) sqs cut in half along diag, 4 x 3in (7.6cm) sqs cut in half along diag

variation 1 [LST2 – 14 1/2in (36.8cm) block]

see other variations page 222

1 Sew the strips into 3 groups of 3, arranging the strips as follows: Orange/pink flowers/pink; pink flowers/pink/orange circles; pink/orange circles/orange check.

2 As for LST1, cut a 45° line, then 8 more 1 1/2in (3.8cm) apart, cutting each set of 3 strips into 8 pieces.

3 Sew 1 of each into sets of 3, following the layout in the block photograph. Make 8.

4 Finish as for LST1 but trimming to 15in (38.1cm) sq.

materials

- **diamonds:** 9 x 1 1/2in x 22in (3.8 x 55.9cm) strips (for the colours starting from the centre of the star: orange, 1 strip; pink flowers, 2 strips; pink, 3 strips; orange circles, 2 strips; orange check, 1 strip)
- **BKG:** 4 x 4in (10.2cm) sqs cut in half along diag, 4 x 5 1/2in (14cm) sqs cut in half along diag

grandmother's flower garden

see other variations page 223
see template page 281

main block [GFG1 — 17 1/2in (44.4cm) block]

1   EPP the 7 flowers using template GFGi. Sew into 7 flowers.

2   Arrange on the BKG as shown in the photograph and appliqué to the BKG fabric.

materials
- **BKG:**
  1 18in (45.7cm) sq
- **flowers:**
  6 x 2 1/2in (6.3cm) sqs per flower (7 flowers) for the petals, 7 x 2 1/2in (6.3cm) sqs for the centres
- **template:** GFGi

---

variation 1 [GFG2 — 12in (30.5cm) block]

1   EPP the 7 flowers using template GFGi. Sew into 2 flowers.

2   Arrange flowers and stems (cut into lengths of 8in and 4in [20.3cm and 10.2cm]) on the BKG as shown in the photograph and appliqué to the BKG fabric.

materials
- **BKG:**
  12 1/2in (31.7cm) sq
- **flowers:** 6 x 2 1/2in (6.3cm) sqs per flower (2 flowers) for the petals, 2 x 2 1/2in (6.3cm) sqs for the centres
- **stems:** 1in x 12in (2.5cm x 30.5cm) bias strip with 1/4in (6mm) edges pressed to middle
- **template:** GFGi

morning star

main block [MST1 — 16in (40.6cm) block]

1 Make 8 HST units pairing A/B 5in (12.7cm) sqs. Trim to 4 1/2in (11.4cm) sq.

2 Sew together the 4 pairs of HST units.

3 Sew A 4 1/2in (11.4cm) sqs onto either end of 2 of these.

4 Sew the other 2 HST units to either side of the 8 1/2in (21.6cm) sq.

5 Assemble the block following the layout in the photograph.

materials

■ **col A (black):**
4 x 5in (12.7cm) sqs, 8 1/2in (21.6cm) sq

■ **col A (white):**
4 x 5in (12.7cm) sqs, 4 x 4 1/2in (11.4cm) sqs

---

variation 1 [MST2 — 16in (40.6cm) block]

see other variations page 224

1 Sash the 8in (20.3cm) sq with the 3/4in (1.9cm) strips using first the shorter for the sides and then the longer for the top and bottom.

2 Finish as for MST1.

materials

■ as for MST1, replacing the 8 1/2in (21.6cm) sq with an 8in (20.3cm) sq, 2 x 3/4in x 8in (1.9cm x 20.3cm) strips, and 2 x 3/4in x 8 1/2in (1.9cm x 21.6cm) strips

prairie flower

main block [PF1 — 12in (30.5cm) block]

1. To each A sq, add 2 C sqs as CSTs to diagonally opposite corners to make block corner sqs.

2. To each B sq, add 2 D sqs as CSTs to both top corners.

3. Arrange and sew as 9-patch using photograph for reference.

materials

- ■ col A (white):
  5 x 4 1/2in (11.4cm) sqs
- ■ col B (pink):
  4 x 4 1/2in (11.4cm) sqs
- ■ col C (dark teal):
  8 x 2 1/2in (6.3cm) sqs
- ■ col D (light teal):
  8 x 2 1/2in (6.3cm) sqs

....

variation 1 [PF2 — 12in (30.5cm) block]

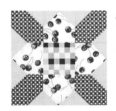

1. Make as for PF1 adding C squares for all CSTs.

see other variations page 225

materials

- ■ col A (red):
  4 x 4 1/2in (11.4cm) sqs
- ■ col B (white):
  4 x 4 1/2in (11.4cm) sqs
- ■ col C (aqua):
  16 x 2 1/2in (6.3cm) sqs
- ■ centre sq:
  4 1/2in (11.4cm) sq

missouri daisy

main block [MD1 — 12in (30.5cm) block]

1 Paper piece 8 of the MDi templates, trim to the dotted lines and remove papers.

2 Piece the 8 petals together, first into pairs, then into halves, then into the daisy.

3 Piece the four triangles of BKG fabric to the four corners of the daisy, press and trim.

materials

- **petals:** 8 x 4in x 5in (10.2cm x 12.7cm) rects
- **center:** 8 x 3in (7.6cm) sqs
- **BKG:** Approx 9in (22.9cm) for paper piecing including 2 x 5in (12.7cm) sqs cut in half on diag
- **template:** MDi

variation 1 [MD2 — 12in (30.5cm)]

1 Sew tog the 2 strips of petal fabric.

2 Make as for MD1 but first aligning the seam on the strips with the point where the tips of the petals meet the sides.

see other variations page 226
see template page 282

materials

- **petals:** 2 x 3in x 32in (7.6cm x 81.3cm) strips
- **center and BKG:** as for MD1 but 2 x 5in (12.7cm) sqs from darker fabric
- **template:** MDi

storm at sea

main block [SAS1 — 12in (30.5cm) block]

1   Add 1 CST to each of the 4 orange 3 1/2in (8.9cm) sqs using the 4 white 2in (5.1cm) sqs.

2   Add 4 CSTs to the 6 1/2in (16.5cm) BKG sq using the 4 blue 3 1/2in (8.9cm) sqs.

3   Paper piece 4 SASi units using the 4 x 3 1/2in x 6 1/2in (8.9cm x 16.5cm) white rects as the centers and the orange and blue 2 1/2in x 5in (6.3cm x 12.7cm) rects cut in half along diag for the corners. Follow the layout in the photograph for these sections.

4   Assemble the block following the layout in the photograph.

materials

- **BKG (white):** 6 1/2in (16.5cm) sq, 4 x 3 1/2in x 6 1/2in (8.9cm x 16.5cm) rects, 4 x 2in (5.1cm) sqs
- **star (blue):** 4 x 3 1/2in (8.9cm) sqs, 4 x 2 1/2in x 5in (6.3cm x 12.7cm) rects cut in half — 2 top right to bottom left, 2 top left to bottom right
- **frame (orange):** 4 x 3 1/2in (8.9cm) sqs, 4 x 1/2in x 5in (1.3cm x 12.7cm) rects cut in half on 2 diff diags (see above)
- **template:** SASi

variation 1 [SAS2 — 12in (30.5cm) block]

1   Add 4 CST to each of the 4 orange 3 1/2in (8.9cm) sqs using the 12 white 2in (5.1cm) sqs. Continue as for SAS1.

see other variations page 227
see template page 282

materials

- as for SAS1, with an additional 12 x 2in (5.1cm) BKG sqs

tulip

main block [TP1 — 5in (12.7cm) block]

1   Make the stamen: Sew sml BKG sq to right edge of stamen sq. Add BKG rect above.

2   Make the tulip: Pair lrg BKG sq/tulip sq sew diagonally, trim, open up to make sq. Place tulip rectangle vertically, add BKG sq to top left corner as CST.

3   Arrange sections as photograph. Join sqs, join to tulip rect.

4   Leaves: Add sml BKG sq to 1 end of each leaf rect to make CSTs. Sew one leaf to left edge of tulip. Add sml BKG sq to 1 1/2in (3.8cm) edge to remaining leaf. Add to bottom of block.

materials

- **tulip:** 2 1/2in (6.3cm) sq, 2 1/2in x 4 1/2in (6.3cm x 11.4cm) rect
- **stamen:** 1 1/2in (3.8cm) sq
- **leaves:** 2 x 1 1/2in x 4 1/2in (3.8cm x 11.4cm) rect
- **BKG:** 4 x 1 1/2in (3.8cm) sml sqs, 2 x 2 1/2in (6.3cm) lrg sqs, 1 1/2in x 2 1/2in (3.8cm x 6.3cm) rect

variation 1 [TP2 — 8in (20.3cm) block]

1   As for TP1 step 1.
2   Pair BKG/tulip 3in (7.6cm) sqs. Make 2 HST units. Trim to 2 1/2in (6.3cm) sq. Sew as 4 patch with stamen and tulip. Repeat steps 1–2 to make 2 tulips. There will be 2 left over HST units.

3   Pair BKG/leaf 5in (12.7cm) sqs. Make 2 HST units. Trim to 4 1/2in (11.4cm) sq. Complete block as 4-patch.

see other variations page 228

materials

- **tulip:** 2 x 2 1/2in (6.3cm) sqs, 3 x 3in (7.6cm) sqs (in 3 prints)
- **stamen:** 2 x 1 1/2in (3.8cm) sqs
- **leaves:** 5in (12.7cm) sq
- **BKG:** 2 x 1 1/2in (3.8cm) sqs, 3 x 3in (7.6cm) sqs, 5in (12.7cm) sq, 2 x 1 1/2in x 2 1/2in (3.8cm x 6.3cm) rects

Tallahassee block

main block [TB1 — 16in (40.6cm) block]

1 Paper piece 16 of template TBi.

2 Sew together following the layout in the photograph.

materials

- **assorted scraps:**
  16 x 4 1/2in (11.4cm) sqs
- **BKG:** 16 x 3 1/2in (8.9cm) sqs cut in half along diag, 16 x 2in x 4in (5.1cm x 10.2cm) rects cut in half along diag (make sure to cut 8 top right to bottom left and 8 top left to bottom right)
- **template:** TBi

---

variation 1 [TB2 — 8in (20.3cm) block]

1 Paper piece 4 of template TBi.

2 Sew together following the layout in the photograph.

see other variations page 229
see template page 283

materials

- **col A (aqua):**
  4 x 4 1/2in (11.4cm) sqs
- **BKG:** 4 x 3 1/2in (8.9cm) sqs cut in half along diag, 4 x 2in x 4in (5.1cm x 10.2cm) rects cut in half along diag (make sure to cut 2 top right to bottom left and 2 top left to bottom right)
- **template:** TBi

diamond star

see base design page 183

variation 2
[DS3 — 12in (30.5cm) block]

materials
from each of 2 fabrics:
2 x 4in x 8in (10.2cm x 20.3cm) rects cut in half along the diag as for DS1, 4in (10.2cm) sq cut in half along the diag, 2 x 5in x 7 1/2in (12.7cm x 19cm) rects cut into isosceles triangles 7 1/2in (19cm) tall

1. Complete as for DS1

variation 3
[DS4 — 12in (30.5cm) block]

materials
as for DS1

1. Make as for DS1 but rotate each block through 180°.

variation 4
[DS5 — 12in (30.5cm) block]

materials
BKG:
4 x 4in x 8in (10.2cm x 20.3cm) rects cut in half along the diag as for DS1
col A (dark):
4in (10.2cm) sq cut in half along diag, 3in x 12in (7.6cm x 30.5cm) strip
col B (medium):
3in x 12in (7.6cm x 30.5cm) strip
col C (light):
4in (10.2cm) sq cut in half along diag, 3in x 12in (7.6cm x 30.5cm) strip

1. Sew the strips together along the long edges in the order A/B/C.

2. Cut 4 x 7 1/2in tall isosceles triangles from the resulting strip, alternating direction so 2 have a dark base and 2 a light base.
3. Sew the light 4in HSTs to the light bottoms and the dark HSTs to the dark bottoms.
4. Assemble as for DS1.

variations
daisy

see base design page 184

variation 1
[DAI2 — 16in (40.6cm) finished]

materials
petals: 3 x 6in x 9in (15.2cm x 22.9cm) rects
center: 9in (22.9cm) sq
BKG: 16 1/2in (41.9cm) sq fusible web

1. Fuse petal and center fabric to fusible web. Cut out 12 x 2in x 4 1/2in (5.1cm x 11.4cm) rects for the petals and an 8in (20.3cm) circle for the center.
2. Fuse petals first and then fuse center to BKG fabric.
3. Finish with zigzag, straight, blanket or other edging stitch.

variation 2
[DAI3 — 18in (45.7cm) block]

materials
petals (dark): 6 x 6in x 5in (15.2cm x 12.7cm) rects
petals (light): 6 x 6in x 4in (15.2cm x 10.2cm) rects
center: 9in (22.9cm) sq
BKG: 18 1/2in (47cm) sq fusible web

1. As for DAI2 but cut out 12 x 2in x 4 1/2in (5.1cm x 11.4cm) rects from the darker petal fabrics and 12 x 2in x 3in (5.1cm x 7.6cm) rects from the lighter petal fabrics.
2. Fuse the darker petals first, then the lighter petals, then the circle to the BKG fabric.
3. Finish as for DAI2.

variation 3
[DAI4 — 11in (27.9cm) block]

materials
petals: 2 x 5in x 6in (12.7cm x 15.2cm) rects
center: 6in (15.2cm) sq
BKG: 11 1/2in (29.2cm) sq fusible web

1. As for DAI2 but cut out 8 x 2in x 2 1/2in (5.1cm x 6.3cm) rects for the petals and a 5in (12.7cm) circle for the center.
2. Finish as for DAI2

variation 4
[DAI5 — 14in (35.6cm) block]

materials
petals: 10in (25.4cm) sq
center: 10in (25.4cm) sq
BKG: 14 1/2in (36.8cm) sq fusible web

1. As for DAI2 but cut out 12in x 2in (30.5cm x 5.1cm) sqs from the petal fabric and a 9in (22.9cm) circle from the center fabric.
2. Finish as for DAI2.

variations
drunkard's path

see base design page 187

variation 2
[DPA3 — 8in (20.3cm) block]

materials
light:
4 x 5 1/2in (14cm) sqs
dark:
4 x 4 1/2in (11.4cm) sqs
templates:
as for DPA1

1. As for DPA1, but using light for all DPAi sections and dark for DPAii.

variation 3
[DPA4 — 8in (20.3cm) block]

materials
col A (dark yellow):
2 x 4 1/2in (11.4cm) sqs
col B (dark green):
2 x 4 1/2in (11.4cm) sqs
col C (light BKG/yellow):
2 x 5 1/2in (14cm) sqs
col D (light BKG/green):
2 x 5 1/2in (14cm) sqs
templates:
as for DPA1

1. As for DPA3.

variation 4
[DPA5 — 8in (20.3cm) block]

materials
print (1/4 circles):
4 x 4 1/2in (11.4cm) sqs
solid colours (frames):
4 x 5 1/2in (14cm) sqs, 1 in each of 4 colours
templates:
as for DPA1

1. As for DPA1.

variations

electric fan

see base design page 188

variation 1
[EF2 — 8 1/2in (21.6cm) block]

materials
col A (peach):
2 x 4 1/2in (11.4cm) sqs,
2 x 3in (7.6cm) sqs
col B (green):
2 x 4 1/2in (11.4cm) sqs,
2 x 3in (7.6cm) sqs
BKG: 4 x 5 1/2in (14cm) sqs, 4 x 2in x 4 1/2in (6.3cm x 11.4cm) rects
center: 3 1/2in (8.9cm) sq
templates: as for EF1
starch: as for EF1

1. Make as for EF1, alternating the blade colour combination as in the photograph.

variation 2
[EF3 — 9 1/2in (24.1cm) block]

materials
fan blades:
4 x 4 1/2in (11.4cm) sqs
BKG (2 diff prints):
4 x 5 1/2in (14cm) sqs,
4 x 2in x 4 1/2in (6.3cm x 11.4cm) rects
center: as for DF1
templates: DPAi frame, DPAii 1/4 circle

1–2. As for DPA1, steps 1 and 2. Sew curved edges together to make sqs.
3–4. As for EF1, steps 3 and 4 using photograph for reference when arranging block.

variation 3
[EF4 — 9 1/2in (24.1cm) block]

materials
fan blades:
4 x 4 1/2in (11.4cm) sqs, 2 each in 2 coordinating prints
BKG and templates:
as for EF3 using 1 print for BKG
center: 2 3/4in (6.9cm) sq

1. Make as for EF3, alternating different colours for blades, as in photograph. For the center, draw a 2 1/4in (5.7cm) circle on 3in (7.6cm) square and continue as for EF1, step 4.

variation 4
[EF5 —12in (30.5cm) block]

materials
fan blades:
4 x 4 1/2in (11.4cm) sqs
BKG: 4 x 5 1/2in (14cm) sqs, 5 x 4 1/2in (11.4cm) sqs
center: as for EF1
fusible web: 3 1/2in (8.9cm) sq
templates: as for EF3

1–2. As for DPA, steps 1 and 2.
3. Arrange and sew 4 1/2in (11.4cm) sqs as 9-patch. Fuse center fabric to web. Draw and cut out 3in (7.6cm) diameter circle and raw edge machine appliqué to center of block.

variations

friendship star

see base design page 189

variation 1
[FST2 — 12in
(30.5cm) block]

materials
as for FST1 x 4

1. Make 16 HST units
as for FST1.
2. Assemble the block
in rows and then sew
the rows together
following the layout
in the photograph.

variation 2
[FST3 — 12in
(30.5cm) block]

materials
as for FST1 x 4

1. Make as for FST2
but following the
layout in the
photograph.

variation 3
[FST4 — 10in
(25.4cm) block]

materials
BKG:
9 x 2 1/2in (6.3cm) sqs,
4 x 3in (7.6cm) sqs
col A (browns):
4 x 2 1/2in (6.3cm) sqs,
8 x 3in (7.6cm) sqs

1. Make 8 HST units
pairing 4 x A/BKG 3in
(7.6cm) sqs. Trim to
2 1/2in (6.3cm) sq.
2. Make 4 HST units
pairing remaining A
3in (7.6cm) sqs. Trim
to 2 1/2in (6.3cm) sq.
3. Assemble the block in
rows and then sew the
rows together following
the layout in the
photograph.

variation 4
[FST5 — 12in
(30.5cm) block]

materials
BKG:
5 x 4 1/2in (11.4cm) sqs,
2 x 5in (12.7cm) sqs
stripes:
2 center fabrics in each HST:
1 x 1 1/2in x 10in (3.8cm x 25.4cm)
strip of each
2 outer fabrics in each HST:
1 x 1 3/4in x 10in (4.4cm x 25.4cm)
strip of each

1. Sew the strips together with the 2
narrower strips in the center and the
wider strips on the top and bottom.
Cut into 2 x 5in (12.7cm) sqs.
2. Make 4 HST units pairing the strip
5in (12.7cm) sqs with the BKG 5in
(12.7cm) sqs. Trim to 4 1/2in (11.4cm) sq.
3. Assemble block following layout
in the photograph.

Dresden plate

see base design page 190

variation 2
[DP3 — 18in
(45.7cm) block]

materials
leaves and center:
6in (15.2cm) sq, 6in x 25in
(15.2cm x 63.5cm) strip
BKG: 18 1/2in (47cm) sq,
6in x 25in (15.2cm x
63.5cm) strip; fusible
web; Darlene Zimmerman
Easy; Dresden Ruler

1. Cut 10 leaves from each
of the 6in (15.2cm)strips
aligning the 1in (2.5cm)
and 7in (17.8cm) lines on
the Easy Dresden Ruler
with edges of the fabric,
and alternating direction
of the ruler with each cut.
2. Assemble Dresden as
for DP1 alternating
leaves.
3. Finish as for DP1.

variation 3
[DP4 — 16in
(40.6cm) block]

materials
BKG: 16 1/2in (14.9cm) sq
center: 6in (15.2cm) sq
leaves: 8 x 1 1/2in x
22in (3.8cm x 55.9cm)
strips (2 of each of 4
colours)
fusible web
freezer paper
Darlene Zimmerman Easy
Dresden Ruler

1. Sew the 4 strips
together along the long
sides. Press all seams in
one direction.
2. Cut 20 Dresden
wedges aligning the 1in
line of the Easy Dresden
Ruler with the edge of
the fabric for each cut.

3. Sew into a circle
and press seams.
4. Cut a 12in (30.5cm)
circle out of the BKG
fabric (to do this, fold
the fabric in half and
in half again. Make a
6in (15.2cm) radius
quarter circle freezer
paper template. Press
onto the BKG fabric
aligning the corner of
the quarter circle with
the folded corner of
the fabric, and cut out.
5. Piece the Dresden
plate into the BKG.
6. Hand-appliqué a
5 1/2in (14cm) center
circle onto the Dresden
plate as for step 4 of
DP1.

variation 4
[DP5 — 8in
(20.3cm) block]

materials
col A (black): 2 x 3 1/2in x 15in
(8.9cm x 38.1cm) strips, 1 1/2in x
15in (3.8cm x 38.1cm) strip
col B (white): 2 x 1 1/2in x
15in (3.8cm x 38.1cm) strips
Darlene Zimmerman Easy
Dresden Ruler

1. Sew the 5 strips tog along
long edges, colours alternating,
blacks outside.
2. Cut 8 wedges with angle of
the ruler as a guide, aiming for
narrow end of wedge to be
1/2in (1.3cm).
3. Sew wedges tog in
alternating directions, matching
seams where black meets white.
Wedges will not match at the
ends.
4. Trim to 8 1/2in (21.6cm) sq.

octagon flower

see base design page 193

variation 2
[OF3 — 22in (55.9cm) block]

materials
as for OF1, replacing the A and B fabrics with 9 x 5 1/2in (14cm) sqs
BKG: As for OF1, replacing the 5 1/2in x 12 1/2in (14cm x 31.7cm) rect with 2 x 4in x 5 1/2in (10.2cm x 14cm) rects

1. Attach 2 adjacent CSTs to 8 of the 5 1/2in (14cm) sqs with 3in (7.6cm) BKG sqs.
2. Sew 2 of the 4in x 5 1/2in (14cm) BGK rects to either side of the remaining 5 1/2in (14cm) sq.
3. Sew 2 of the CST units to each end of step 2 unit.
4. Make as for OF1 from step 4 using CST units in place of flying geese units.

variation 3
[OF4 — 22in (55.9cm) block]

materials
as for OF1, replacing the A and B fabrics with 9 x 5 1/2in (14cm) sqs, plus 4 x 4in x 5 1/2in (10.2cm x 14cm) rects (orange fabric in the photograph)
BKG: as for OF1, omitting the 5 1/2in x 12 1/2in (14cm x 31.7cm) rect, the 2 x 4in x 5 1/2in (10.2cm x 14cm) rects and the 16 x 3in (7.6cm) sqs

1. Sew 2 of the 4in x 5 1/2in (10.2cm x 14cm) rects to either side of 1 of the 5 1/2in (14cm) sqs.
2. Make as for OF1 from step 3 onwards with the 8 remaining 5 1/2in (14cm) sqs replacing the flying geese + rect units.

variation 4
[OF5 — 22in (55.9cm) block]

materials
as for OF2 with additional 32 x 3in (7.6cm) BKG sqs

1. Add CSTs to the 8 print 5 1/2in (14cm) sqs using the 32 x 3in (7.6cm) BKG sqs.
2. Make as for OF1 from step 3 using the sqs made at step 1 in place of the flying geese and rect units.

variations

grandma's fan

see base design page 194

variation 2
[GF3 — 10in
(25.4cm) block]

materials
as for GF2 x 4

1. Make 4 GF2 blocks.
Arrange as shown in
photo, sew as 4-patch.

variation 3
[GF4 — 7in
(17.8cm) block]

materials
petals:
3 x 3in x 5in (7.6cm x 14cm) rects
circle:
4 1/2in (11.4cm) sq
BKG:
12in (30.5cm) sq for DAli
templates:
DAli, DPAii 1/4 circle

1. Print DAli foundation template. Foundation paper
piece DAli. Trim retaining SA including the inner curve
SA. Remove paper.

2. On reverse of 4 1/2in (11.4cm) sq draw around
template DPAii in pencil, cut out adding 1/4in (6mm) SA
all round. Join 1/4 circle to inner curve of DAli block.

variation 4
[GF5 — 14in
(35.6cm) block]

materials
petals/circles:
as for GF4 x 2
BKG:
FQ for DAli BKG sections;
from same FQ cut
2 x 7 1/2in (19cm) sqs
templates: DAli, DPAii
1/4 circle

1–2. As for GF4, steps
1–2. Make 2.
3. Arrange and sew as
4-patch with BKG sqs.

lemoyne star

see base design page 195

variation 2
[LS3 — 9 1/2in (24.1cm) block]

materials
diamonds:
4 x 1 1/2in x 20in
(3.8cm x 50.8cm) strips
(2 of each colour)
BKG: as for LS1

1. Sew the 20in (50.8cm) strips into pairs along the long edges. Cut 4 diamonds from each resulting strip.
2. Finish as for LS1 following the layout in the photograph.

variation 3
[LS4 — 9 1/2in (24.1cm) block]

materials
diamonds:
4 x 1 1/2in x 20in
(3.8cm x 50.8cm) strips
(2 of each colour)
BKG: as for LS1

1. Sew the 20in (50.8cm) strips into pairs along the long edges. Cut 4 diamonds from each resulting strip making sure to cut one set top right to bottom left and the other set top left to bottom right.
2. Finish as for LS1 following the layout in the photograph.

variation 4
[LS5 — 12in (30.5cm) block]

materials
as for LS1 plus
4 x 1 3/4in x 10in
(4.4cm x 25.4cm)
rects, 4 x 1 3/4in
(4.4cm) sqs

1. Make as for LS1.
2. Finish by sewing main block, sashing and cornerstones together as if making a 9-patch, following the layout in the photograph.

variations

georgetown carnival

see base design page 196

variation 1
[GC2 — 17 1/2in
(44.4cm) block]

materials
as for GC1, omitting 12
scrap sqs.

1. Make as for GC1 but
without the 12 outer sqs.

variation 2
[GC3 — 15in
(38.1cm) block]

materials
BKG:
15 1/2in (39.4cm) sq
col A (dark blue):
8 x 2 1/2in (6.3cm) sqs
col B (lightw blue):
2 1/2in (6.3cm) sq,
12 x 3in (7.6cm) sqs
template: GCii

1. Apply fusible web to
the back of the A/B sqs.
2. Cut 12 triangles out
of the B 3in (7.6cm) sqs
using template GCii.
3. Fuse to the BKG
following the layout in
the photograph.

variation 3
[GC4 — 17 1/2in
(44.4cm) block]

materials
BKG:
18in (45.7cm) sq
col A (orange):
12in (30.5cm) sq
col B (grey scraps):
36 x 3in (7.6cm) sq
templates: GCi, ii, and iii

1. Make as for GC1 and
sew the outer ring
together using the
photograph for reference.
2. Appliqué to the col A
sq then cut away the
edges from the back.
3. Appliqué to the BKG.

variation 4
[GC5 — 9 1/2in
(24.1cm) block]

materials
BKG:
10in (25.4cm) sq
star:
5in sq, 6 x 3in (7.6cm) sqs
templates: GCi, ii, and iii

1. Make as for GC1 but
using the photograph for
reference.

variations
pictures in the stairwell

see base design page 199

<table>
</table>

### variation 2 [PS3 — 8in (20.3cm) block]	### variation 3 [PS4 — 8in (20.3cm) block]	### variation 4 [PS5 — 10in (25.4cm) block]
materials **col A (blue):** 4 x 2 1/2in (6.3cm) sqs, 2 x 5 1/2in (14cm) sqs **col B (yellow):** 2 x 2 1/2in (6.3cm) sqs, 2 x 4 1/2in (11.4cm) sqs **col C (green):** 2 x 2 1/2in (6.3cm) sqs **templates:** as PS1	**materials** **col A (black):** 4 x 2 1/2in (6.3cm) sqs, 2 x 5 1/2in (14cm) sqs **col B (grey):** 2 x 3in (7.6cm) sqs, 4 1/2in (11.4cm) sq **col C (pink):** 2 x 3in (7.6cm) sqs, 4 1/2in (11.4cm) sq **templates:** as for PS1	**materials** **col A (grey):** 4 x 5 1/2in (14cm) sqs **col B (navy):** 4 x 4 1/2in (11.4cm) sqs **yellow/red/green:** 9 x 2 1/2in (6.3cm) sqs (3 in each colour) **templates:** as for PS1
1. Make as for PS1 using photograph for placement.	**1.** Pair B/C 3in (7.6cm) sqs and make 4 HST units. Trim to 2 1/2in (6.3cm) sq. Continue as for PS1.	**1.** Make DPAi/DPAii sections from A and B. Sew 4 x 2 1/2in (6.3cm) squares in 2 rows of 2. Place rows between DPAi/DPAii sections. **2.** Sew remaining 5 x 2 1/2in (6.3cm) squares into a row. Join sections completed in step 1 above and below row.

memory

see base design page 200

variation 2
[ME3 — 12in (30.5cm) block]

materials
center sq:
4 1/2in (11.4cm) lrg sq
col A (white):
8 x 2 1/2in (6.3cm) sqs
col B (scraps):
12 x 2 1/2in (6.3cm) sqs, 4 x 3in (7.6cm) sqs, 4 x 2 1/2in (6.3cm) x 4 1/2in (11.4cm) rects
col C (light blue):
4 x 2 1/2in (6.3cm) sqs, 4 x 3in (7.6cm) sqs, 4 x 2 1/2in x 4 1/2in (6.3cm x 11.4cm) rects

1. Make as ME1.

variation 3
[ME4 — 12in (30.5cm) block]

materials
center sq:
4 1/2in (11.4cm) lrg sq
col A (cream):
8 x 2 1/2in (6.3cm) sqs, 4 x 3in (7.6cm) sqs
col B (pink):
8 x 2 1/2in (6.3cm) sqs, 4 x 2 1/2in x 4 1/2in (6.3cm x 11.4cm) rects
col C (grey):
4 x 2 1/2in (6.3cm) sqs, 4 x 3in (7.6cm) sqs, 4 x 2 1/2in x 4 1/2in (6.3cm x 11.4cm) rects

1. As for ME1 step 1.
2. As for ME1 step 2, with A/C replacing B/C. Complete as for ME1.

variation 4
ME5 — 12in (30.5cm) block

materials
center sq:
4 1/2in (11.4cm) lrg sq
col A (white):
8 x 2 1/2in (6.3cm) sqs
col B (pink):
8 x 2 1/2in x 4 1/2in (6.3cm x 11.4cm) rects
col C (navy):
4 x 2 1/2in (6.3cm) sqs, 4 x 3in (7.6cm) sqs
col D (aqua):
4 x 2 1/2in (6.3cm) sqs, 4 x 3in (7.6cm) sqs

1. As for ME2 step 1.
2. As for ME1 joining HST units to C sqs and D sqs. Complete as for ME1.

variations

lone star

see base design page 201

variation 2
[LST3 — 12 1/4in (31.1cm) block]

materials
diamonds:
as for LST1 but 2 of each colour
BKG:
4 x 3 1/2in (8.9cm) sqs cut in half along diag, 4 x 5in (12.7cm) sqs cut in half along diag, 8 x 1in x 5in (2.5cm x 12.7cm) strips, 8 x 1in x 6in (2.5cm x 15.2cm) strips

1. Make 8 diamonds as in LST1, making sure the same colour fabric is always in the points of the diamonds.
2. Sash two sides of each diamond using first the shorter BKG strips, and then the long BKG strips. Trim as you go.
3. Assemble block as for LST1 and trim to 12 3/4in (32.4cm) sq.

variation 3
[LST4 — 13 1/2in (34.3cm) block]

materials
diamonds: as for LST3
frames: 16 x 3/4in x 5in (1.9cm x 12.7cm) strips, 16 x 3/4in x 6in (1.9cm x 15.2cm) strips
BKG: 4 x 3 1/2in (8.9cm) sqs cut in half along diag, 4 x 5in (12.7cm) sqs cut in half along diag, 4 x 1in x 12in (2.5cm x 30.5cm) strips, 2 x 1in x 7in (2.5cm x 17.8cm) strips, 1in x 14in (2.5cm x 35.6cm) strip

1. Make 8 diamonds as in LST3. Sash two sides of each diamond using the shorter BKG strips and then the other two sides using the long BKG strips. Trim as you go.
2. Sew triangles to the sides of each diamond as in LST1. Sash each pair of traingles together along the diag using the 1 x 12in (30.5cm) BKG strips.
3. Sash those units together using the 1in x 7in (2.5cm x 17.8cm) strips.
4. Sash the 2 halves of the block together using the 1in x 14in (2.5cm x 35.6cm) strip.
5. Assemble block as for LST1 and trim to 14in (35.6cm) sq.

variation 4
[LST5 — 12in (30.5cm) block]

materials
from each of 2 colours:
2 x 1 1/2in x 22in (3.8cm x 55.9cm) strips, 2 x 4in (10.2cm) sqs cut in half along diag, 2 x 3in (7.6cm) sqs cut in half along diag

1. Make as for LST1 but following the colour placement in the photograph.

variations

grandmother's flower garden

see base design page 202

variation 2
[GFG3 — 12in (30.5cm) block]

materials
BKG:
12 1/2in (31.7cm) sq
flowers:
6 x 2 1/2in (6.3cm) sqs for petals, 2 1/2in (6.3cm) sq for the center
circles:
6 x 3in (7.6cm) sqs
template: GFGi

1. EPP the flower using template GFGi. Appliqué to center of BKG fabric.
2. Appliqué 6 x 2 1/4in (5.7cm) diameter circles in a circle around the flower.

variation 3
[GFG4 — 18in (45.7cm) block]

materials
BKG:
18 1/2in (47cm) sq
flowers:
6 x 2 1/2in (6.3cm) sqs per flower (6 flowers) for petals, 6 x 2 1/2in (6.3cm) sq for the centers
template: GFGi

1. EPP each flower using template GFGi. Appliqué to center of BKG fabric.

variation 4
[GFG5 — 11in (27.9cm) block]

materials
BKG:
7 1/2in (19cm) sq
sashing: 2 x 2 1/2in x 7 1/2in (6.3cm x 19cm) strips, 2 x 2 1/2in x 11 1/2in (6.3cm x 29.2cm) strips
flowers: 6 x 2 1/2in (6.3cm) sqs for the petals
template: GFGi

1. EPP the flower using template GFGi. Appliqué to center of BKG fabric.
2. Sash the sides using the shorter strips and the top and bottom using the longer strips.

morning star

see base design page 204

variation 2
[MST3 — 16in (40.6cm) block]

materials
as for MST1 but with 4 x 4 1/2in (11.4cm) sqs (pale pink)

1. Add 4 CSTs to the 8 1/2in (21.6cm) sq using the 4 x 4 1/2in (11.4cm) sqs pale pink fabric.
2. Finish as for MST1.

variation 3
[MST4 — 16in (40.6cm) block]

materials
BKG: 2 x 5 1/2in (14cm) sqs, 8 1/2in (21.6cm) sq, 4 x 4 1/2in (11.4cm) sqs
col A (dark): 2 x 5 1/2in (14cm) sqs, 4 x 4 1/2in (11.4cm) sqs
col B (medium): 4 x 5in (12.7cm) sqs

1. Make 4 HST units pairing A/BKG 5 1/2in (14cm) sqs. Trim to 5in (12.7cm) sq.
2. Pair each unit with a col B 5in (12.7cm) sq; sew 2 lines each 1/4in (6mm) from diag to make 8 HST with QST units. Trim to 4 1/2in (11.4cm) sq.
3. Finish as for MST1 following the photograph.

variation 4
[MST5 — 12in (30.5cm) block]

materials
col A (black): 4 x 3 1/2in x 6 1/2in (8.9cm x 16.5cm) rects, 4 x 3 1/2in (8.9cm) sqs
col B (green): 6 1/2in (16.5cm) sq, 8 x 5in (12.7cm) sqs

1. Lay a B sq aligned with 1 corner of an A rect so that some of the green sq hangs over the edge of the rect.
2. Draw a wonky diagonal line to mark the seam of one of the points of the stars — this point should be placed in the corner of the rect where the green fabric is aligned, not in the corner where it overhangs.
3. Sew the seam, flip, press, trim the rectangle back to 3 1/2in x 6 1/2in (8.9cm x 16.5cm), then cut off excess fabrics beyond seam allowance.
4. Repeat for the second point of the star on that rectangle, making sure that the second star point seam crosses through the point where the first star point seam will meet the 1/4in (6mm) seam allowance.
5. Repeat for the remaining rects.
6. Assemble the block following the layout in the photograph.

variations
prairie flower

see base design page 205

variation 2
[PF3 — 12in
(30.5cm) block]

materials
col A (cream):
5 x 4 1/2in (11.4cm) sqs
col B (blue):
4 x 4 1/2in (11.4cm) sqs
col C (red):
8 x 2 1/2in (6.3cm) sqs
col D (grey):
8 x 2 1/2in (6.3cm) sqs

1. Make as for PF1 but
using D for the CSTs on
the A sqs and C for the
CSTs on the B sqs.

variation 3
[PF4 — 12in
(30.5cm) block]

materials
col A (multi):
4 x 4 1/2in (11.4cm) sqs
col B (light green):
4 x 4 1/2in (11.4cm) sqs,
8 x 2 1/2in (6.3cm) sqs
center sq:
4 1/2in (11.4cm) sq

1. As for PF1 step 2 with
A sqs and using B 2 1/2in
(6.3cm) sqs as CSTs.
2. Arrange and sew as
9-patch.

variation 4
[PF5 — 12in
(30.5cm) block]

materials
col A (rust):
4 x 4 1/2in (11.4cm) sqs
col B (yellow):
4 1/2in (11.4cm) center sq
col C (light grey):
4 x 4 1/2in (11.4cm) sqs
col D (dark grey):
12 x 2 1/2in (6.3cm) sqs

1. As for PF1 step 2
with A sqs and D 2 1/2in
(6.3cm) sqs as CSTs.
2. Add D 2 1/2in (6.3cm)
sqs as CSTs to each
corner of the center sq.
3. Arrange and sew as
9-patch.

missouri daisy

see base design page 206

variation 2
[MD3 — 12in
(30.5cm) block]

materials
petals and centers:
as for MD1 but with 5
instead of 8
stem: 1in x 7in (2.5cm
x 17.8cm) strip
BKG:
As for MD1 but 3 wedges
cut using outline of MDi
template

1. Piece 5 MDi templates.
2. Cut 1 of the BKG
wedges in half vertically.
Sash back together using
the 7in (17.8cm) stem
strip.
3. Finish block as for
MD1 following the layout
in the photograph.

variation 3
[MD4 — 12in
(30.5cm) block]

materials
petals:
4 x 4in x 7in (10.2cm
x 17.8cm) rects
BKG:
As for MD1 plus 4
wedges cut using outline
of MDi template

1. Paper piece 4 MDi
templates using the petal
fabric to cover sections
1 and 2.
2. Finish as MD1 but
following the layout in
the photograph.

variation 4
[MD5 — 12in
(30.5cm) block]

materials
petal and center:
as for MD1 but with 1 instead of 8
stem: 1in x 7in (2.5cm x 17.8cm) strip
leaf: 2in x 6in (5.1cm x 15.2cm) rect
BKG:
As for MD1 but with 7 wedges cut using outline of
MDi template
fusible web

1. Piece 1 MDi template.
2. Cut a 1/4in (6mm) strip off the long side of 2 of the
BKG wedges. Sash them together using the 7in
(17.8cm) stem strip.
3. Finish block as for MD1 following the layout in
the photograph.
4. Cut out a leaf shape approx 2in x 6in (5.1cm x
15.2cm). You can use the sides of a dinner plate to draw
a template.
5. Fuse leaf to BKG. Finish with zigzag, straight, blanket,
or other edging stitch.

variations
storm at sea

see base design page 207

variation 2
[SAS3 — 12in (30.5cm) block]

materials
as for SAS1, omitting the 4 x 3 1/2in (8.9cm) squares framing the center section

1. As for SAS1, skipping step 2.

variation 3
[SAS4 — 12in (30.5cm) block]

materials
as for SAS1 omitting the 4 x 2in (5.1cm) squares which add CSTs to the corner 3 1/2in (8.9cm) sqs

1. As for SAS1, skipping step 1.

variation 4
[SAS5 — 12in (30.5cm) block]

materials
as for SAS1, with an additional 2 x 6in (15.2cm) sqs cut in half along the diag

1. Make as for SAS1 then add the 4 x 6in (15.2cm) HSTs onto the sides, top and bottom of the block, centering the triangle on each side to turn the block on point.
2. Trim to 12 1/2in (31.7cm) sq.

stars, circles, curves, flowers **227**

variations
tulip

see base design page 208

variation 2
[TP3 — 5in (12.7cm) block]

materials
tulip/stamen:
as for TP1 using 2 colours for tulip
leaves:
1 1/2in x 4 1/2in (3.8cm x 11.4cm) sml rect, 1 1/2in x 5 1/2in (3.8cm x 14cm) lrg rect
BKG:
3 x 1 1/2in (3.8cm) sml sqs, 2 x 2 1/2in (6.3cm) lrg sqs, 1 1/2in x 2 1/2in (3.8cm x 6.3cm) rect

1. As for TP1 steps 1–3.
2. Add CSTs to leaves as in TP1 step 4. Sew sml leaf to bottom of block and lrg leaf to side.

variation 3
[TP4 — 4in (10.2cm) block]

materials
tulip/BKG:
as for TP1 but with 4 sml BKG 1 1/2in (3.8cm) sqs
leaves:
as for TP3
stamen:
2 x 1 1/2in (3.8cm) sq in 2 prints

1. Stamen: Sew stamen sqs together across diagonal. Trim excess. Open out to make sq. Continue as TP1 steps 2–3.
2. As TP3 step 2 but adding CST to both ends of the lrg leaf.

variation 4
[TP5 — 8in (20.3cm) block]

materials
tulip:
3 x 4 1/2in (11.4cm) sqs
stamen:
2 1/2in (6.3cm) sq
BKG:
2 1/2in (6.3cm) sq, 3 x 5 1/2in (14cm) sqs, 2 1/2in x 4 1/2in (6.3cm x 11.4cm) rect
templates:
DPAi frame, DPAii 1/4 circle embroidery thread

1. Make stamen as in TP1.
2. Make 3 DPA sqs as in DPA1.
3. Arrange and sew as 4-patch as photograph. Add stem by hand if you like, using embroidery thread and stem stitch.

tallahassee block

see base design page 209

variation 2
**[TB3 — 9in
(22.9cm) block]**

materials
as for TB2, plus:
col A: 5 x 1 1/2in (3.8cm) sqs
BKG: 4 x 1 1/2in x 2 1/2in
(3.8cm x 6.3cm) rects,
4 x 1 1/2in (3.8cm) sqs

1. Paper piece 4 of
template TBi.
2. Sew 4 together
following the layout in the
photograph adding in
sashing between the TB
blocks using the 1 1/2in x
2 1/2in (3.8cm x 6.3cm) BKG
rects, the 1 1/2in (3.8cm)
BKG sqs and 1 1/2in
(3.8cm) dark sqs. Use the
BKG sqs to join the prints
in the TB block and 1 more
in the center of the block.

variation 3
**[TB4 — 10in
(25.4cm) block]**

materials
as for TB2, plus:
2 x 5 1/2in (14cm) BKG
sqs cut in half along
the diag

1. Paper piece 4 of
template TBi.
2. Sew 4 together and
add 4 HSTs to the sides,
top and bottom to turn
the block on point.
3. Trim to 10 1/2in
(26.7cm) sq.

variation 4
**[TB5 — 9in
(22.9cm) block]**

materials
as for TB2, plus:
red:
4 x 1 1/2in x 4 1/2in
(3.8cm x 11.4cm) rects
BKG:
1 1/2in (3.8cm) sq

1. Paper piece 4 of
template TBi.
2. Arrange blocks, red
rects and BKG sq as per
photograph. Sew
together as a 9-patch.

pictures and patterns

Picture blocks such as animals, letters, numbers and houses can be found in this chapter alongside dynamic pattern based blocks like Whirligig and Wonky Cross. All the projects have a pictorial theme. There are quilt projects with two children's quilts: Baby Love and Stars and Stripes. The Book Bag is an ideal make for any bibliophile and the projects bag and spool thread pot are both perfect for storing your crafty goodies. The potholder and needle book are useful items that could easily be made in a couple of hours and would make lovely gifts.

boat at sea

see other variations page 260

main block [BS1 — 8in (20.3cm) block]

1   Pair sail/sky 3in (7.6cm) sqs. Make 4 HST units. Trim to 2 1/2in
    (6.3cm) sq. Join in 4-patch as photograph. Sew sky rects to
    side edges.

2   Sew sky 2 1/2in (6.3cm) sqs to both ends of boat rect as CSTs using
    photograph for placement. Join bottom edge of boat to sea rect.

3   Join sails/sky to boat/sea.

    note: block pictured left at top.

materials
- **sails:** 2 x 3in (7.6cm) sqs
- **sky:** 2 x 2 1/2in (6.3cm) sqs, 2 x
  3in (7.6cm) sqs, 2 x 2 1/2in x
  4 1/2in (6.3cm x 11.4cm) rects
- **boat:** 2 1/2in x 8 1/2in (6.3cm
  x 21.6cm) rect
- **sea:** 2 1/2in x 8 1/2in (6.3cm
  x 21.6cm) rect

variation 1 [BS2 — 8in (20.3cm) block]

1   Pair sail/sky 4 1/2in (11.4cm) sqs RS tog.
    Sew across diagonal, trim excess fabric
    1/4in (6mm) away from the seam, open out
    to make HST unit.

2   Join mast to right sail edge of HST unit.
    Add sky sml rect to left vertical edge and
    lrg rect to right.

3   Continue as for BS1.

materials
- **boat/sea:** as BS1
- **sails:** 4 1/2in (11.4cm) sq
- **sky:** 2 x 2 1/2in (6.3cm) sqs,
  4 1/2in (11.4cm) sq, 1in x 4 1/2in
  (2.5cm x 11.4cm) sml rect,
  3 1/2in x 4 1/2in (8.9cm x
  11.4cm) lrg rect
- **mast:** 3/4in x 4 1/2in (1.9cm
  x 11.4cm) rect

abc

see other variations page 261

main block [AB1 — 6in (15.2cm) block]

1 Place letter lrg rects vertically, sew BKG sqs as CSTs to the top corners of letter strips using photograph for diagonal placement.

2 Arrange a 2 1/2in (6.3cm) wide column: Letter rect 1; BKG sml rect; letter rect 2; BKG lrg rect. Join to make the central letter section.

3 Using photograph for reference, arrange block in 5 columns. Join columns.

materials:

- **BKG:** 2 x 1 1/2in (3.8cm) sqs, 2in x 2 1/2in (5.1cm x 6.3cm) sml rect, 2 1/2in x 3in (6.3cm x 7.6cm) lrg rect
- **BKG sashing:** 2 x 1 1/2in x 6 1/2in (3.8cm x 16.5cm) strips
- **letter:** 2 x 1 1/2in x 6 1/2in (3.8cm x 16.5cm) strips, 2 x 11/2in x 2 1/2in (3.8cm x 6.3cm) rects

variation 1 [AB2 — 6in (15.2cm) block]

1 Place letter lrg rects vertically, sew BKG sqs as CSTs to the top and bottom corners of each letter lrg rects using photograph for placement. Join rects together at short edges.

2 Arrange in rows to make a 2 1/2in (6.3cm) wide column: Letter sml rect 1; BKG rect. 1; letter sml rect 2; BKG rect. 2; letter sml rect 3. Join to make the central letter section.

3 Complete as for AB1.

materials

- **BKG:** 4 x 1 1/2in (3.8cm) sqs, 2 x 2in x 2 1/2in (5.1cm x 6.3cm) rects
- **BKG sashing:** 2 x 1 1/2in x 6 1/2in (3.8cm x 16.5cm) strips
- **letter:** 1 1/2in x 6 1/2in (3.8cm x 16.5cm) strip, 3 x 1 1/2in x 2 1/2in (3.8cm x 6.3cm) sml rects, 2 x 1 1/2in x 3 1/2in (3.8cm x 8.9cm) lrg rects

cup and saucer

see others variations page 262

main block [CU1 — 6in (15.2cm) block]

1 For the handle: Join 1 handle/1 BKG sml rect at 1 1/2in (3.8cm) edges. Place 2nd handle rect horizontally, add BKG 1in (2.5cm) sq as CST to right edge sewing diagonal seam from top left to bottom right. Join above 1st section. Repeat with 3rd handle rect/BKG sq, sewing CST diagonal in opposite direction. Join below 1st section. Add BKG sml rects to top and bottom edges.

2 For the cup: Sew handle section right 3 1/2in (8.9cm) edge of cup and BKG med rect to left edge.

3 Saucer: Sew BKG 1 1/2in (3.8cm) sqs to both ends of saucer rect as CSTs. Join to cup.

4 Add BKG lrg rects to top and bottom.

materials

- **BKG:** 2 x 1in (2.5cm) sqs, 2 x 1 1/2in (3.8cm) sqs, 3 x 1in x 1 1/2in (2.5cm x 3.8cm) sml rects, 1 1/2in x 3 1/2in (2.5cm x 8.9cm) med rect, 2 x 1 1/2in x 6 1/2in (2.5cm x 16.5cm) lrg rects
- **cup:** 3 1/2in x 4 1/2in (8.9cm x 11.4cm)
- **handle:** 3 x 1in x 1 1/2in (2.5cm x 3.8cm) rects
- **saucer:** 1 1/2in x 6 1/2in (3.8cm x 16.5cm)

....

variation 1 [CU2 — 6in (15.2cm) block]

1 As for CU1.

2 For the cup: Join cup rects along 4 1/2in (11.4cm) edges with light rect in centre. Continue blocks as CU1.

materials

- as for CU1, except cup
- **cup:** 1 1/2in x 4 1/2in (3.8cm x 11.4cm) light rect, 2 x 1 1/2in x 4 1/2in (3.8cm x 11.4cm) dark rects

house

main block [HB1 — 12in (30.5cm) block]

1 House top floor: Sew windows to either side of wall sq. Add wall rects to window side edges.

2 House bottom floor: Sew walls to either side of door. Repeat steps 1 and 2 to make 4 houses.

3 Pair roof sqs, make 2 HST units. Cut each in half diagonally, choose 1 half from each original HST and sew together to make central sq of block. Trim to 5 1/2in (14cm) sq.

4 Sew 1 sky sq to either side of 1 house block to make top row. Repeat for bottom row. Sew the two remaining houses to opposite edges of the centre sq.

5 Arrange 3 rows as block photograph. Join rows.

materials:

- **roof:** 2 x 6 1/2in (16.5cm) sqs (in 2 shades of red)
- **sky:** 4 x 4in (10.2cm) sqs
- **4 x house top floor:**
  walls: 2 x 1in x 2in (2.5cm x 5.1cm) rects, 2in (5.1cm) sq; windows: 2 x 1 3/4in x 2in (4.4cm x 5.1cm)
- **4 x house bottom floor:** walls: 2 x 2 1/4in x 2 1/2in (5.7cm x 6.3cm) rects; door: 2in x 2 1/2in (5.1cm x 6.3cm) rect

variation 1 [HB2 — 5in (12.7cm) block]

see other variations page 263

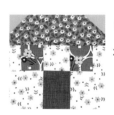

1 Make house as HB1 steps 1/2.

2 Add roof to top of house. Sew sky sqs as CSTs to both top corners of roof.

materials

- **roof:** 2in x 5 1/2in (5.1cm x 14cm) rect
- **sky:** 2 x 1 1/4in (3.2cm) sqs
- **house:** as HB1

string block

main block [STB1 — 12in (30.5cm) block]

1 Cut out 4 x 6 1/2in (16.5cm) paper sqs. In pencil on WS, draw diag lines 1in (2.5cm) apart starting with 2 lines each 1/2in (1.3cm) away from centre diag.

2 Lay the one of the light 10in (25.4cm) strips covering the central diag on the RS side of the paper with the RS of the fabric facing away from the paper and pin in place.

3 Foundation paper piece the remaining strips as follows: The 9in (22.9cm) dark strips on either side of the diag strip, then the 7in (17.8cm) light strips, then the 5in (12.7cm) dark strips, then the 3in (7.6cm) light strips. Repeat x 4.

4 Trim off excess fabric to the edge of the paper and remove paper.

5 Sew the four sections together following the layout in the photograph.

materials:

■ **light:** 4 x 1 1/2in x 10in (3.8cm x 25.4cm) strips, 8 x 1 1/2in x 7in (3.8cm x 17.8cm) strips, 8 x 1 1/2in x 3in (3.8cm x 7.6cm) strips

■ **dark:** 8 x 1 1/2in x 9in (3.8cm x 22.9cm) strips, 8 x 1 1/2in x 5in (3.8cm x 12.7cm) strips

....

variation 1 [STB2 — 12in (30.5cm) block]

1 Make as for STB1 but instead using fewer strips and the HSTs.

see other variations page 264

materials

■ **dark and light:** 2 x 5in (12.7cm) sqs of each cut in half along diag

■ **blue strips:** 4 x 1 1/2in x 7in (3.8cm x 17.8cm) strips light, 4 x 1 1/2in x 10in (3.8cm x 25.4cm) strips med, 4 x 1 1/2in x 7in (3.8cm x 17.8cm) strips dark

heart

see other variations page 265

project: baby love quilt [36in (91.4cm) square]

1 Make 2 HE5 blocks and 1 each of all AB and NU blocks using blue BKG throughout (12 blocks total).

2 Make 9-patch blocks using ABC blocks and pastel squares. Repeat for Numbers.

3 Sew quilt top sections tog as 4-patch. Back, quilt, and bind as desired.

materials

- as for HE5 x 2, plus:
- materials as for AB1–5 and NU1–5
- 8 x 6 1/2in (16.5cm) sqs using variety of pastel colours
- **batting:** 40in (102cm) sq
- **backing:** 40in (102cm) sq
- **binding:** 1/2in yd (0.46m) pink fabric; **note:** 3/4 yd (0.69) blue BKG is sufficient for all BKG used in this project

main block [HE1 — 6in (15.2cm) block]

1 Place A sml rects horizontally. At both ends of each rect sew BKG 1 1/2in (3.8cm) sqs diagonally to make CSTs using photo for placement. Join rects to make top row of block.

2 Sew lrg BKG sqs as CSTs to lower corners on A lrg rect 6 1/2in (16.5cm) edge.

3 Arrange as photo, join tog.

materials

- **col A (heart):** 2 x 1 1/2in x 3 1/2in (3.8cm x 8.9cm) rects, 5 1/2in x 6 1/2in (14cm x 16.5cm) lrg rect
- **BKG:** 4 x 1 1/2in (3.8cm) sml sqs, 2 x 3 1/2in (8.9cm) sqs

numbers

see other variations page 266

main block [NU1 — 6in (15.2cm) block]

1 Pair BKG/number 1 1/2in (3.8cm) sqs, join diagonally, trim excess, open out to make HST unit.

2 Sew the number 1 1/2in (3.8cm) sq to BKG lrg rect. Repeat to BKG sml rect adding HST to the top of BKG sml rect.

3 Using photograph for ref, arrange block in 5 columns. Join.

materials

■ **BKG:** 1 1/2in (3.8cm) sq, 1 1/2in x 4 1/2in (3.8cm x 11.4cm) sml rect, 1 1/2in x 5 1/2in (3.8cm x 14cm) lrg rect

■ **BKG sashing:** 2 x 2in x 6 1/2in (5.1cm x 16.5cm) strips

■ **number:** 3 x 1 1/2in (3.8cm) sqs, 1 1/2in x 6 1/2in (3.8cm x 16.5cm) rect

variation 1 [NU2 — 6in (15.2cm) block]

1 Place the number sml rect vertically, add BKG 1 1/2in (3.8cm) sq to top left corner as CST, sewing diag seam from bottom left to top right. Repeat for the number lrg rect and BKG sml rect. Join underneath.

2 Arrange in rows: The number sml rect; BKG med rect; the number sml rect; BKG med rect. Join along 2 1/2in (6.3cm) edges.

3 Place the number lrg rect vertically, add BKG 1 1/2in (3.8cm) sq as CST to top right corner, sewing diag seam from bottom left to top right. Use same method to add BKG med rect to bottom right corner of the number, diag running the opposite direction. Join to right edge of step 2 section. Sew the number med rect underneath. Add to right edge of step 1 section. Add sashing strips.

materials

■ **BKG:** 2 x 1 1/2in (3.8cm) sqs, 2 x 1 1/2in x 2in (3.8cm x 5.1cm) sml rects, 2 x 2in x 2 1/2in (5.1cm x 6.3cm) med rects, 1 1/2in x 3in (3.8cm x 7.6cm) lrg rect

■ **BKG sashing:** 2 x 1 1/2in x 6 1/2in (3.8cm x 16.5cm) strips

■ **number:** 3 x 1 1/2in x 2 1/2in (3.8cm x 6.3cm) sml rects, 1 1/2in x 3 1/2in (3.8cm x 8.9cm) med rect, 2 x 1 1/2in x 4in (3.8cm x 10.2cm) lrg rects

modern spool

see variations page 267

project: modern spool thread pot [6in (15.2cm) cube]

1 Cut out 5 x 5 3/4in (14.6cm) sqs of cardboard. Glue 5 x 5 3/4in (14.6cm) sqs of batting onto them.

2 Sew together the 4 spool blocks and 1 of the sq of coloured fabric into a cross shape so coloured fabric will make the bottom of the pot and the spool blocks the sides.

3 Sew together the remaining sq into the same cross shape to make the lining of the pot.

4 Pin the ribbons onto the top corners of the spool cross blocks.

5 Sew the spool cross to the lining cross, RST using a 1/4in (6mm) SA, leaving one end seam open.

6 Turn inside out, clip corners, press. Slide cardboard sqs into the pot with the batting facing towards the spool blocks.

7 Hand sew final seam and tie the ties to make thread pot.

materials

- as for MS1 x 4, plus:
- 6 x 6 1/2in (16.5cm) sq coloured fabric for bottom and lining of pot
- 8 x 6in (15.2cm) narrow strips of ribbon or binding
- card stock
- batting

main block [MS1 — 6in (15.2cm) block]

1 Sew the 2 x 1in x 1 1/4in (2.5cm x 3.2cm) C rects to 2 opposite sides of the 1in (2.5cm) B sq.

2 Sew the 1in x 2 1/2in (2.5cm x 6.3cm) C rect to the top of the piece made at step 1.

3 Sew the 2 1/2in x 4 1/2in (6.3cm x 11.4cm) A rect to the bottom of the piece made at step 2.

4 Sew the 2 x 3/4in x 5 1/2in (1.9cm x 14cm) C rects to either side of the spool.

5 Sew the 1in x 3in (2.5cm x 7.6cm) B rect to the bottom of the spool then the 1in x 3in (2.5cm x 7.6cm) C rect to the bottom of that.

6 Sew the 2 x 2 1/4in x 6 1/2in (5.7cm x 16.5cm) rects onto either side of the spool to complete the block.

materials

- col A (striped thread): 1 x 2 1/2in x 4 1/2in (6.3cm x 11.4cm) rect
- col B (grey): 1in (2.5cm) sq, 1in x 3in (2.5cm x 7.6cm) rect
- col C (cream): 2 x 1in x 1 1/4in (2.5cm x 3.2cm) rects, 1in x 2 1/2in (2.5cm x 6.3cm) rect, 2 x 3/4in x 5 1/2in (1.9cm x 14cm) rects, 1in x 3in (2.5cm x 7.6cm) rect, 2 x 2 1/4in x 6 1/2in (6mm x 16.5cm) rects

note: block shown at right as part of project.

pets

see other variations page 268

main block [PT1 — 6in (15.2cm) block]

1   Make the nose/chin by joining cream rects either side of pink rect.
    Cut into 4 QSTs, choose one 'nose' triangle, keep other for another
    block, discard the other two. Sew nose QST to cream QST along bias
    edge. Sew white QST to remaining cream QST. Join QST pairs tog
    along bias. Open out, trim to 3 1/2in (8.9cm) sq.

2   Face: Add cream rect above nose section and collar below. Sew
    cream rect to base of face section and BKG rect to top.

3   Ears: Add 2 BKG sqs as CSTs to each ear rect. Sew ears either side of
    face. Sew on eyes.

materials

- **face:** cream 2 x 1 1/2in x 3 1/2in (3.8cm x 8.9cm) sml rects, cream 4 1/2in (11.4cm) sq cut into 4 QSTs
- **nose:** pink 2 3/4in x 4 1/2in (6.9cm x 11.4cm) rect, cream 2 x 1 3/8in x 4 1/2in (3.5cm x 11.4cm) lrg rects
- **chin:** white 4 1/2in (11.4cm) sq cut into 4 QSTs
- **collar:** 1 x 3 1/2in (8.9cm) rect
- **ears:** 2 x 2in x 6 1/2in (5.1cm x 16.5cm) rects
- **BKG:** 4 x 2in (5.1cm) sqs, 1in x 3 1/2in (2.5cm x 8.9cm) rect
- **eyes:** buttons or felt circles

variation 1 [PT2 — 6in (15.2cm) block]

1   As for PT1. Sew face rect above nose/chin.

2   Cheeks: Add BKG sq to each cheek rect as
    CSTs. Sew either side of face.

3   Ears: Sew ear sqs as CSTs to BKG rect. Join
    to top of block. Add eyes.

materials

- **face:** black 2 1/2in x 3 1/2in (6.3cm 8.9cm) rect, 4 1/2in (11.4cm) sq cut into 4 QSTs
- **nose:** pink 2 3/4in x 4 1/2in (6.9cm x 11.4cm) rect, white 2 x 1 3/8in x 4 1/2in (3.5cm x 11.4cm) lrg rects
- **chin; eyes:** as PT1
- **cheeks:** 2 x 2in x 5 1/2in (5.1cm x 14cm) rects
- **ears:** 2 x 2in (5.1cm) sqs
- **BKG:** 2 x 2in (5.1cm) sqs, 2in x 6 1/2in (5.1cm x 16.5cm) rect

raw edge appliqué

project: stars and stripes quilt
[37 1/2in (95.2cm) square]

1   Make the 13 x 7 1/2in (19cm) finished stripe blocks by sewing together 3 strips of blue fabric and 2 of cream alternating blue, cream, blue, cream, blue.

2   Make 12 REA1 star blocks.

3   Sew the blocks into rows and the rows into a quilt top following the layout in the quilt photograph.

4   Back, quilt and bind.

see variations page 269

see template page 284

materials

- as for REA1 x 12, plus:
- **fabric A (cream):** 12 x 8in (20.3cm) sqs, 26 x 2in x 8in (5.1cm x 20.3cm) strips
- **fabric B (blue):** 12 x 8in (20.3cm) sqs, 39 x 2in x 8in (5.1cm x 20.3cm) strips, 12 x 8in (20.3cm) sqs fusible web
- batting, backing and binding

main block [REA1 — 7 1/2in (19cm) block]

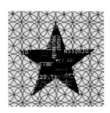

1   Trace star shape from template REAi onto fusible web. Fuse the fusible to the back of the dark fabric, cut out star shape then remove fusible paper.

2   Fuse to background fabric.

3   Finish with the stitch of your choice around the edge of the star shape.

materials

- 8in (20.3cm) dark and light sqs
- 8in (20.3cm) sq fusible web
- **template:** REAi

pots and pans

see other variations page 270

project: kettle pot holder [8 1/2in (21.6cm) square]

1 Make block as for PP4. Add sml sashing strips to sides and lrg to top/bottom.

2 Make quilt sandwich of backing fabric on bottom/batting/heat resistant insulated batting reflective side up/block on top. Baste and quilt. Trim and square the edges.

3 Round the corners by drawing around a cup or other circular object and trimming the potholder corners. Make hanging loop using 5in (12.7cm) of binding, fold and press in half long ways, bringing raw edges to centre fold, press and stitch along edges. Sew loop to top right corner with loop facing inwards and stitching in SA.

4 Add bias binding using single fold technique. Turn hanging loop outwards and stitch to binding.

main block [PP1 — size 6in (15.2cm) block]

1 Knob: Sew BKG rects C either side of knob. Add BKG rect E above.

2 Lid: Sew rects B either side of lid rect.

3 Handles: Add lrg BKG sq as CST to each handle rect. Sew rect A above each handle and rect D below. Sew casserole cream rect between the 2 orange rects. Add sml BKG sqs to casserole lower corners as CSTs. Sew handles/BKG to casserole sides.

4 Join sections as shown in photograph.

---

materials

- as for PP4 (but can be made with any PP block), plus:
- **BKG sashing:** 2 x 1 1/2in x 6 1/2in (3.8cm x 16.5cm) sml rects, 2 x 1 1/2in x 8 1/2in (3.8cm x 21.6cm) lrg rects
- **backing fabric:** 9in (22.9cm) sq
- **cotton batting:** 9in (22.9cm) sq
- **heat-resistant insulated cotton batting:** 9in (22.9cm) sq
- **binding:** 1 1/2in x 50in (3.8cm x 127cm) bias cut strip or ready made bias binding

materials

- **BKG:** 2 x 1in (2.5cm) sml sqs, 2 x 1 1/4in (3.2cm) lrg sqs, 2 3/4in x 1 1/4in (6.9cm x 3.2cm) rects A, 2 x 1in x 1 1/2in (2.5cm x 3.8cm) rects B, 2 x 1in x 3in (2.5cm x 7.6cm) rects C, 2 x 1 1/4in x 2 1/4in (3.2cm x 5.7cm) rects D, 1 1/2in x 6 1/2in (3.8cm x 16.5cm) rect E
- **knob:** 1in x 1 1/2in (2.5cm x 3.8cm)
- **lid:** 1in x 4 1/2in (2.5cm x 11.4cm)
- **handles:** 2 x 1 1/4in x 1 1/2in (3.2cm x 3.8cm) rects
- **casserole:** 2 x 1 1/2in x 5in (3.8cm x 12.7cm) orange rects, 1 1/2in x 5in (3.8cm x 12.7cm) cream rect
- **worktop:** 1 1/2in x 6 1/2in (3.8cm x 16.5cm)

school house

main block [SHB1 — 8in (20.3cm) block]

1. Make sky/chimney: Join chimney to base edge of sky sml sq. Repeat. Arrange 3 lrg sky sqs alternating with 2 chimneys as in photograph. Sew tog.

2. Make roof: Place house gable so 4 1/2in (11.4cm) edge is horizontal. Add lrg sky sq to top left corner of house gable to make CST. Repeat with roof rect, placing CST to top right corner. Place roof at right angles to gable and join using CST/rectangle technique.

3. Make door: Sew rects B either side of door along 3 1/2in (8.9cm), add 1 rect C to the top.

4. Make window: Sew rects A either side of window. Add rect C above and rect D below.

5. Join door/window sections of house tog. Add roof above and sky/chimney to the top of the block.

materials

- **sky:** 2 x 1 1/2in (3.8cm) sml sqs, 5 x 2 1/2in (6.3cm) lrg sqs
- **chimney:** 2 x 1 1/2in (3.8cm) sqs
- **house gable:** 2 1/2in x 4 1/2in (6.3cm x 11.4cm)
- **roof:** 2 1/2in x 6 1/2in (6.3cm x 16.5cm)
- **house:** 2 x 1 3/4in x 2in (4.4cm x 5.1cm) rects A, 2 x 1 3/4in x 3 1/2in (4.4cm x 8.9cm) rects B, 2 x 1 1/2in x 4 1/2in (3.8cm x 11.4cm) rects C, 2in x 4 1/2in (5.1cm x 11.4cm) rect D
- **door:** 2in x 3 1/2in (5.1cm x 8.9cm)
- **window:** 2in (5.1cm) sq

---

variation 1 [SHB2 — 8in (20.3cm) block]

see other variations page 272

1. Make sky/chimney: Join chimney/sky sml sq as SHB1 step 1. Sew sky rect to left edge and sky lrg sq to right.
2. Make roof: As SHB1 step 2.
3. Make door: Sew house med rects either side of door. Add house lrg rect above.
4. Make window: Sew house sml rects either side of window. Add house lrg rects above and below.
5. Assemble as for SHB1.

materials

- **sky:** 1 1/2in (3.8cm) sml sq, 3 x 2 1/2in (6.3cm) lrg sqs, 2 1/2in x 5 1/2in (6.3cm x 14cm) rect
- **chimney:** 1 1/2in (3.8cm) sq
- **house gable:** 2 1/2in x 4 1/2in (6.3cm x 11.4cm)
- **roof:** 2 1/2in x 6 1/2in (6.3cm x 16.5cm)
- **house:** 2 x 1 1/2in x 2 1/2in (3.8cm x 6.3cm) sml rects, 2 x 1 1/2in x 3 1/2in (3.8cm x 8.9cm) med rects, 3 x 1 1/2in x 4 1/2in (3.8cm x 11.4cm) lrg rects
- **door:** 2 1/2in x 3 1/2in
- **window:** 2 1/2in sq

whirligig

see variations page 273

main block [WGG1 — 14in (35.6cm) block]

1 Place rects horizontally, mark points 2 1/4in (5.7cm) down in from the top left and 2 1/4in (5.7cm) in from the bottom right. Draw line connecting points, cut along line.

2 Sew into pairs pairing a print/BKG.

3 Sew into the block following the layout in the photograph.

materials

■ **BKG:**
  8 x 4in x 4 1/2in (10.2cm x 11.4cm) rects

■ **prints:**
  8 x 4in x 4 1/2in (10.2cm x 11.4cm) rects (2 of each print if desired)

spool block

see other variations page 274
see template page 283

project: craft bag [12in x 15in (30.5cm x 38.1cm) not including handles]

1 To make bag front, make 9 x SB5 blocks. Arrange and sew as 9-patch alternating centre strip direction as in photograph. Add sashing strips to top and bottom.

2 Apply fusible fleece to bag front/back. Quilt it as desired.

3 Measure inner handle + 1/2in (1.3cm) and cut handle fabric this width x 7in (17.8cm) length. Fold in half along 7in (17.8cm) edges RS tog, sew side seams, turn through. Repeat to make 2 handle holders. Fold over handles for snug fit, baste long edges together and trim any excess.

4 Pin handle holders to centre of bag front and back top edges with handles facing down. Sew in SA as close to handles as possible. A zipper foot helps with this and moving the machine needle.

5 Place bag front/back RS tog, sew side/bottom edges. Press side seams open. Repeat with lining, but use scant 3/8in (9mm) seam and leave 5in (12.7cm) opening on bottom edge for turning.

6 Turn bag outer RS out, place inside lining RS tog, match side seams, stitch around top edges.

7 Turn bag through lining opening. Close opening with slip stitch. Press.

materials

- as for SB5 x 9, plus:
- **backing:** 12 1/2in x 15 1/2in (31.7cm x 39.4cm)
- **lining:** 2 x 12 1/2in x 15 1/2in (31.7cm x 39.4cm)
- **sashing strips:** 2 x 2 1/2in x 12 1/2in (6.3cm x 31.7cm)
- **handle holders:** 7in (17.8cm) x width of inner wooden handles + 1/2in (1.3cm)
- **wooden handles:** pair
- **fusible fleece:** 2 x 12in x 15in (30.5cm x 38.1cm)

main block [SB1 — 6in (15.2cm) block]

1 Sew 1 BKG sq diag to make CST at corner of spool rect. Repeat at other end of rect (see photo). Repeat with 2nd spool rect.

2 Join BKG sqs either side of thread sq. Join rows.

materials

- **spool:** 2 x 2 1/2in x 6 1/2in (6.3cm x 16.5cm) rects
- **thread:** 2 1/2in (6.3cm) sq
- **BKG:** 6 x 2 1/2in (6.3cm) sqs

sunshine and stained glass

main block [SSG1 — 8in (20.3cm) block]

1   Make as for DPA1 to make 4 sqs.

2   On the 1/4 circle inner corner of each sq, add contrasting 1 1/2in (3.8cm) sq as CSTs. On the outer frame corner of each sq, add contrasting 2 1/2in (6.3cm) sqs to make CSTs in the same way.

3   Arrange as in photograph. Join as 4-patch.

materials

■ **col A:** 2 x 1 1/2in (3.8cm) sqs, 2 x 2 1/2in (6.3cm) sqs, 2 x 4 1/2in (11.4cm) sqs, 2 x 5 1/2in (14cm) sqs
■ **col B:** 2 x 1 1/2in (3.8cm) sqs, 2 x 2 1/2in (6.3cm) sqs, 2 x 4 1/2in (1.4cm) sqs, 2 x 5 1/2in (14cm) sqs
■ **templates:** DPAi frame, DPAii 1/4 circle

---

variation 1 [SSG2 — 8in (20.3cm) block]

see other variations page 275
see template page 280

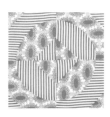

1   Make as for SSG1 but swapping the position of the 1 1/2in (3.8cm) and 2 1/2in (6.3cm) CSTs.

materials

■ as for SSG1

wonky crosses

main block [WC1 — 12in (30.5cm) block]

1   Cut 1 x 5in (12.7cm) dark sq in half on a wonky angle. Sash the 2 halves back together using a light strip.

2   Cut in half again perpendicular to the first cut and sash the 2 halves back together using a light strip.

3   Trim to 4 1/2in (11.4cm) sq.

4   Repeat for the remaining 4 dark blocks and 4 light blocks.

5   Sew together into the finished block following the layout in the photograph.

materials

- **dark:** 5 x 5in (12.7cm) sqs, 8 x 1in x 6in (2.5cm x 15.2cm) strips
- **light:** 4 x 5in (12.7cm) sqs, 10 x 1in x 6in (2.5cm x 15.2cm) strips

variation 1 [WC2 — 7in (17.8cm) block]

1   Make as for WC1, trimming to 5 1/2in (14cm) sq.

2   Sash the sides using the shorter strips and then the top and bottom using the longer.

see other variations page 276

materials

- **col A (yellow):** 6in (16.5cm) sq
- **BKG:** 2 x 1in x 7in (2.5cm x 17.8cm) strips, 2 x 1in x 5 1/2in (2.5cm x 14cm) strips, 2 x 1in x 7 1/2in (2.5cm x 19cm) strips

basket

see other variations page 277
see template page 283

project: button basket needle book (4in x 4in [10.2cm x 10.2cm] closed)

1 Make BA5 block. Join BKG sq to left side edge of block to make needle book front.

2 Apply fusible batting to reverse leaving 1/4in (6mm) gap around SA of needle book front.

3 Sew buttons as flowers to needle book front.

4 Place needle book front/lining fabric RS tog. Stitch around edge leaving 2 1/2in (6.3cm) gap for turning. Clip corners, turn through and press. Close opening with slip stitch. Fold to create book, press and open out.

5 Fold felt in half bringing short edges together, press, and open out. Pin to lining side of needle book. Stitch through book front and felt along centre fold.

materials

■ as for BA5 (this project could also be made with any 4in (10.2cm) quilt block), plus:
■ **BKG:** 4 1/2in (11.4cm) sq
■ **lining fabric:** 4 1/2in x 8 1/2in (11.4cm x 21.6cm) rect
■ **fusible fleece:** 4in x 8in (11.4cm x 21.6cm) rect
■ **felt/wool fabric:** 3 1/2in x 7in (8.9cm x 17.8cm) rect (cut with pinking shears)
■ **template:** SBi
■ small flower buttons
■ spray starch (optional)

basket main block (BA1 – 5in (12.7cm) block)

1 Draw diagonal on WS of BKG 4 1/2in (11.4cm) sq. On RS sew rickrack for basket handle in one triangle half with handle starting/ending 1in in from each corner and ends extending 1/4in (6mm) into SA (see BA1 diagram).

2 Pair basket/BKG 4 1/2in (11.4cm) sq RS tog. Sew across diagonal, trim excess fabric 1/4in (6mm) away from the seam and reserve for step 4.

3 Sew basket sml HST to 1 BKG rect, lining up right angle and rect corner to start seam. Repeat. Join to basket sides as per photograph.

4 Take BKG HST created in step 2 and add to block lower right corner. Trim to 5 1/2in (14cm) sq.

materials

■ **basket:** 4 1/2in (11.4cm) sq, 1 7/8in (4.8cm) sq cut in half diagonally to make 2 sml HSTs
■ **BKG:** 4 1/2in (11.4cm) sq, 2 x 1 1/2in x 3 1/2in (3.8cm x 8.9cm) rects
■ **handle:** rickrack 3/8in x 6in (9mm x 15.2cm)

books

see other variations page 278

project: book bag [14in x 16in (35.6cm x 40.6cm) not including straps]

1   Make BK5. Add BKG sashing strips to top and bottom edges. Apply interfacing to WS of bag front and back.

2   For each handle: Press fabric in half long ways, apply interfacing next to centre fold crease. Bring long edges to centre, press to make double fold strip. Stitch along edges with 1/8in (3mm) SA.

3   On top edge of bag front/back mark 3in (7.6cm) inwards from side edges. Pin handles inside marks and with handle loops facing downwards. Stitching in SA, sew handle ends to bag top edge.

4   Place bag front/back RS tog, sew side and bottom edges. Press side seams open. Repeat with lining, using scant 3/8in (9mm) seam and leaving 5in (12.7cm) opening on bottom edge for turning. Leave lining WS outwards.

5   Turn bag outer RS out, place inside lining RS tog, match side seams, pin and stitch around top.

6   Turn bag through lining opening. Close with slip stitch. Press. Top stitch around bag opening with 1/8in (3mm) SA.

book main block [BK1 — 14in (35.6cm) block]

1   Assemble each book plus BKG piece into column and arrange in order left to right following block photograph. Join columns.

2   Sew shelf fabric to bottom long edge.

258   pictures and patterns

materials

- as for BK5 (but any BK block will work for this project), plus:
- **BKG (linen):** 2 x 1 1/2in x 14 1/2in (3.8cm x 36.8cm) sashing strips, 14 1/2in x 16 1/2in 36.8cm x 41.9cm) bag back
- **lining:** 2 x 14 1/2in x 16 1/2in (36.8cm x 41.9cm)
- **handles:** 2 x 4 1/4in x 26in (11.4cm x 66cm)
- **medium weight woven interfacing:** 2 x 14in x 16in (35.6cm x 40.6cm) (front/back), 2in x 26in (5.1cm x 66cm) (handles)

materials

- **A:** 2 1/2in x 11 1/2in (6.3cm x 29.2cm), BKG 1 1/2in x 2 1/2in (3.8cm x 6.3cm)
- **B:** 2 1/2in x 10 1/2in (6.3cm x 26.7cm), BKG 2 1/2in (6.3cm) sq
- **C:** 1 3/4in x 11in (4.4cm x 27.9cm), BKG 1 3/4in x 2in (4.4cm x 5.1cm)
- **D:** 3in x 10in (7.6cm x 25.4cm), BKG 3in (7.6cm) sq
- **E:** 2in x 9in (5.1cm x 22.9cm), BKG 2in x 4in (5.1cm x 10.2cm)
- **F:** 2 1/4in x 8 1/4in (5.7cm x 21cm), BKG 2 1/4in x 4 3/4in (5.7cm x 12.1cm)
- **G:** 2 1/2in x 6 1/2in (6.3cm x 16.5cm), BKG 2 1/2in x 6 1/2in (6.3cm x 16.5cm)
- **H:** 1 1/2in x 5in (3.8cm x 14cm), BKG 1 1/2in x 8in
- **shelf:** 2 1/2in x 14 1/2in (6.3cm x 36.8cm)

variations

boat at sea

see base design page 231

variation 2
[BS3 — 8in (20.3cm) block]

materials
boat/sea/mast: as BS1
sails: 3 3/4in (9.5cm) sq
fusible web: 3 3/4in (9.5cm) sq
sky: 2 x 2 1/2in (6.3cm) sqs, 3 1/2in x
4 1/2in (8.9cm x 11.4cm) sml rect,
4 1/2in x 5 1/4in (11.4cm x 13.3cm)
lrg rect

1. Sew sky lrg rect to left 4 1/2in (11.4cm)
edge of mast and sky sml rect to the right.
2. Fuse sail fabric to web. Cut in half
diagonally. Keep 1 of these triangles for
right sail. Trim remaining triangle to
make a narrower triangle for left sail.
Fuse sails either side of mast placing
sails 1/2in (1.3cm) above the bottom
edge of this section. Use sewing machine
raw edge appliqué to sew sails to block.
3. Continue as for BS1.

variation 3
[BS4 4in (10.2cm) — block]

materials
boat: 2in x 4 1/2in (5.1cm x 11.4cm) rect
sail: 2 3/4in (6.9cm) sq
sky: 2 x 1 1/4in x 3in (3.2cm x 7.6cm)
sml rects, 3/4in x 2 3/4in (1.9cm x 6.9cm)
med rect, 2 1 1/2in x 3 1/2in (3.8cm x
8.9cm) lrg rects, 2 3/4in (6.9cm) sq
mast: 3/4in x 3in (1.9cm x 7.6cm) rect
foundation pattern: SBi

1. Pair sail/sky 2 3/4in (6.9cm) sqs RS tog,
make HST unit as BS2 step 1. Sew sky
med rect to bottom edge of sail triangle
and mast to the right. Add sky sml rects
either side.
2. Print/trace pattern SBi. Use boat
fabric and 2 sky lrg rects to make boat
using foundation piecing technique.
Trim, retaining SA. Remove paper. Join
under sail.

variation 4
[BS5 — 4in (10.2cm) block]

materials
boat: 2in x 4 1/2in
(5.1cm x 11.4cm) rect
sail: 3in (7.6cm) sq
sky: 3in (7.6cm) sq, 1in
x 3in (2.5cm x 7.6cm) sml
rect, 1 1/2in x 3in (3.8cm
x 7.6cm) med rect, 2 x
1 1/2in x 3 1/2in (3.8cm
x 8.9cm)lrg rects
foundation pattern: SBi

1. Pair sail/sky 3in sqs.
RS tog. Make HST unit as
per BS2 step 1. Sew sky
sml rect to right edge
and med rect to left.
2. Complete block as
per BS4.

variations

abc

see base design page 232

variation 2
[AB3 — 6in (15.2cm) block]

materials
BKG: 4 x 1 1/2in (3.8cm) sqs, 1 1/2in x
2 1/2in (3.8cm x 6.3cm) sml rect, 2 1/2in
x 4 1/2in (6.3cm x 11.4cm) lrg rect
BKG sashing: 2 x 1 1/2in x 6 1/2in
(3.8cm x 16.5cm) strips
letter: 1 1/2in x 6 1/2in (3.8cm x
16.5cm) strip, 4 x 1 1/2in x 2 1/2in
(3.8cm x 6.3cm) rects

1. Place letter strip vertically, sew BKG
sqs as CSTs to the top and bottom
corners of letter strip using photograph
for placement.
2. Sew BKG sqs to horizontal letter rects
adding 1 CST to each. Arrange in a column
with BKG sml rect between them. Join
together at short edges.
3. Arrange a 2 1/2in (6.3cm) wide column:
Letter rect 1; BKG lrg rect; letter rect 2.
Join to make the central letter section.
4. Complete as for AB1.

variation 3
[AB4 — 6in (15.2cm) block]

materials
BKG: 2 x 1 1/2in (3.8cm) sqs, 2 1/2in
x 4 1/2in (6.3cm x 11.4cm) lrg rect
BKG sashing: 2 x 1 1/2in x 6 1/2in
(3.8cm x 16.5cm) strips
letter: 2 x 1 1/2in x 6 1/2in (3.8cm x
16.5cm) strips, 2 x 1 1/2in x 2 1/2in
(3.6cm x 6.3cm) sml rects

1. Place letter strip vertically, sew BKG
sqs as CSTs to the top and bottom
corners of 1 letter strip using
photograph for placement.
2. Arrange a 2 1/2in (6.3cm) wide
column: Letter sml rect 1; BKG lrg rect;
letter sml rect 2. Join to make the
central letter section.
3. Complete as for AB1.

variation 4
[AB5 — 6in (15.2cm) block]

materials
BKG: 1 1/2in (3.8cm) sq,
2 x 2in x 3 1/2in (5.1cm x 8.9cm)
rects
BKG sashing: 2 x 1 1/2in
x 6 1/2in (3.8cm x 16.5cm) strips
letter: 1 1/2in x 6 1/2in
(3.8cm x 16.5cm) strip,
1 1/2in x 2 1/2in (3.8cm x 6.3cm)
sml rect, 2 1/2in x 3 1/2in
(3.8cm x 8.9cm) lrg rects

1. Sew BKG sq to letter sml
rect along 1 1/2in (3.8cm) edge.
2. Arrange a 3 1/2in (8.9cm)
wide column: Letter lrg rect 1;
BKG rect 1; rect from step 1;
BKG rect 2; letter lrg rect 2.
Join to make the central
letter section.
3. Complete as for AB1.

variations

cup and saucer

see base design page 235

variation 2
[CU3 — 6in (15.2cm) block]

materials

BKG: 1in (2.5cm) sq, 4 x 1 1/4in (3.2cm) sqs, 3/4in x 1 1/2in (1.9cm x 3.8cm) rect A, 1in x 1 1/2in (2.5cm x 3.8cm) rect B, 1 1/2in x 1 3/4in (3.8cm x 4.4cm) rect C, 1 1/2in x 3 1/4in (1.9cm x 8.3cm) rect D, 1 1/2in x 6 1/2in (3.8cm x 16.5cm) rect E, 1 3/4in x 6 1/2in (4.4cm x 16.5cm) rect F.
cup: 3 1/4in x 4 1/2in (8.3cm x 11.4cm).
handle: 1 1/2in x 1 1/4in (3.8cm x 3.2cm).
saucer: 1 1/4in x 6 1/2in (3.2cm x 16.5cm)

1. For the handle: Sew BKG 1in (2.5cm) sq as CST to handle on right corner lower 1 1/4in (3.2cm) edge. Join BKG rect A to right long edge. Sew rect B to top edge and rect C to lower edge.
2. For the cup: Add 2 x BKG 1 1/4in (3.2cm) sqs to both corners along lower 4 1/2in (11.4cm) edge as CSTs. Sew rect D to left side edge and handle to right.
3. Complete as for CT1, adding rect E to bottom of block and rect F to top.

variation 3
[CU4 — 6in (15.2cm) block]

materials
as for CU3, except cup
cup:
1 1/4in x 4 1/2in (3.2cm x 11.4cm) light rect, 2 1/2in x 4 1/2in (6.3cm x 11.4cm) dark rect

1. As for CU3.
2. For the cup: Sew rects tog along 4 1/2in (11.4cm) edges, placing light rect at lower edge. Continue and complete as for CU3.

variation 4
[CU5 — 6in (15.2cm) block]

materials

BKG: 3 x 1in sqs (2.5cm), 1in x 2in (2.5cm x 5.1cm) rect A, 1 1/2in x 2in (3.8cm x 5.1cm) rect B, 1 1/2in x 2 1/2in (3.8cm x 6.3cm) rect C, 1 1/2in x 4 1/2in (3.8cm x 11.4cm) rect D, 1 1/2in x 6 1/2in (3.8cm x 16.5cm) rect E
mug: 4 1/2in x 5 1/2in (11.4cm x 14cm)
handle: 2 x 1in x 1 1/2in sml rect (2.5cm x 3.8cm), 1in x 2in (2.5cm x 5.1cm) med rect

1. For the handle: Join handle med rect/BKG rect A at 2in (5.1cm) edges. Place handle sml rect horizontally, add BKG 1in (2.5cm) sq as CST to right edge, sewing diagonal seam from top right to bottom left. Join below 1st section. Add 2nd handle sml rect to the top of section along 1 1/2in (3.8cm) edges. Join BKG rect B to bottom edge of handle and rect C to top edge.
2. For the mug: Sew BKG sqs to both corners along lower 4 1/2in (11.4cm) edge as CSTs. Add BKG rect D along top 4 1/2in (11.4cm) edge. Sew handle section to right edge and BKG rect E to left edge.

variations
house

see base design page 236

variation 2
[HB3 — 7in (17.8cm) block]

materials
house: as HB1
roof: as HB2
sky: 2 x 1 1/4in (3.2cm) sqs, 2 x 1 1/2in x 5 1/2in (3.8cm x 14cm) sml rects, 1 1/2in x 7 1/2in (3.8cm x 19cm) lrg rect
grass:
1 1/2in x 7 1/2in (3.8cm x 19cm) strip

1. Make house as HB2. Add sky sml rects to block side edges, sky large rect to top and grass to block bottom.

variation 3
[HB4 — 4in (10.2cm) block]

materials
sky: 2 x 2in (5.1cm) sqs, 2 x 1in x 4 1/2in (2.5cm x 11.4cm) rects
roof: 2in x 3 1/2in (5.1cm x 8.9cm)
house top floor:
walls: 2 x 3/4in x 1 1/2in (1.9cm x 3.8cm) rects, 1 1/2in (3.8cm) sq
windows: 2 x 1 1/4 in x 1 1/2in
house bottom floor:
walls: 2 x 1 1/2in x 2in (3.8cm x 5.1cm)
door: 1 1/2in x 2in (3.8cm x 5.1cm)

1. Roof: Add sky sqs to roof as CSTs.
2. House top floor: Sew windows to either side of wall sq. Add wall rects to window side edges.
3. House bottom floor: Sew walls either side of door.
4. Sew rows together. Add sky rects to block sides.

variation 4
[HB5 — 6in (15.2cm) block]

materials
sky: 2 x 3 1/2in (8.9cm) sqs, 2 x 1 1/4in x 3 1/2in (3.2cm x 8.9cm) rects
roof: 3 1/2in x 6 1/2in (8.9cm x 16.5cm) rect
house top floor:
walls: 2 x 1in x 1 3/4in (2.5cm x 4.4cm) sml rects, 1 3/4in x 2in (4.4cm x 5.1cm) lrg rect
windows: 2 x 1 1/2in x 1 3/4in (3.8cm x 4.4cm) rects
house bottom floor:
walls: 2 x 2 1/4in (5.7cm) sqs
door: 1 1/2in x 2 1/4in (3.8cm x 5.7cm) rect

1. Roof: Add sky sqs to roof rect as CSTs.
2. House top floor: Sew windows either side of wall lrg rect along 1 3/4in (4.4cm) edges. Add wall sml rects to window side edges.
3. House bottom floor: Sew wall sqs either side of door rect. Join window/door house sections together.
3. Add sky rects to sides of house. Sew roof section above.

variations
string block

see base design page 237

heart

variation 2
[STB3 — 12in (30.5cm) block]

materials
pale: 4 x 3 1/2in x 10in (8.9cm x 25.4cm) strips, 4 x 4in (10.2cm) sqs cut in half along diag
prints:
8 x 1 1/2in x 7in (3.8cm x 17.8cm) strips

1. Make as for STB1, using first the 4 x 3 1/2in x 10in (8.9cm x 25.4cm) strips along the central diag line and then using the print strips and pale HSTs.

variation 3
[STB4 — 12in (30.5cm) block]

materials
white: 12 x 1 1/2in x 10in (3.8cm x 25.4cm) strips
prints:
8 x 1 1/2in x 9in (3.8cm x 22.9cm) strips, 4 x 3 1/2in (8.9cm) sqs cut in half along the diag

1. Make as for STB1, using 1 of the white strips as the centre strip then piecing using the print strips, white strips, and print triangles.

variation 4
[STB5 — 12in (30.5cm) block]

materials
charcoal: 4 x 2 1/2in x 10in (6.3 x 25.4cm) strips, 8 x 1in x 7in (2.5cm x 17.8cm) strips, 8 x 1in x 5in (2.5cm x 12.7cm) strips, 4 x 2 1/2in (6.3cm) sqs cut in half along diag. **prints:** 8 x 1in x 7in (2.5cm x 17.8cm) strips, 8 x 1in x 6in (2.5cm x 15.2cm) strips, 8 x 1in x 4in (2.5cm x 10.2cm) strips

1. As for STB1 step 1, adding extra lines 1/2in (1.3cm) between the 1in (2.5cm) lines.
2. Make as for STB1, using the wider charcoal strips for the centre lines, then alternating the print and charcoal strips in diminishing order of length and ending with HSTs.

variation 1
[HE2 — 6in (15.2cm) block]

materials
stripes: 2 x 3 1/2in x 6 1/2in (8.9cm x 16.5cm) rects cut on bias. **BKG:** 4 x 2in (5.1cm) sqs, 2 x 3 1/2in (8.9cm) sqs

1. Place 1 rect with long edges vertical. To top corners, sew BKG 2in (5.1cm) sqs diagonally to make CSTs using photograph for directions. To lower left corner, add BKG 3 1/2in (8.9cm) sq as CST.
2. Repeat step 1 with other rect to make mirror image. Join rects together.

variations

see base design page 238

variation 2
[HE3 — 6in (15.2cm) block]

materials
col A: 2 x 1 1/2in x 3 1/2in (3.8cm x 8.9cm) rects
cols B/C/D/E/F: 1 1/2in x 6 1/2in (3.8cm x 16.5cm) rect (1 for each colour)
BKG: 4 x 1 1/2in (3.8cm) sml sqs, 2 x 3 1/2 (8.9cm) lrg sqs

1. As HE1 step 1 using BKG sml sqs and col A rects.
2. Sew Rows B–F. Join under A.
3. Add lrg BKG squares to block lower corners as CSTs to make heart shape.

variation 3
[HE4 — 5 1/2in (14cm) block]

materials
heart (scraps): 3 x 1 1/2in (3.8cm) sqs, 2 x 1 1/2in x 2 1/2in (3.8cm x 6.3cm) sml rects, 2 x 1 1/2in x 3 1/2in (3.8cm x 8.9cm) med rects, 1 1/2in x 4 1/2in (3.8cm x 11.4cm) lrg rects
BKG: 2 1/2in (6.3cm) sq, 3 1/4in (8.3cm) sq halved diagonally, 4 1/2in (11.4cm) sq halved diagonally

1. Place BKG 2 1/2in (6.3cm) sq on point. Add heart sml rect to left lower edge. Join heart sq to remaining heart sml rect and add to right lower edge in the style of Scots plaid block (see SP1).
2. Continue with remaining heart scraps using photograph for reference. Trim off top of BKG sq 1/4in (6mm) above the top points of the heart.
3. Add smaller BKG triangles to make the top corners and larger triangles to make the bottom corners. You will have a rectangle shape. Trim to 6in (15.2cm) sq.

variation 4
[HE5 — 18in (45.7cm) block]

materials
col A (pink prints): 20 x 3 1/2in (8.9cm) sqs, 5 x 3 7/8in (9.8cm) sqs — cut in half diagonally
BKG: 2 x 3 7/8in (9.8cm) sqs — cut in half diagonally, 9 7/8in (25.1cm) sq — cut in half diagonally
diagram: heart HE5

1. Arrange sqs and triangles into rows following diagram. For the 1st row, sew blue/pink triangles together and then join remaining sections.

2. Sew the remaining heart following diagram. Join rows then add lrg BKG triangles.

variations

numbers

see base design page 241

variation 2
[NU3 — 6in (15.2cm) block]

materials
BKG: 6 x 1 1/2in (3.8cm) sqs, 2 x 2in x 2 1/2in (5.1cm x 6.3cm) sml rects, 1 1/2in x 4 1/2in (3.8cm x 11.4cm) lrg rect. **BKG Sashing:** as NU2. **number:** 1 1/2in x 2 1/2in (3.8cm x 6.3cm) sml rect, 4 x 1 1/2in x 3 1/2in (3.8cm x 8.9cm) lrg rects

1. Add BKG sml rects above/below 2 1/2in (6.3cm) edges of number sml rect. Sew BKG lrg rect to left side edge of this.
2. Place number lrg rect horizontally. Add BKG 1 1/2in (3.8cm) sq as CST to left edge, sewing diagonal seam from bottom left to top right. Join above section created in step 1. Repeat with other number lrg rect with diagonal running opposite direction. Join below section.
3. Place number lrg rect vertically. Add 2 BKG 1 1/2in (3.8cm) sqs as CSTs to number lrg rect to make CSTs at both ends using photo for ref. Repeat. Join together at 1 1/2in (3.8cm) edges and sew to the right edge of block. Add sashing strips.

variation 3
[NU4 — 6in (15.2cm) block]

materials
BKG: 1 1/2in x 2in (3.8cm x 5.1cm) rect A, 2in x 2 1/2in (5.1cm x 6.3cm) rect B, 1 1/2in x 2 1/2in (3.8cm x 6.3cm) rect C, 2 x 1 1/2in x 4in (3.8cm x 10.2cm) rects D
BKG Sashing: as NU2
number: 2 x 1 1/2in x 2in (3.8cm x 5.1cm) sml rects, 1 1/2in x 3 1/2in (3.8cm x 8.9cm) med rect, 1 1/2in x 5in (3.8cm x 38.1cm) lrg rect

1. Place BKG rect C and number sml rect vertically, join along 1 1/2in edges with number rect under BKG. Join BKG rect D's to both side edges. Add number med rect to the bottom and number lrg rect to the left of this section.
2. Place number sml rect vertically, add BKG rect A to right edge and rect B to left. Join to the bottom of the section completed in step 1. Add sashing strips to sides of block.

variation 4
[NU5 — 6in (15.2cm) block]

materials
BKG: 2 x 1 1/2in (3.8cm) sqs, 2 x 2in x 3 1/2in (5.1cm x 8.9cm) rects. **BKG Sashing:** as NU2. **number:** 1 1/2in x 2in (3.8cm x 5.1cm)rect A, 2 x 1 1/2in x 3 1/2in (3.8cm x 8.9cm) rects B, 1 1/2in x 4in (3.8cm x 10.2cm) rect C, 1 1/2in x 4 1/2in (3.8cm x 11.4cm) rect D

1. Join BKG rect under 1st number rect B along 3 1/2in (8.9cm) edges.
2. Place 2nd number rect B horizontally, add BKG 1 1/2in (3.8cm) sq to right edge sewing diagonal seam from top left right to bottom right. Join under rect B/BKG rect from step 1. Join rect C to left side edge.
3. Join number rect A to right side of BKG rect along 2in (5.1cm) edges. Sew under section from steps 1 and 2. Sew BKG 1 1/2in (3.8cm) sq as CST to number rect D as in step 2 with diagonal sewn top right to bottom left. Join to bottom of section. Add sashing strips to side edges.

variations

modern spool

see base design page 242

variation 1
[MS2 — 12in (30.5cm) block]

materials
as for MS1 x 4

1. Make as for MS1 4 times.
Sew together as if making a 4-patch.

variation 2
[MS3 — 6in (15.2cm) block]

materials
as for MS1 without the 2 x 2 1/4in x 6 1/2in (6.3cm x 16.5cm rects, plus:
col C (orange): 1in x 3in (2.5cm x 7.6cm) rect, 1in x 5in (2.5cm x 12.7cm) rect. **BKG:** 2 x 1 1/4in x 5in (3.2cm x 12.7cm) rects, 1in x 2 1/2in (2.5cm x 6.3cm) rect, 2 x 3/4in x 5 1/2in (1.9cm x 14cm) rects, 1in x 3in (2.5cm x 7.6cm) rect, 1in x 6 1/2in (2.5cm x 16.5cm)rect, 2 x 3/4in x 6 1/2in (1.9cm x 16.5cm) rects

1. Sew the 2 x 1 1/4in x 5in (3.2cm x 12.7cm) BKG rects to sides of 1in x 5in (2.5cm x 12.7cm) rect C fabric.
2. Follow steps 2, 4 and 5 from MS1. Sash the two spools together using the 1in x 6 1/2in (2.5cm x 16.5cm) BKG rect.
3. Sew the 2 x 3/4in x 6 1/2in (1.9cm x 16.5cm) rects to either side of the block to finish.

variation 3
[MS4 — 6in (15.2cm) block]

materials
as for MS1, omitting the 1in x 3in (2.5cm x 7.6cm) BKG rect and the 2 x 2 1/4in x 6 1/2in (6.3cm x 16.5cm) BKG rects, plus:
BKG: 3 1/2in (8.9cm) sq cut in half along diag, 5 1/2in (14cm) sq cut in half along diag

1. Make as for MS1 from steps 1–5, omitting the second half of step 5.
2. Sew the 3 1/2in (8.9cm) HSTs onto the top and bottom of the spool. Trim off excess sides.
3. Sew the 5 1/2in (14cm) HSTs onto the sides of the spool. Trim block to 6 1/2in (16.5cm)sq.

variation 4
[MS5 — 12in (30.5cm) block]

materials
col A (striped thread): 4 1/2in x 8 1/2in (11.4cm x 21.6cm) rect. **col B (green):** 1 1/2in (3.8cm) sq, 1 1/2in x 5 1/2in (3.8cm x 14cm) rect
col C (cream): 2 x 1 1/2in x 2in (3.8cm x 5.1cm) rects, 1 1/2in x 4 1/2in (3.8cm x 11.4cm) rect, 2 x 1in x 10 1/2in (2.5cm x 26.7cm) rects, 1 1/2in x 5 1/2in (3.8cm x 14cm) rect, 2 x 4in x 12 1/2in (10.2cm x 31.7cm) rects

1. Make as for MS1, using each larger piece listed above in place of each piece listed in MS1.

variations

pets

see base design page 245

variation 2
[PT3 — 6in (15.2cm) block]

materials
face/nose/chin: as PT2 with grey replacing black
ears/cheeks: grey 2 x 2in x 6 1/2in (5.1cm x 16.5cm) rect
BKG: 4 x 2in (5cm) sqs, 2 1/2in (6.3cm) sq, 1 1/2in x 3 1/2in (3.8cm x 8.9cm) rect
eyes: as PT1

1. As for PT2.
2. Sew face rect above nose/chin. Add BKG rect above face rect.
3. As for PT1. Join to either side of face. Add eyes.

variation 3
[PT4 — 6in (15.2cm) block]

materials
face/nose/chin/collar/ eyes: as for PT1
ears: 2 x 2in x 3in (5cm x 7.6cm) rects
BKG: 1in x 3 1/2in (2.5cm x 8.9cm) sml rect, 2 x 2in x 5 1/2in (5cm x 14cm) lrg rects

1–2. As for PT1 but swapping position of cream rect and collar at bottom of block.
3. Ears — place ear rects perpendicular to BKG rects, join diagonally (see diagram page 19). Join to sides of face. Add eyes.

variation 4
[PT5 — 6in (15.2cm) block]

materials
face/nose/chin/collar/ eyes: as for PT1
ears: 2 x 2in x 5in (2.5cm x 12.7cm) rects
BKG: 2 x 2in (5cm) sqs, 1in x 3 1/2in (2.5cm x 8.9cm) sml rect, 2 x 2in x 3 1/2in (2.5cm x 8.9cm) lrg rects

1–2. As for PT3.
3. Ears — Place ear rects vertically. To top end of each ear rect, add BKG sq as CST. To the other end, place BKG lrg rect perpendicular and join diagonally (see diagram page 19). Add eyes.

variations

raw edge appliqué

see base design page 246

variation 1
[REA2 — 15in (38.1cm) block]

materials
BKG: 15 1/2in (39.4cm) sc
stars: 4 x 8in (20.3cm) sqs

1. Prepare 4 stars as for REA1. Fuse and then sew to BKG following the layout in the photograph.

variation 2
[REA3 — 9 1/2in (24.1cm) block]

materials
as for REA1, plus:
2 x 1 1/2in x 8in (3.8cm x 20.3cm) and 2 x 1 1/2in x 10in (3.8cm x 25.4cm) strips
template: REAii

1. Make as for REA1 but using the heart template REAii.
2. Sash the sides using the shorter and then the top and bottom using the longer strips.

variation 3
[REA4 — 12in (30.5cm) block]

materials
BKG: 12 1/2in (31.7cm) sq
hearts: 4 x 8in (20.3cm) sqs

1. Prepare 4 hearts as for REA3. Fuse and then sew to BKG following the layout in the photograph.

variation 4
[REA5 — 15in (38.1cm) block]

materials
BKG: 15 1/2in (39.4cm) sq
orange segments: 4 x 8in (20.3cm) sqs of 4 different colours
template: REAiii

1. Prepare 3 orange segments per fabric colour as for REA1 but using template REAiii. Fuse and then sew to BKG following the layout in the photograph.

pots and pans

variation 1
[PP2 — 6in (15.2cm) block]

materials
BKG: as PP1 (you will not need the sml sqs)
knob/lid/handles/ worktop: as PP1
casserole:
3 1/2in x 5in (8.9cm x 12.7cm) rect

1. Make as for PP1 without CSTs at bottom of casserole.

variation 2
[PP3 — 6in (15.2cm) block]

materials
BKG: 3 x 1in (2.5cm) sml sqs, 2 x 1 1/4in (3.2cm) med sqs, 1 1/2in (3.8cm) lrg sq, 2 x 1in x 3in (2.5cm x 7.6cm) rects A, 2 x 1 1/4in x 1 1/2in (3.2cm x 3.8cm) rects B, 1 1/2in x 2 1/4in (3.8cm x 5.7cm) rect C, 1 1/2in x 2 3/4in (3.8cm x 6.9cm) rect D.
knob/lid/worktop: as PP1
spout: 1 1/2in x 2in (3.8cm x 5.1cm) rect
handle: 1 1/2in x 2 1/2in (3.8cm x 6.3cm) rect
teapot: 4 1/2in (11.4cm) sq

1. Knob: Sew BKG rects A either side of knob.
2. Lid/teapot: Add 2 BKG sml sqs as CSTs to lid rect top corners. Add 2 BKG med sqs as CSTs to teapot rect bottom corners. Join teapot under lid.
3. Spout/handles: Add BKG lrg sq as CST to spout rect. Add rect B above and rect D below. Add BKG sml sq as CST to handle. Add rect B above, rect C below. Join spout and handle to teapot sides.
4. Add lid to top and worktop to bottom of block.

variations

see base design page 249

variation 3
[PP4 — 6in (15.2cm) block]

materials

BKG: 4 x 1 1/2in (3.8cm) sqs, 1 1/2in x 2in (3.8cm x 2.5cm) sml rect, 1 1/2in x 5 1/2in (3.8cm x 14cm) lrg rect
handle: 1 1/2in x 5 1/2in (3.8cm x 14cm) rect, 1 1/2in (3.8cm) sq
spout: 1 1/2in x 2in (3.8cm x 2.5cm) rect
kettle: 3 1/2in x 5 1/2in (8.9cm x 14cm) rect
flames: 6 x 2in (5.1cm) sqs — 3 yellow, 3 orange

1. Handle, row 1: Sew 2 BKG sqs to handle rect as CST. Sew BKG sq to left side of handle.
2. Handle, row 2: Sew handle sq to right edge of lrg BKG rect.
3. Spout/Kettle: Sew BKG sq to spout sml rect as CST. Join to sml BKG rect. Join spout/BKG to left edge of kettle rect.
4. Flames: Pair yellow/orange sqs. Make 6 HST pairs. Trim to 1 1/2in (3.8cm) sq. Join in a row.
5. Join rows together.

variation 4
[PP5 — 6in (15.2cm) block]

materials

BKG: 4 x 1in (2.5cm) sqs, 1in x 2 1/2in (2.5cm x 6.3cm) sml rect, 1 3/4in x 2 1/2in (4.4cm x 6.3cm) med rect, 3 1/4in x 6 1/2in (8.3cm x 16.5cm) lrg rect
pan: 2 x 1in x 2 1/2in (2.5cm x 6.3cm) sml rects, 2 1/4in x 4 1/2in (5.7cm x 11.4cm) lrg rect
handle: 1in (2.5cm) sq, 1in x 2 1/2in (2.5cm x 6.3cm) rect
flames: as for PP4

1. Handle: Sew handle sq to BKG sml rect as CST. Join underneath handle rect along 2 1/2in (6.3cm) edges. Sew BKG med rect below.
2. Pan: Sew BKG sq to pan sml rect as CST. Repeat and join rects at CSTs to make spout. Sew BKG sqs to pan lrg rect lower corners as CSTs. Join under pan/spout. Add handle to right side of pan and lrg BKG rect above pan.
3. Flames: As for PP4. Add to base of block.

school house

see base design page 250

variation 2
[SHB3 — 8in (20.3cm) block]

materials
sky/chimney/house gable (using house fabric A) /roof/door: all as SHB2
house fabric A (yellow): 2 x 1 3/4in x 3 1/2in (4.4cm x .8.9cm)rects C, 1 1/2in x 4 1/2in (3.8cm x 11.4cm) rect D
house fabric B (peach): 2 x 1in x 2 1/4in (2.5cm x 5.7cm) rects A, 1 1/2in x 2 1/4in (3.8cm x 5.7cm) rect B, 1 1/2in x 4 1/2in (3.8cm x 11.4cm) rect D, 1 3/4in x 4 1/2in (4.4cm x 11.4cm) rect E
window: 2 x 1 1/2in x 2 1/4in (3.8cm x 5.7cm)

1–2. As for SHB2 steps 1–2.
3. make door: Sew rects C either side of door along 3 1/2in (8.9cm) edges. Add rect D above door.
4. Make window: Sew both windows either side of rect B along 2 1/4in (5.7cm) edges. Add rects A either side of windows. Sew rect D above, rect E below.
5. Assemble as for SHB1.

variation 3
[SHB4 — 8in (20.3cm) block]

materials
sky/chimney/house gable/roof: as for SHB1
house: 2 x 1 3/4in (4.4cm) sqs, 2 x 1 3/4in x 3 1/4in (4.4cm x 8.3cm) sml rects, 2 x 1 1/4in x 4 1/2in (3.2cm x 11.4cm) lrg rects
door: 2in x 3 1/4in (5.1cm x 8.3cm)
window: 1 3/4in x 2in (4.4cm x 5.1cm)
grass: 1 3/4in x 8 1/2in (4.4cm x 21.6cm)

1. Make sky/chimney: As SHB1 step 1.
2. Make roof: As SHB1 step 2.
3. Make door: Sew sml rects either side of door.
4. Make window: Sew 1 3/4in (4.4cm) house sqs either side of window. Sew lrg rects above and below.
5. Assemble as for SHB1 adding grass strip to bottom of block.

variation 4
[SHB5 — 8in (20.3cm) block]

materials
sky/chimney/house gable/roof: as SHB2
house: 3 x 1in x 1 3/4in (2.5cm x 4.4cm) sml rects, 2 x 1 3/4in x 3 1/4in (4.4cm x 8.3cm) med rects, 2 x 1 1/4in x 4 1/2in (3.2cm x 11.4cm) lrg rects
door: as SHB4
window: 2 x 1 3/4in (4.4cm) sq
path: 1 3/4in x 4 1/4in (4.4cm x 10.8cm)
grass: 1 3/4in (4.4cm) sq, 1 3/4in x 5 3/4in (4.4cm x 14.6cm)

1. Make sky/chimney: As for SHB2 step 1.
2. Make roof: As for SHB1 step 2.
3. Make door: Sew med rects either side of door.
4. Make window: Sew 2 windows between 3 sml rects. Add lrg rects above and below.
5. Make path: Place path horizontally. Add grass sq as CST to left lower corner. Add grass rect as CST with rectangles to path right edge. Assemble as for SHB1 adding path strip to bottom of block.

variations

whirligig

see base design page 251

variation 1
[WGG2 — 14in (35.6cm) block]

materials
as for WGG1

1. Make as for WGG1 but following the layout in the photograph.

variation 2
[WGG3 — 10in (25.4cm) block]

materials
BKG: 2 x 4in x 4 1/2in (10.2cm x 16.5cm) rects, 2 x 6 1/2in (16.5cm) sqs cut in half along the diag
print: 2 x 4in x 4 1/2in (10.2cm x 11.4cm) rects

1. Make 1 block as in WGG1.
2. Add the HSTs to the sides, top, and bottom to set the block on point, and trim to 10 1/2in (26.7cm) sq.

variation 3
[WGG4 — 9in (22.9cm) block]

materials
BKG: 2 x 4in x 4 1/2in (10.2cm x 11.4cm) rects, 2 x 1 1/2in x 7 1/2in (3.8cm x 19cm) strips, 2 x 1 1/2in x 9 1/2in (3.8cm x 24.1cm) strips
print: 2 x 4in x 4 1/2in (10.2cm x 11.4cm) rects

1. Make 1 block as in WGG1.
2. Add the shorter sashing strips to the sides and the longer to the top and bottom.

variation 4
[WGG5 — 18in (45.7cm) block]

materials
4 x requirements for WGG4

1. Make 4 blocks as in WGG4. Sew together as 4-patch.

variations
spool block

see base design page 252

variation 1
[SB2 — 6in (15.2cm) block]

materials
spool: 2 x 2 1/2in (6.3cm) sqs, 2 x 3in (7.6cm) sqs
thread: 2 1/2in (6.3cm) sq
BKG: 2 x 2 1/2in (6.3cm) sqs, 2 x 3in (7.6cm) sqs

1. Pair spool and BKG 3in sqs. Make 4 HST units. Trim to 2 1/2in (6.3cm) sq. Sew either side of spool to 2 1/2in (6.3cm) sqs using photograph for direction.
2. Continue as for SB1.

variation 2
[SB3 — 6in (15.2cm) block]

materials
spool: 4in (10.2cm) sq (directional print cut on point)
thread: 4 x 2in (5.1cm) sqs
BKG: 2 x 3 1/2in (6.3cm) sqs, 4in (10.2cm) sq

1. Pair spool and BKG 4in (10.2cm) sqs. Make 2 HST units. Trim to 3 1/2in (6.3cm) sq. Sew 1 thread sq diagonally to make CST on each spool corner HST sq. Repeat with other HST sq.
2. Sew 1 thread sq diagonally to make CST on 1 corner of BKG 2in (5.1cm) sq. Repeat with other sq.
3. Sew tog as 4-patch.

variation 3
[SB4 — 6in (15.2cm) block]

materials
BKG: 2 x 3 1/2in (6.3cm) sqs
bowtie (striped): 2 x 2in (5.1cm) sqs stripes cut on point, 2 x 3 1/2in (6.3cm) sqs

1. Sew 1 bowtie sq diagonally to make CST at bottom right corner of BKG sq. Repeat with other BKG sq with CST in top left corner.
2. Arrange as in photograph. Join as 4-patch.

variation 4
[SB5 — 4in (10.2cm) block]

materials
spool: 2 x 2in x 4 1/2in (5.1cm x 11.4cm)
centre strip: 1 1/2in x 4 1/2in (3.8cm x 11.4cm)
BKG: 4 x 1 1/2in x 3 1/2in (3.8cm x 6.3cm) sml rects
template: SBi

1. Print/trace 2 x SBi patterns. Use spool fabric and 2 BKG sml rects to make half a spool using foundation piecing technique. Trim, retaining SA. Remove paper. Repeat with 2nd pattern.
2. Arrange and sew together as block photograph with strip in the centre.

variations

sunshine and stained glass

see base design page 254

variation 2
[SSG3 — 8in (20.3cm) block]

materials
dark: 4 x 5 1/2in (14cm) sqs
light: 4 x 4 1/2in (11.4cm) sqs (2 in each of 2 colours)
stripes: 4 x 2in (5.1cm) sqs bias cut for diagonal stripes
templates: as for SSG1

1. Make as for SSG1 but adding CSTs to 1/4 circle inner corner of each sq only.

variation 3
[SSG4 — 8in (20.3cm) block]

materials
col A: 2 x 4 1/2in (11.4cm) sqs, 2 x 5 1/2in (14cm) sqs
col B: 2 x 4 1/2in (11.4cm) sqs, 2 x 5 1/2in (14cm) sqs
col C: 4 x 2in (5.1cm) sqs
col D: 4 x 2in (5.1cm) sqs
templates: as for SSG1

1. Make as for SSG1 using photograph for reference with colour placement.

variation 4
[SSG5 — 8in (20.3cm) block]

materials
scrappy mid/light mix:
4 x 2in (5.1cm) sqs, 4 x 5 1/2in (14cm) sqs, 4 x 4 1/2in (11.4cm) sqs
templates: as for SSG1

1. Make as for SSG1 but placing the CSTs on the frame outer corner of each sq only.

variations

wonky crosses

see base design page 255

variation 2
[WC3 — 12 1/2in (31.7cm) block]

materials
4 x 6in (15.2cm) sqs (1 from each of 4 colours)
BKG: 8 x 1in x 7in (2.5cm x 17.8cm) strips, 2 x 1in x 6in (2.5cm x 15.2cm) strips, 3 x 1in x 12in (2.5cm x 30.5cm) strips, 2 x 1in x 13in (2.5cm x 33cm) strips

1. Lay out all 4 sqs next to each other as they will be in the final block. Make 2 wonky vertical cuts from top to bottom, each cut running through 2 of the sqs.
2. Sash the 2 halves of each sq tog using 2 x 7in (5.1cm x 17.8cm) strips.
3. Lay the 4 sqs out again on the table and make 2 wonky cuts from left to right, each cut running through 2 sqs.
4. Sash the 2 halves of each sq tog using 2 x 7in (5.1cm x 17.8cm) strips, and trim to 6in sq.
5. Sash 2 pairs of sqs tog using the 6in strips and then the 2 halves of the block tog using 1 of the 12in (30.5cm) strips.
6. Sash the sides using the remaining 12in (30.5cm) strips and then the top and bottom using the 13in (33cm) strips.

variation 3
[WC4 — 10 1/2in (26.7cm) block]

materials
col A (red): 6 1/2in (16.5cm) sq
BKG:
3 x 2 1/2in x 7in (6.3cm x 17.8cm) strips, 2 1/2in x 8in (6.3cm x 20.3cm) strip, 2 x 2 1/2in x 11in (6.3cm x 27.9cm) strips

1. Make a WC sq using 1 of the 7in (17.8cm) strips then the 8in (20.3cm) strip. Trim to 7in (17.8cm) sq.
2. Sash the sides using the remaining 7in (17.8cm) strips then the top and bottom using the 11in strips.

variation 4
[WC5 — 12in (30.5cm) block]

materials
BKG: 7in x 8in (17.8cm x 20.3cm) rect, 2 x 2in x 7 1/2in (5.1cm x 19cm)strips, 2 x 3in x 12 1/2in (7.6cm x 31.7cm) strips
green: 1 1/2in x 8in (3.8cm x 20.3cm) strip, 3 1/2in x 7 1/2in (8.9cm x 19cm) strip

1. Placing the BKG rect horizontally on the cutting mat, cut it in half horizontally and sash back tog using the green 1 1/2in x 8in (3.8cm x 20.3cm)strip.
2. Cut in half vertically and sash back tog using the 3 1/2in x 7 1/2in (8.9cm x 19cm) strip.
3. Sash the sides using the BKG 2in x 7 1/2in (5.1cm x 19cm)strips and then the top and bottom using the 3in x 12 1/2in (7.6cm x 31.7cm) strips.

variations
basket

see base design page 257

variation 1
(BA2 — 6in (15.2cm) block)

materials
basket: 4 1/2in (11.4cm) sq, 2 7/8in (7.3cm) sq cut in half diagonally to make 2 HSTs
handle: rickrack 3/8in x 6in (9mm x 15.2cm)
BKG: 4 1/2in (11.4cm) sq, 4 7/8in (12.4cm) sq cut in half diagonally to make 2 HSTs, 2 x 2 1/2in (6.3cm) sqs

1. As BA1, with BKG sqs replacing BKG rect in step 2.

variation 2
(BA3 — 6in (15.2cm) block)

materials
basket: 3 1/2in x 6 1/2in (8.9cm x 16.5cm) rect
handle: 1 1/2in x 2 1/2in (3.8cm x 6.3cm) rect
BKG: 1 1/2in (3.8cm) sml sq, 2 x 2 1/2in (6.3cm) lrg sqs, 2 x 3in x 3 1/2in (7.6cm x 8.9cm) rects

1. Join handle to BKG sml sq. Sew BKG rects either side of handle along 3 1/2in (8.9cm) edges.
2. Sew BKG lrg sqs as CSTs to both bottom corners of the basket rect. Join to handle.

variation 3
(BA4 — 4in (10.2cm) block)

materials
BKG: 2 x 1 1/2in x 3 1/2in (3.8cm x 8.9cm) sml rects, 2 x 2 1/4in x 3in (5.7cm x 7.6cm) med rect, 1in (2.5cm) sq
basket: 2in x 4 1/2in (5.1cm x 11.4cm) rect
handle: 1in x 2 1/2in (2.5cm x 6.3cm) rect
foundation pattern: SBi

1. Print/trace pattern SBi. Use basket fabric and 2 BKG sml rects to make basket using foundation piecing technique. Trim, remove paper.
2. Join handle and BKG sq at 1in edges. Sew BKG med rects either side of handle/BKG. Join handle/ BKG to basket.

variation 4
(BA5 — 4in (10.2cm) block)

materials
BKG: 2 1/2in x 3 1/2in (3.8cm x 8.9cm) sml rects, 3in x 4 1/2in (7.6cm x 11.4cm) med rect
basket: 2in x 4 1/2in (5.1cm x 11.4cm) rect
handle: 1in x 6in (2.5cm x 15.2cm) bias strip
spray starch (optional)
foundation pattern: SBi

1. As BA4 step 1.
2. To make handle, spray bias strip with starch. Fold and press 1/4in (6mm) both long edges. Find centre point along length of bias strip, press lightly to crease.
3. On BKG med rect long lower edge make 2 pencil marks in SA 1/2in (1.3cm) in from outer edges. On top long edge, find centre point and measure 1/2in (1.3cm) down, mark by placing a pin. Starting at bottom edge, pin ends of bias strip on the inside of pencil marks. Match centre of bias strip with pin mark on BKG. Curve, press and gently stretch the strip between the pins to form handle shape. Hand-appliqué handle to BKG rect.
4. Join basket to handle/BKG to make block. The handle ends will be enclosed in the seam.

variations

books

variation 1
[BK2 — 14in (35.6cm) block]

materials
(in order of construction, left to right)
books A–D/BKG as for BK1
book E: 2 1/2in x 6 3/4in (6.3cm x 17.1cm)
book F: 1 1/2in x 5in (3.8cm x 12.7cm), BKG
1 1/2in x 2 1/4in (3.8cm x 5.7cm)
shelf: 2 1/2in x 14 1/2in (6.3cm x 36.8cm)
BKG: 6 3/4in x 9 1/2in (17.1cm x 24.1cm) lrg rect

1. Make books A–D as for BK1 step 1.
2. Sew BKG and book F tog along 1 1/2in (3.8cm) edges.
Join long edge to book E so book F sits above book E.
Add BKG lrg rect above this so the books E and F are
arranged horizontally. Sew section to books A–D.
3. Complete as for BK1.

variation 2
[BK3 — 14in (35.6cm) block]

materials
book A: 2 1/2in x 10 1/2in (6.3cm x 26.7cm), BKG
2 1/2in (6.3cm) sq
book B: 2 1/2in x 11 1/2in (6.3cm x 29.2cm), BKG
1 1/2in x 2 1/2in (3.8cm x 6.3cm)
book C: 3in x 9 1/2in (7.6cm x 24.1cm), BKG 3in x
3 1/2in (7.6cm x 8.9cm)
book D: 2in x 9in (5.1cm x 22.9cm), BKG 2in x 4in
(5.1cm x 10.2cm)
bookends: 2 x 1 1/2in x 2 1/2in (3.8cm x 6.3cm)sml
rects, 2 x 1 1/2in x 4 1/2in (3.8cm x 11.4cm) lrg rects
BKG: 2 x 2 1/2in x 3 1/2in (6.3cm x 8.9cm) sml rects,
2 x 3 1/2in x 8 1/2in (8.9cm x 21.6cm) lrg rects
shelf: 2 1/2in x 14 1/2in (6.3cm x 36.8cm)

1. Make books A–D as for BK1, step 1.
2. Join 2 1/2in (6.3cm)edges of bookend sml rect and
BKG sml rect so the bookend is underneath the BKG.
Sew bookend lrg rect to right side and BKG lrg rect to
top. Repeat for other bookend, sewing bookend lrg rect
to left side. Sew bookend strips to sides of books A–B.
3. Complete as for BK1.

see base design page 258

variation 3
[BK4 — 14in (35.6cm) block]

materials
(listed in order of construction)
top row 1: BKG 1 1/4in x 14 1/2in (3.2cm x 36.8cm)
row 2: BKG 2 1/4in x 5 1/4in (5.7cm x 13.3cm), book A 2 1/4in x 6 1/2in (5.7cm x 16.5cm), BKG 2 1/4in x 3 3/4in (5.7cm x 9.5cm)
row 3: BKG 2in x 2 1/4in (5.1cm x 5.7cm), book B 2in x 9in (5.1cm x 22.9cm) BKG 2in x 4 1/4in (5.1cm x 10.2cm)
row 4: BKG 3in x 3 1/2in (7.6cm x 8.9cm), book C 3in x 10in (7.6cm x 25.4cm), BKG 2in x 3in (5.1cm x 7.6cm)
row 5: BKG 1 3/4in x 2in (4.4cm x 5.1cm), book D 1 3/4in x 11in (4.4cm x 27.9cm), BKG 1 3/4in x 2 1/2in (4.4cm x 6.3cm)
row 6: BKG 2 1/2in x 4in (6.3cm x 10.2cm), book E 2 1/2in x 10 1/2in (6.3cm x 26.7cm) BKG 1in x 2 1/2in (2.5cm x 6.3cm)
row 7: BKG 2 1/2in (6.3cm) sq, book F 2 1/2in x 11 1/2in (6.3cm x 29.2cm), BKG 1 1/2in x 2 1/2in (3.8cm x 6.3cm)
shelf: 2 1/2in x 14 1/2in (6.3cm x 36.8cm)

1. Assemble each row and arrange in order. Join rows.
2. Complete as for BK1.

variation 4
[BK5 — 14in (35.6cm) block]

materials
(in order of construction left to right)
books A–D/BKG: as for BK1
book E: 2 1/4in x 9in (5.7cm x 22.9cm), BKG 2 1/4in x 4in (5.7cm x 10.2cm)
book F: 2 1/4in x 8 1/4in (5.7cm x 21cm), BKG 2in x 3 1/2in (5.1cm x 6.3cm) sml rect, 2 1/4in x 3in (5.7cm x 7.6cm) med rect, 3 1/2in x 8 3/4in (8.9cm x 22.2cm) lrg rect, 6in (15.2cm) sq
shelf: 2 1/2in x 14 1/2in (6.3cm x 36.8cm)
diagram: BK5

1. Make books A–E as for BK1, step 1.
2. Add BKG med rect to top 2 1/4in (5.7cm) edge of book F. Place BKG lrg rect vertically, cut in half from top left to bottom right corners. Sew triangles either side of book F/BKG piece following BK5 diagram.
3 Add BKG sml rect to bottom of book F using 1/2in (1.3cm) seam and trim to square off top/bottom of book F section to measure 5in x 8in (12.7cm x 20.3cm). Add BKG 6in (15.2cm) sq to top edge and trim whole section to 5in x 12 1/2in (12.7cm x 31.7cm). Join to side of books A–E.
4. Complete as for BK1.

Start seam with triangle corner placed

Line up corners to start seam here

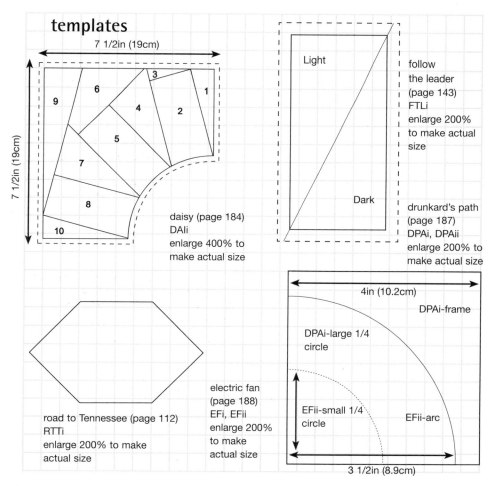

templates

7 1/2in (19cm)

7 1/2in (19cm)

3
6
1
9
4
2
5
7
8
10

daisy (page 184)
DAIi
enlarge 400% to
make actual size

Light

Dark

follow
the leader
(page 143)
FTLi
enlarge 200%
to make actual
size

drunkard's path
(page 187)
DPAi, DPAii
enlarge 200% to
make actual size

road to Tennessee (page 112)
RTTi
enlarge 200% to make
actual size

electric fan
(page 188)
EFi, EFii
enlarge 200%
to make
actual size

4in (10.2cm)

DPAi-frame

DPAi-large 1/4
circle

EFii-small 1/4
circle

EFii-arc

3 1/2in (8.9cm)

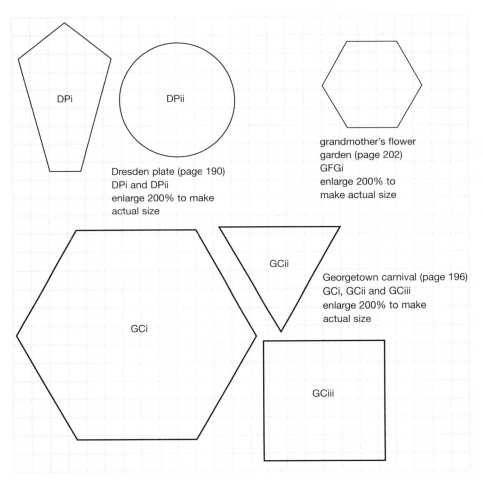

DPi

DPii

Dresden plate (page 190)
DPi and DPii
enlarge 200% to make
actual size

grandmother's flower
garden (page 202)
GFGi
enlarge 200% to
make actual size

GCi

GCii

Georgetown carnival (page 196)
GCi, GCii and GCiii
enlarge 200% to make
actual size

GCiii

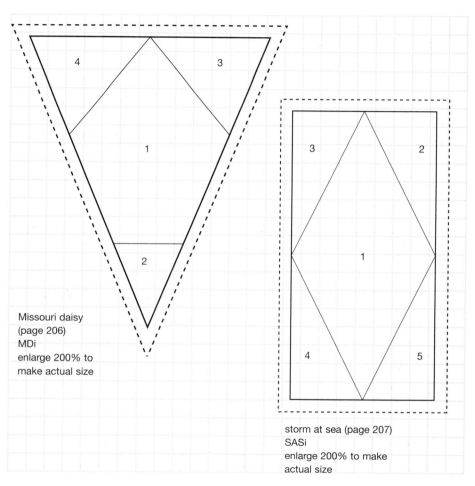

Missouri daisy
(page 206)
MDi
enlarge 200% to
make actual size

storm at sea (page 207)
SASi
enlarge 200% to make
actual size

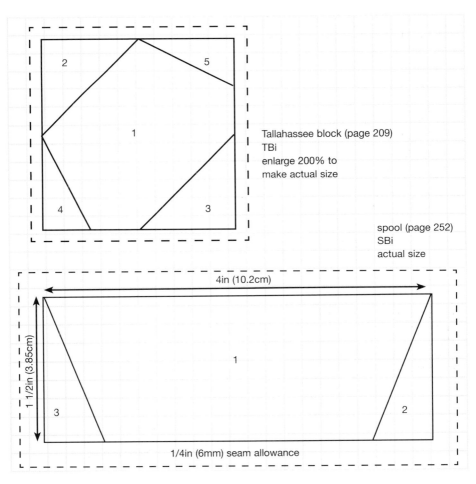

Tallahassee block (page 209)
TBi
enlarge 200% to
make actual size

spool (page 252)
SBi
actual size

4in (10.2cm)

1 1/2in (3.85cm)

1/4in (6mm) seam allowance

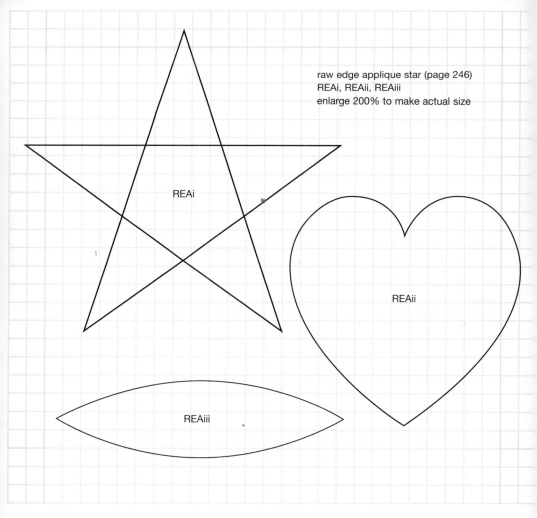

raw edge applique star (page 246)
REAi, REAii, REAiii
enlarge 200% to make actual size

REAi

REAii

REAiii

Suppliers and manufacturers

Fabric shops

Amitie Textiles, Australia
www.amitie.com.au

Backstitch, UK
www.backstitch.co.uk

Celtic Fusions Fabrics, UK
www.celticfusionfabrics.com

Contemporary Cloth, US
www.contemporarycloth.com

Eclectic Maker, UK
www.eclecticmaker.co.uk

Eternal Maker, UK
www.eternalmaker.com

Fat Quarter Shop, US
www.fatquartershop.com

Gone to Earth, UK
www.gonetoearth.co.uk

Hyggeligt Fabrics, Canada
www.hyggeligt.ca

Marmalade Fabrics, US
www.marmaladefabrics.com

M is for Make, UK
www.misformake.co.uk

Pink Castle Fabrics, US
www.pinkcastlefabrics.com

Sew Fresh Fabrics, US
www.sewfreshfabrics.com

Sew Me a Song, US
www.etsy.com/shop/sewmeasong

Simply Solids, UK
www.simplysolids.co.uk

Village Haberdashery, UK
www.thevillagehaberdashery.co.uk

Manufacturers of products used in this book

Andover Fabrics
www.andoverfabrics.com

Art Gallery Fabrics
www.artgalleryquilts.com

Aurifil Threads
www.aurifil.com

Blueberry Park
www.blueberry-park.co.uk

Ellison — manufacturers of the Sizzix die-cutting range
www.sizzix.co.uk

Free Spirit Fabrics
www.freespiritfabric.com

Liberty Art Fabrics
www.liberty.co.uk

Moda Fabrics
www.unitednotions.com

Oakshott Shot Cottons
www.oakshottfabrics.com

Riley Blake Fabrics
www.rileyblakedesigns.com

Robert Kaufman Fabrics
www.robertkaufman.com

Rowan Fabrics
www.westminsterfabrics.com

Superior Titanium Topstitch Needles
www.superiorthreads.com

Windham Fabrics
www.windhamfabrics.net

index

Page numbers in **bold** type
refer to templates

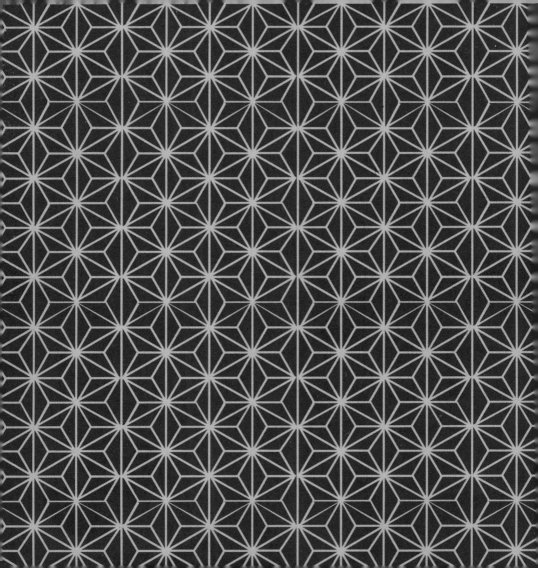